BEGINNING

SPEECH

Allyn and Bacon, Inc.   *Boston, 1964*

BEGINNING SPEECH

SPEECH

An Introduction to Intelligent

Speaking and Listening

Thomas H. Napiecinski   *Randall C. Ruechelle*

COLORADO STATE UNIVERSITY

Library of Congress Catalogue Card Number: 64–18555

PREFACE

THIS BOOK IS written for the student learning public speaking, not for the instructor teaching the course; but we emphasize at the outset that no one can learn how to speak from this or any other text or workbook. Public speaking is learned through diligent practice and experience. A course in beginning public speaking can only start the student in the right direction, with the instructor as his guide, and his text as a map of the territory he will traverse in his first venture into the exciting and rewarding experience of speaking before an audience.

This book does not attempt to say everything that a public speaker ultimately needs to know, but rather to provide some helpful materials and directions for the beginning student. The rest must be left to other books, other courses, and the lessons of experience.

Rapidly developing communication devices are making communication easier, more prevalent, and more necessary. But they can also make the spoken word a cheaper commodity. Although we are now able to speak to more people more easily, the worth of what we have to say should not be lessened. Our primary emphasis throughout this work is upon the *quality* of the message, of its utterance, and of the listening which is accorded it.

The book is designed for a single-term course of instruction. It is organized in a progressive series of units, each unit being constructed as a coordinated learning experience in intelligent speaking and listening. The prepared speeches assigned in the five regular units provide only a minimum of experience for the student. If more time is available in the term, inclusion of some or all of the assignments listed in the optional units, and the assignment of additional speeches provided for in the regular units would be desirable.

The inclusion of all materials, from background material to the specifics of any one given assignment, make it not only helpful but imperative that the student use both the text and the accompanying workbook constantly

v

in class meetings, in preparation of speaking and listening assignments, and for review.

We are indebted to our colleagues at Colorado State University for their valuable contributions and suggestions. We are even more indebted to our students for their contributions to our instruction over the past nine years during which this book has evolved.

T. H. N.

R. C. R.

CONTENTS

Unit III: *Information and Abstract Materials*

BACKGROUND: Speaking to a general audience, Purposes of the assignment

THE ASSIGNMENT

SUBJECT AND MATERIALS: Choose a subject area, Abstractions, A sample subject area, Investigate the subject area, Materials for definition, Special means of definition, Use of reasoning materials

APPLICATION TO AUDIENCE AND OCCASION

CONSTRUCTION OF THE SPEECH: Moving up by going down, The necessity for being interesting, The factors of attention, Organizing the speech, Wording the speech

PREPARATION FOR DELIVERY

REVIEW OF PREPARATION. SAMPLE STUDENT OUTLINE. REFERENCES

Unit IV: *Persuasion and Intellectual Appeals*

BACKGROUND: A rationale for persuasion, Purposes of the assignment, The nature of persuasion

THE ASSIGNMENT

SUBJECT AND MATERIALS: Choose a subject area, Investigate the subject area, The process of reflective thinking, Evaluating your materials, Methods of reasoning and their tests, A final word on evaluating your materials

APPLICATION TO AUDIENCE AND OCCASION: Action and belief, Attitudes and beliefs, Determining the purpose

CONSTRUCTION OF THE SPEECH: Accomplishing the specific purpose, Kinds of propositions, The speaker's character, Intellectual and psychological appeals, Relationship of audience and materials of the speech, Organizing and wording the speech

PREPARATION FOR DELIVERY

REVIEW OF PREPARATION. SAMPLE STUDENT OUTLINE. REFERENCES

Unit V: *Persuasion and Psychological Appeals*

BACKGROUND: The ethics of persuasion, Purposes of the assignment

ORGANIZATION OF THE BOOK

AND THE COURSE

THE ORGANIZATION OF this book has been coordinated with a pattern of course instruction designed to make it easier for you to learn the basic theory of public speaking and to guide you steadily and surely toward excellence in public speaking through the meaningful application of that theory. Your entire experience in the course will follow the normal, natural progression from the simple to the complex. The first assignments introduce the more basic concepts and the more elementary kinds of public speaking performances; in the final assignments, you will be tackling relatively profound theory and, in the speeches you give, some of the most difficult jobs the public speaker has. You will want to do your best work on each unit as it comes. The design of the instruction is such that, if you do your very best, you will always be ready for the next unit coming up.

This book is divided into five basic units and three optional units. Assignments in the optional units will be given at the discretion of your instructor and in accordance with the over-all pattern of your course. The general sequence of your work in each unit may be outlined as follows:

1. Read all the information, instructions, and supplementary materials in the unit. In the light of what you have read, start preparations for the speaking assignment of the unit.
2. Listen the introductory lecture or the class discussion conducted by your instructor before each unit. Be sure to take notes carefully on the material that supplements what you have read. Continue preparations for your speaking assignment, revising where necessary in the light of what you have learned from the lecture or discussion.
3. Complete preparations for your speaking assignment, so that you will be ready to deliver your speech on the day you are scheduled to do so.

4. On that day, have ready to turn in to your instructor any outline, comment page, inventory page, or other materials asked for in connection with completing the assignment for the particular unit. These pages are provided in the workbook which accompanies the text.

5. Whenever speeches are given, both before and after you give yours, listen carefully to the speaking of your classmates. You will learn a great deal of useful general information from hearing what they have to say in their speeches, and you will get much valuable instruction in public speaking from observing how they solve, or fail to solve, problems in speaking similar to your own.

6. Each time that there is class evaluation and criticism of your speaking performances or those of your classmates, make contributions to it, listen carefully, and note the contributions of your classmates. Keeping records of your performance can be an important aid to your learning.

Each of these tasks is of vital importance to you in accomplishing the work of this course and in getting the most from your experience in it. Do not neglect a single one of them.

The last section of the book is devoted to the evaluation of speeches and contains information about listening, criticism, and the composition of speech reports. You will doubtless be asked to read this section carefully early in the term, and will want to refer to it rather frequently, since the information given there applies to the work you do in each of the other units. In that section directions are also given for the composition of reports that your instructor may assign during the term.

Some additional general advice about your reading and listening in connection with your course work can be given at this time.

CREATIVE READING AND LISTENING

It is commonplace, when speaking of the learning of any art or skill, to say that one learns best by doing. Modern educational theory, as well as the instruction in this course, are based upon this truth. But one must understand the full implications of the statement. It must not be taken at face value. One learns to speak by speaking, but not alone by speaking. It is no exaggeration to say that one could speak several times a day throughout his life and yet never learn to speak. Numberless speakers of the past and present give testimony to this. You have undoubtedly heard some of the worst examples yourself—any college campus has more than its fair share of them. Doing must be combined with reading, listening, observing, and critical examination, if it is to lead to learning and consequent improvement. That is why this book and the course are organized so that each unit prepares you for doing by reading, listening, and observing. They also allow for criticism by your instructor, your classmates, and yourself. You learn what you should do, you try to do it, and then you determine how well you succeeded.

Advice at this point about how to accomplish the speaking assignments of the course would be feeble and futile. The entire book is designed to give you that advice in the proper dosage as needed. But some general advice about how to accomplish your reading, listening, observation, and critical tasks may not be amiss.

All the reading and listening you do should be creative. By "creative" we mean reading and listening that derives more out of the experience than what is contributed by the writer or speaker. We mean that you should first get as much as possible from what is read or said, and then supplement it with your own thinking and organizing skills.

Creative reading and listening require more from you than just attention to what is being said. First, they require purpose. Your purpose in reading this textbook or in listening to lectures in this course should be to receive and comprehend ideas about the nature of public speaking and practical suggestions that you can apply not only in the speaking assignment of the moment but in every speech that you will give for the rest of your life. Second, creative reading and listening require an inquiring mind. You should approach each such experience with questions in your own mind about what exactly might be learned and applied. Third, they require discipline and orderliness. You should take careful and systematic notes, not just because textbook and lecture materials might be covered in quizzes and examinations, but as a means of reinforcing your memory of what you learn. Fourth, creative reading and listening require a skeptical mind. You should not assume that what you have read or heard provides the final answers to all of your questions. Instead, you should use the ideas given you as stimuli to further thought, investigation, and application to any and all speaking assignments you may have.

We have already said that observing other speakers can be helpful to you as a means of learning something about public speaking. You are fortunate in a public speaking course of this kind to have, as an additional source of learning, the observations of your instructor and your classmates on both your speaking efforts and those of your fellow students. May we now suggest a word or two of advice about how to adapt and use the criticism, direct and indirect, that you will be receiving.

CLASSROOM CRITICISM

First of all, develop the ability to take and profit from adverse criticism. Most of the negative criticism that will be sent in your direction in this course will be extremely well meant; but even that which is not, even that which may seem capricious or possibly even malicious, can be helpful to you. It does not matter what the source of the criticism or the motives behind it may be, as long as it is valid. If it is a true criticism, you will want to know it in order to correct the fault. George Bernard Shaw once said that there is no worthwhile criticism that is not destructive in nature. He meant that, while compliments are good to hear, they do not help much in improving your skills. Welcome negative criticism from any and all sources, take it in good spirit, and *take it to heart.*

The major portion of the criticism, positive or negative, that you will receive will probably come from your instructor. After you have given a speech your instructor may return to you a completed comment page [1] on which he has noted items that pertain just to you, your speech, and your delivery of it. This can be one of the most valuable aids you will get in the course. Save the comment page, using it as the basis for completion of your speech inventory, and refer to both of these in preparing for each new speech assignment. In addition, as class time allows, your instructor may lead discussions of the speeches delivered during that period. His comments on each speech and his general criticisms are intended to be applied for the benefit of the entire class.

Using criteria based upon his own extensive knowledge and experience in public speaking, your instructor's evaluation will take this approach: first, to point out what was done; second, to indicate criteria by which it should be evaluated; and finally, to offer suggestions for improvement of a fault or advice on how everyone can use a successful technique. The comments, then, serve as an evaluation of what progress is being made by the class and as a program for continuing development applicable to each member of the class. Listen carefully to what your instructor has to say in these evaluation sessions: you will be amazed at how many times the shoe is just your size and width.

Although your instructor is a trained and skillful observer, he is neither omniscient nor infallible. Because he realizes that, he will welcome ques-

---

[1] The use of these materials is explained more fully in the workbook.

tions, comments, and suggestions from the class during the evaluation period. You may want to back him up or to disagree with him; either will please him, if what you say demonstrates accurate observation and sound reasoning. You may have noticed something that he missed; by all means speak up and give the class the benefit of your observation. Everyone must work at the job of criticism if the class is to make the maximum amount of improvement in the time allotted for this course. Try to contribute often and contribute well. General statements such as "good speech" or "nice delivery" mean nothing. Be specific in your criticisms; give examples. The harder you work at helping your classmates improve, the more you yourself will improve. The successes that you achieve will be shared and appreciated by other members of the class, just as you will share their successes. Your learning effort in this course is in every sense of the word a cooperative effort.

ORGANIZATION OF ASSIGNMENTS

The specific organization of the course assignments will be determined by the nature of the course in which you are enrolled. The total number of class meetings, the size of your class, and the particular instructional devices used at your institution may differ in some details from similar courses taught at other institutions. Some colleges and universities give each instructor sole responsibility for teaching his section. Other institutions have large, combined lecture sessions which then divide into smaller groups for the speaking performances. A number of institutions are now using a system of televised lectures and demonstrations to present a common body of materials to all those taking the course and to help standardize the assignments that are given.

This book and the organization of instruction it sets forth are applicable to any of these situations. The total amount of work assigned and the inclusion of some or all of the optional units depend mainly on the total number of meetings allotted to the course. The twenty or so members of your class should have full and equal opportunity to perform and time should still be available for class discussion and evaluation of the speeches, and for the scheduling and reviewing of assignments.

We shall list some possible sequences of assignments likely to fit most class situations. These suggestions cover the organizations typical of most beginning speech courses. Should the total number of class meetings of your particular course fall somewhere in the range between 36 and 42, a selection of optional units and an arrangement of sequences of these and of the regular units can easily be made to accommodate the circumstances.

Courses Having 30 to 35 Class Meetings

Suggested Sequence of Units	*Suggested Hours For Each Unit*	*Possible Assignments*
* Optional Unit A	3	Orientation lecture and speeches of introduction
Unit I	5	Introductory lecture and single-unit speeches
* Optional Unit B	3	Introductory lecture and recording sessions or oral readings
Unit II	5	Introductory lecture and student speeches
Unit III	5	Introductory lecture and student speeches
Unit IV	5	Introductory lecture and student speeches
* Optional Unit C	3	Introductory lecture and playback of recorded group discussions
Unit V	5	Introductory lecture and final student speeches

Two or three hours will probably be reserved for examinations and review. We suggest that a minimum of two written reports on speeches heard outside the classroom and one written report on a classroom speech be assigned, and that these assignments be spaced throughout the term. Your instructor may prefer to assign the report of a student speech first—perhaps for the Unit II speeches—and schedule the other two for later in the term.

* Any one or possibly a combination of two of these optional units may be assigned.

Courses Having 43 to 47 Class Meetings

Suggested Sequence of Units	Suggested Hours For Each Unit	Possible Assignments
Optional Unit A	3	Orientation lecture and speeches of introduction
Unit I	5	Introductory lecture and single-unit speeches
Optional Unit B	5	Introductory lecture and recording sessions or oral readings
Unit II	5	Introductory lecture and student speeches
* Unit III	6	Introductory lecture and student speeches
* Unit IV	6	Introductory lecture and student speeches
* Unit V	6	Introductory lecture and student speeches
Optional Unit C	5	Introductory lecture and group discussions

Again, two or three hours will probably be reserved for examinations and review. We suggest here that a minimum of four written speech reports be assigned during the term, and that at least one of them be assigned for a student speech, preferably early in the term.

* Each of these units allows for the possibility of more than one speech to be given in the unit, selected from the various options described in the unit assignments; therefore, the suggested hours listed for each unit are entirely variable.

BEGINNING

SPEECH

Introduction

REASONS FOR STUDYING SPEECH

Most of us give no conscious thought to our speech until such time as we are called upon to demonstrate it in public. We then come to the sudden realization that speaking is not the perfectly natural act that we had always assumed it to be. The least of our worries suddenly becomes one of the greatest. If something important to our welfare hinges on a successful speaking performance, as it very often does, the worry may assume awesome proportions.

What is wrong with this entirely too pervasive attitude, of course, is that it prevents people from doing anything about improving their speaking abilities until it is too late. The attitude might very well be compared with the one we have toward breathing. We take breathing for granted as necessary to physical existence, not thinking about it until our ability to breathe effectively is curtailed. Then we become panicky with the realization that this act, so long taken for granted, is really a life-and-death matter. Although physical existence is not often threatened by our inability to speak effectively (although even that can happen on occasion), our social existence is continually conditioned for the better or worse by this neglected skill.

Human society began when man learned to communicate with his fellows well enough to band together with them for mutual advantage. It grew and advanced to its present size and complexity as man perfected his communicative powers and developed new agencies for extending them. Think, for example, of the impact of the printing press on the world. The telegraph,

1

the telephone, the radio, and most recently the television receiver are more recent illustrations of the extension of man's ability to communicate. Today, space satellites permit messages to be flashed in an instant throughout the world. Only the most active imaginations can suggest the possibilities for communication that lie ahead. The smaller societies and groups into which the world is subdivided and the individuals who in their turn comprise these components of societal structure are equally dependent on communication. The individual becomes a part of the society and groups in which he lives and performs as he learns to communicate with the other members. If he is deprived of even one of his communicative abilities—speaking, listening, reading, or writing—he is to a considerable degree denied participation. Inability to communicate in any way means complete social isolation.

We normally begin to use speech in our second year of life and continue to use it to express ourselves, to learn from others, and to get things done in all kinds of daily activities. We would be quite literally lost without it. Even public speaking is a far more common experience than might be supposed. The business or professional man, especially, is besieged by public speaking opportunities, but the value of learning to speak well is a necessary part of anyone's education. The possession of some measure of public speaking skill has become practically mandatory for success in many occupations, and highly desirable in almost all. This course in public speaking is going to have more relevance to your future than you may realize. Learning to communicate has always been a vital concern of your education; learning to speak well in public will now assume a special importance for you.

Speech in Education

The study of public speaking has been a significant part of the entire educational tradition of the Western world. Its beginnings date back at least as far as any other kind of organized formal instruction in our civilization, and it has been accorded an important role in the educational system of almost every age and every nation.

Over two thousand years ago, teachers and philosophers in the early Greek city-states devoted a great part of their teaching and writing to the subject of public speaking. They used the term "rhetoric" to describe this study. Aristotle's *Rhetoric,* the teachings of the great orator-statesman Isocrates, and Plato's *Gorgias* and *Phaedrus* are among the contributions to public speaking theory made by the Greeks. Ancient Rome gave us the names of Cicero and Quintilian as writers on the subject. Quintilian's *Institutes of Oratory* remains a standard reference in modern courses in educational theory as well as in courses in speech. The study of rhetoric was in many instances the only one pursued by Greek and Roman students. According to George Kennedy, the study of rhetoric was paramount in ancient education.[1]

Rhetoric continued to be a standard part of the school curriculum in medieval times and increased in importance with the Renaissance. The Renaissance interest in almost all things Greek and Roman included the study of rhetoric. As an ordinary rural schoolboy in sixteenth-century England, William Shakespeare studied rhetoric; at Eaton a few years later a more privileged scholar, John Milton, was also instructed in the art. No less estimable a person than Francis Bacon was among the numerous men of the period who contributed to the literature of the study.

In the eighteenth and nineteenth centuries, rhetoric continued to hold its honored place. The great interest during the nineteenth century fostered the production of a number of classical works on the subject, notably those of George Campbell, Hugh Blair, and Richard Whately. John Quincy Adams, sixth President of the United States, was the author of a book on public speaking and also at one time Professor of Rhetoric at Harvard University. Abraham Lincoln, in his eminently successful quest for self-education, studied various books on the subject.

In twentieth-century America, the subject of speech is taught in almost every high school and college. Most American colleges and universities now offer undergraduate degrees, and many offer graduate degrees, in one or more of the various aspects of speech.

Speech is an ancient study; it is also a modern one. It is as modern as the ever-increasing space-age demands for improved communication. From its beginnings in ancient Greece until the present day, it has always been a major study engaging the attention of some of the greatest minds.

Speech in a Democratic Society

Speech Training Necessary for Leaders. One very good reason for the prominent role of public speaking in education is that skill in speech is necessary for leaders in law, religion, business, and most especially politics. Leadership, as Franklyn Haiman pointed out, most frequently requires the medium of speech.[2] Possibly nowhere is this more true than in the legislative halls of a democratic society. The history of political oratory in democratic societies mirrors the history of political action.

In our own country, we can see how statesmanship and public speaking

[1] George Kennedy, *The Art of Persuasion in Greece* (Princeton, New Jersey: Princeton University Press, 1963), p. 7.
[2] Franklyn S. Haiman, *Group Leadership and Democratic Action* (Cambridge, Massachusetts: Houghton Mifflin Company, 1951), pp. 4 ff.

ability have been closely connected. The speeches of Patrick Henry, James Otis, Alexander Hamilton, and the Adamses had great influence on the thinking and events of the Revolutionary period. The oratory of Henry Clay, Daniel Webster, John Calhoun, the elder Thomas Hart Benton, Stephen A. Douglas, and Abraham Lincoln helped shape our country's destiny. In more modern times, the careers of Theodore and Franklin Roosevelt, Woodrow Wilson, Adlai Stevenson, Dwight Eisenhower, Richard Nixon, John F. Kennedy, and Lyndon Johnson have been closely identified with their accomplishments in public speaking. Public opinion, national decisions, and events that intimately affect the lives of all of us depend in large part upon the caliber of public speaking in our society.

Speech Training Necessary for Everyone.   The great speeches of great leaders are not only results of public speaking training, but are often one of the means of instruction used in that training. Such speeches have always been used by teachers as models of excellence. The study of the public speaking careers of prominent public figures can teach us much about the inherent values and particular uses of public address. Immensely valuable as it may be, however, great oratory is neither the usual nor the most necessary aim of speech training in a democracy. Rather, such training is meant for all the citizens, the humble as well as the great, the followers as well as the leaders; and it is designed to make every one of them better able to participate in the workings of society and make contributions to it.

The ancient Greeks realized in their time, as we do now, that education in public speaking helps insure the successful workings of a society and contributes to the intellectual development of the individual. As the Greek teachers and philosophers maintained, universal speech training is an absolute necessity in a democracy, since the success of a democracy depends on the deliberations of the many rather than on the mandates of the few. It is not by accident that so many of the current textbooks in public speaking use the words *democracy* or *democratic* in stressing the values of public speaking, or that William N. Brigance subtitled his outstanding work in speech "Techniques and Disciplines in a Free Society." [3]

Speech Training Necessary for You.   You should not think of this course only in terms of such great speakers as Demosthenes, Cicero, Edmund Burke, William Jennings Bryan, Clarence Darrow, or Winston Churchill. Think of it also in terms of your high-school mathematics teacher delivering a slide lecture on her trip to Europe, the mechanical engineer explaining his complicated blueprints to an audience of shop foremen, the sales manager

[3] William Norwood Brigance, *Speech: Its Techniques and Disciplines in a Free Society* (New York: Appleton-Century-Crofts, Inc., 1961).

trying to whip up the enthusiasm of his salesmen, or the aroused citizen trying to persuade the city council not to pass a discriminatory zoning ordinance. Visualizing such applications may enable you to breathe a little easier about this course. Perhaps you can more easily visualize yourself in these roles.

Think of this course, too, as providing you with the opportunity to work with significant ideas and gain proficiency in communicating them well. The issues of our times should be matters of concern to each educated, thinking citizen of a democratic nation. Issues such as racial discrimination, world peace, disarmament, atomic testing, economic policy, social welfare, and human rights affect each individual profoundly. You need to care about them. You should acquire enough understanding of these problems to be able to talk about them, even though you may not now have the means to solve any of them. Time goes on, one generation replaces another, and the same or similar issues are still perplexing the world. The cumulative body of knowledge that comprises our civilization survives as it is communicated from one generation to another, and its persisting issues are understood, deliberated, and eventually solved, if they ever are to be, largely by means of men communicating with each other.

What You Will Gain

An Immediately Useful Tool. Even as a student, although admittedly you listen more than you speak, you do some speaking in public. If you think of every question you ask in class, as well as every answer you give and every comment you make as being—what they by all rights are—public speeches, the extent of your "public" speaking is considerable. Brief as each such contribution may be, its value in aiding your learning and that of the class (and sometimes even of the instructor) is immeasurable. Present as well as future success may be urged as a reason for studying public speaking. Oral reports that you are called upon to present in some of your courses and talks that you make in the organizations and clubs to which you belong present further opportunities for you to make this course pay immediate dividends.

A Part of Your General Education. Further, the study of public speaking comprises a necessary adjunct to your general education in an institution of higher learning. For it is one thing to understand an idea and quite another to be able to communicate it and thereby aid the understanding of others. Equally important is the need for intelligent listening that gives you not only the means to appreciate the contributions of the outstanding speakers you may be privileged to hear, but the everyday opportunity to understand better the thoughts and feelings of your fellowmen. One reason why a course in public speaking is required of students in so many colleges and universities is that those institutions realize the necessity for their graduates to communicate well and to understand the communication of others, if they are to succeed in whatever profession they enter. Another is that they realize full well that practice in intelligent speaking and listening is a necessary part of the entire intellectual development which is the aim of higher education.

Basic Training in Learning and Communication Skills.   In addition to accomplishing its specific purpose of making you a better speaker and listener, this course in public speaking can give you training so basic that it applies to much of the learning that you are doing and to every kind of communication that you attempt.

Whenever you give a speech in this course, you will be asking some 20 or more persons to give you their undivided time and attention. It is not a small thing to ask. To justify their doing it, you should have a message for them that is worth their time and effort. In producing a message of such worth, you will have to think long and hard in order to find the right subject for yourself, the audience, and the assignment, and to recall all that you presently know about it; you will have to observe and interview and read in order to expand your knowledge; you will have to rack your brain again in order to choose the right things to say in your speech and to organize them so that the audience will be able to follow you; you will have to rehearse aloud often enough to feel easy with your speech, your body, and your voice; and finally, while under the pressure of communicating to listeners in the same room with you, you will have to present the result of all your work and thought in a poised, vital, and winning manner, using the very best language, vocal expression, and bodily action you can command. Thus it can be seen that any speech that is well prepared and well presented provides rigorous exercise in original thought, the investigation and evaluation of the thought of others, the organization of ideas, and the communication of a message under unsettling circumstances. Thinking, investigating, evaluating, and organizing can be said to be the basic means by which all learning is accomplished. Moreover, the adjustments forced upon you by having to communicate under trying circumstances should result in general improvement of all your communication skills.

Personality Gains.   We have stressed that study in this course will add to your general knowledge, that it will be an asset to you as a professional person and a citizen, and that learning to speak well can help you greatly in your present educational career. There are some additional dividends to consider: substantial gains in self-confidence, and a measure of personality improvement. The addition to your knowledge about matters you already know and care about will come from preparing your own speeches; additions to your knowledge about other matters will come from hearing the speeches of your classmates. Both can increase your confidence in your ability and potential as a student.

Probably the only thing that can be said for certain about what will be accomplished in gaining further self-confidence is that, if you give the assigned speeches and always do your best job with them, you will be far more confident as a speaker and a person at the end of the course than you were at the beginning. The exceptions to this rule are so few as to be negligible. In its turn, increased self-confidence tends to have a salutary effect on the whole personality. The constant necessity of putting your best self forward in public speaking can also have a beneficial effect on your personality.

ATTITUDES AND SPECIAL PROBLEMS

What attitudes should you as a student of public speaking have in approaching that study? You may have dreaded taking the course, but most of you now expect that public speaking will be a valuable learning experience for you. Regardless of your past training or experience, you have already come a long way, and probably know much more about the study than you realize. What you now will be learning will in many ways culminate much of your previous knowledge, adding to it new dimensions that will continue to help you in years to come.

Public Speaking as a Natural Gift

We hope you are not now discouraged by the notion that the ability to speak well in public is a natural attribute that some have and others do not. Of course some students in your class may have more natural aptitude or may have already had more work and practice in public speaking than others; for these, the learning, at least at the start, may come easier. However, this could also be said about any of the subjects you are now taking. You do not often despair completely of ever learning anything about chemistry, history, or French. There is no more reason to despair in public speaking. Any person of ordinary intelligence, we submit, can through study and experience become an acceptable public speaker.

Even those with some special personality traits that make them more adaptable to the speaking platform begin only a very short step ahead of anyone else. Public speakers have to study their craft and have to practice long and hard at it to gain their competence. Those who do not have the advantage of getting speech instruction in a special course must learn the hard way, through trial and error and concentrated individual effort. Learn they must. Biographies of all great public speakers show that they have studied their art either in school or on their own. Intelligent speaking of the kind you will be doing in this course demands a great deal more than a knack for public speaking.

The same advice holds for those who, whether they possess special talent or not, might feel that their prior training and experience has given them special advantage. Previous experience and training in high school or in organizations should prove valuable, but it has not taught you everything that you need to know about speech. Even the greatest teachers and most proficient speakers of the past and present, nearing the ends of their careers, have admitted that they still had much to learn.

Unless handicapped by some physical or mental disability, everyone can speak. The ability to speak well is not an inborn talent nor is it gained by sudden inspiration. It is an art and a skill that is more complex than most arts and skills, and it must be learned through study and hard work.

Public Speaking as Social Control

Giles W. Gray and Claude M. Wise discuss differences between the functions of speech in "social integration," and "social control." [4] In one instance, they say, oral communication binds society together; speech is a vital part of human social behavior. In the other instance, oral communication becomes the means by which society functions. Speech is used to influence human social behavior, and thereby becomes an instrument through which society controls itself or is controlled. We can add to these two dimensions by suggesting a third: oral communication is also a means by which the civilization of a society perpetuates. We become educated in the sciences and arts, history, and customs that constitute our cultural traditions. We learn from the past as it communicates to us, and we contribute to the new traditions and learning now being communicated. The effects of this communication will be felt by generations to come. The great speeches of history are part of our cultural tradition; the ideas they contain have been perpetuated. However, the concern in this course is not with the history of public speaking, but with its present uses as a means of social control.

You have been talking most of your life, and most of what you have been saying and listening to has been used for social integration, for accom-

---

[4] Giles Wilkeson Gray and Claude Merton Wise, *The Bases of Speech* (New York: Harper & Brothers, 1959), pp. 21–24.

modating yourself to the society into which you were born. One of the first and primary ways by which you learned this social accommodation was through learning a common language, so that you could make your wants and feelings known to your family, neighbors, and playmates, and so that you learned to understand what they were thinking and feeling when they expressed themselves to you. Then, as you started to school, you began to acquire more formal knowledge of language and its uses mainly through learning to read and write. As your education progressed, you continued to learn the uses of language, mainly in its written form, and have gradually become acquainted with some of the writings that constitute part of our cultural tradition. This learning will continue during your college career and, it is hoped, will be an important part of your continuing education following graduation. Much of your learning about written communication has been in the so-called "practical" uses of language: finding out ways of expressing yourself clearly, accurately, and with some measure of style. This study has included first learning letters and words; then sentences and larger units; then spelling, syntax, and grammar; and then the various forms and styles of writing. Simultaneously you have learned to read, first becoming acquainted with words that constitute language, then with ideas contained in the literature you encountered.

What you have learned about oral communication, for the most part, has been less systematized. The greater part of the actual work done in the classroom has consisted of your listening to what the teacher has to say. From time to time you have responded by asking or answering questions, and there may also have been some group discussions or creative uses of speech in acting or reciting. Nevertheless, the greater part of your speech training has been incidental to the instruction in the various subjects to which you have been exposed.

However, the "socializing" nature of communication has continued as part of your total experience. Generally speaking, there is nothing most human beings like better than the chance to make known to others their thoughts and feelings about matters that affect their lives. Human communication is the principal way of socializing, of recognizing the identity of other human beings, and of being recognized by them. You use speech constantly not only in your everyday conversation, but in the everyday conducting of your affairs.

All of these experiences have contributed to what you now know about speech. Public speaking, you will discover, is in many respects nothing more than enlarged conversation. It is one of the most natural of human acts. Your present study, then, can be thought of as an opportunity to broaden the scope of your enjoyment of conversation. In a sense, you will be learning how to "converse" with many instead of just a few.

Yet in broadening the scope of your conversation, in making it public rather than private speaking, you should realize that you do give it different emphases. The public speaker's aim is not socializing or even just expressing himself. He expresses himself, yes, but for the purpose of exercising a degree of social control. He plays an active role, transmitting a specific message to a group of listeners in a deliberate effort to teach them something, or in some measure to influence their attitudes, beliefs, or subsequent actions.

The listener's role is the more passive one. His listening behavior places him at a different level from those who take part in conversation, yet he, having a mind of his own, becomes a judge of what is said, and the extent to which he is influenced depends largely on the degree of acceptance he accords the speaker and his message.

Your Present Resources in Public Speaking

What you are now about to learn about public speaking brings to a climax much of what you have learned so far. All your accumulated experiences in speaking with and listening to others will be drawn upon as you learn to speak in public. All you have learned or are presently learning in your college composition courses about language in its written form, including grammar and style, organization and outlining, and clear and accurate means of expressing ideas, will be of great value to you as you now begin communicating orally. All that you have learned, are now learning, and will be learning from your reading has contributed to your store of knowledge and will serve you well as resource material for your speeches. Whatever experiences you have had in public performance or in high-school speech instruction will also be most useful to you. It may be that the greater emphasis in your past learning and experience, whether it has been in report-giving, acting, debate, or speeches given in class, has been on "expressing yourself" well in public. This is only part of a public speaker's job, but it is an important part. Such learning should also serve you well.

THE STUDY DEFINED

Of the two principal means of communication, oral and written, the first is by far the more common. Ralph G. Nichols and Leonard A. Stevens report studies of the time spent by the average person in sending and receiving messages.[5]

[5] Ralph G. Nichols and Leonard A. Stevens, *Are You Listening?* (New York: McGraw-Hill Book Company, Inc., 1957), pp. 6 ff.

The greatest portion of time is spent in listening, the next in speaking; comparatively little total time is spent in reading or writing. Certainly, although speaking and listening occupy a far greater proportion of time than writing or reading, the generally higher levels of artistry and profundity possible in written communication, as well as its permanence, make it at least as important as oral communication. But the irony is obvious: we study least extensively and systematically that means of communication which we use the most and which ordinarily has the greatest effect upon our lives. Although writing is probably more permanent and exact, being a more "fixed" means of communication, the recipients of the message are seldom physically present. The communication is far less personal. In oral communication, the recipients are usually physically present. The principle of "confrontation," a term discussed by Gray and Wise,[6] means that functions of speaking and listening blend together in an immediate, dynamic process of communication; the speaker and listener both contribute simultaneously to the process of oral communication.

We can thus see that speech is both a type and a process of human communication. The elements of oral communication are the *speaker*, including his resources of knowledge, thought, and feeling, his management of materials, and his instruments of voice and action; the medium of language that conveys the *message* of the speech; and the reception of the speech on the part of the *listeners*. These elements, when combined in an action of coinstantaneous speaking and listening through which meaning is transmitted, constitute the particular human behavior we call speech. They apply fundamentally to all speaking and listening, including that done in private conversation, discussion, oral reading, acting, and public speaking.

Public speaking is a special kind of oral communication: one particular speaker communicating purposefully a particular message to a particular group of listeners. The speaker is the sender, the audience is the recipient. By *purposeful* communication we mean that the speaker communicates his thoughts and feelings in order to get a response. He employs the total behavior of speech that includes thought, feeling, voice, action, and language in order to transmit a message to a group of listeners. Their listening behavior includes the sensory perceptions of hearing and seeing, their thought (comprehension and interpretation) and feeling, and their retention of the message. The kind of response given by the listeners determines the degree of the speaker's success. If the response is in accord with what he intended to achieve, his communication has been successful.

Details about preparation and performance, about responsibilities and measurements of success or failure, about values and judgments, all of which

[6] Gray and Wise, *op. cit.*, pp. 24–35.

are part of public speaking, are developed throughout this book. Throughout, public speaking is considered a useful art, one that requires continuing study, skill, and practice.

NATURE OF THE COURSE

For most of you a course in public speaking is an entirely new experience. However, you need not fear it. It can and most probably will be pleasurable for you. We assume that most of you have had little or no formal training in the preparation and delivery of speeches and perhaps even less experience speaking in public. So it is that this course begins with simple, relatively undemanding assignments. As you gain in knowledge and skill, however, the assignments become increasingly difficult and exacting. You are expected to improve as a speaker because literally millions of other students who have come before you have demonstrated that, with reasonable effort, you can do so. Lack of significant progress in the course is an almost sure sign that you have not worked to the limits of your ability. Everyone is expected to improve. There has never been a perfect speaker; each one of you can stand improvement.

One thing likely to make this course pleasant will be the relative informality characteristic of a class in public speaking. The course is essentially a laboratory course. While there may be some formalities similar to what you experience in so-called lecture courses, the greater part of the learning you accomplish comes from your own direct participation. In your class sessions, you will get to know your instructor and your fellow students as you seldom get to know them in other classes, and you should make friends and learn a great deal about people in the process. In these sessions, too, you and your fellow students will do most of the talking; your instructor will guide you, not force upon you his ideas about the content of what you should say or listen to.

Responsibility is Stressed

A public speaking course, however, would have little educational value if enjoyment were its sole object. Greater satisfaction will come from doing a difficult job well.

A rather common and most unfortunate misunderstanding about the nature of a course in public speaking is that it is merely the study and practice of the skills of performance. Some misguided speech training, it is true, stresses just that. In many commercial "success" courses in public speaking the emphasis is on the polished performance, the message of the speech being purely incidental. Speech training need not be and often is not of this kind, fortunately. While delivery of a speech—the use of voice and action—is important, the lasting effect of a speech depends more on the value of what is said. A speaker must learn to use voice and bodily action well so that he can communicate significant ideas to others. Good modern speech training is not satisfied with teaching you to say nothing gracefully. While this textbook, your instructor, and your experiences in the speech class will endeavor to improve your speech delivery, they will also aim at improving the quality of your materials, your thought, and your language.

Also unlike the commercial "success" courses in public speaking, this one does not guarantee you the moon. We are realistic enough to realize that you cannot become an accomplished public speaker in ten easy lessons. The lessons are many more than ten, they are not all learned in a classroom, and they are anything but easy. In this course we will stress your lifelong responsibility to continue learning the skills of public speaking and, more importantly, the knowledge and wisdom that those skills will be used to communicate.

Still another way in which we differ from "success" courses is that we abhor the idea that speech should be learned as a tool by which you manipulate the minds of others to your own personal advantage. Such hypocritical use of public speaking is misuse. We believe that the speaker has at all times a moral obligation to his listeners to inform them on matters and direct them toward courses of action which he sincerely believes will benefit them. Throughout this course, the recognition of your social responsibility will be stressed.

Unscrupulous individuals realize that speech is a powerful tool for manipulating the minds of men and use it to that end. This fact argues all the more strongly for learning about speech. Just as Aristotle, hundreds of years ago, described public speaking at its highest level as a means of giving effective voice to the truth, and as the Roman rhetorician, Quintilian, emphasized the necessity of the orator being the "good man skilled in speaking," so we today should realize the necessity of concerning ourselves with the values and consequences of what we say. If good is to win out over evil, it should have every weapon that the enemy has, and preferably better weapons. The surgeon's scalpel can be used for murder, but we do not outlaw it for that reason. An announcer using his speech skills to extol the virtues of brand Z cigarettes over brand X can make anyone distrustful of those skills. But skillful speaking can be used to sell sound ideas as well as menthol cigarettes. The ethics of public speaking is part of our study. The speaker must learn to assume responsibility for what he says, just as the listener must learn to take responsibility for accepting or rejecting what he hears. Learning public speaking is not just learning to say something, not just learning to say something well, but learning also that the honesty and truth of what is said is as much a part of the judgment of a speech as of a speaker.

We want you to be challenged. We want you to culminate your learning the particular uses of oral communication in the public speaking situation, and further to broaden your horizons of acquaintance with new ideas and significant issues with which to challenge the thinking of others.

Extemporaneous Speaking is Stressed

One thing we most especially do *not* want you to do in beginning public speaking is to write out your speech word for word and deliver it from memory or manuscript. Most of the public speaking done today is done extemporaneously; that is, with the speaker, after having made careful preparations, going to the platform knowing exactly what ideas he is going to develop in his speech, in what order he will bring them up, and how he will develop them, but trusting in some measure to the inspiration of the moment for the wording he will use. Many contemporary public speakers have found that while their language may suffer a bit in extemporaneous presentation, this mode of delivery is preferable for most occasions. It is certainly, of the modes calling for advance preparations, the one in which the speaker is best able to achieve spontaneity and a strong sense of communication, both of which are essential aspects of delivery.

Impromptu speaking, the kind of spontaneous speaking done with little or no warning and no advance systematic preparation, does subject a speaker to a severe test of his ability to think on his feet and to gain effective communication simultaneously. However, its uses are limited, and the occasions for it as public speaking are few indeed. Although Optional Unit A calls for some impromptu speaking, all the other speeches of this course require thorough and extensive preparation.

Since all of this is true, the only mode of delivery that will be used or that is acceptable for the principal units of this course is what is called the extemporaneous mode. Speeches are not to be memorized, read from manuscript, or thought up on the spur of the moment.

Coordinated Learning is Stressed

You will be doing considerable writing in this course, and considerable reading as well. Writing is involved in your preparation of speeches as well as in examinations and in reporting on speeches you have heard. Examinations assure both you and you instructor that you are gaining the knowledge of speech-making which can be found in a textbook, knowledge which, if employed, will help to make you a better speaker. Written outlines are assigned because they require you to go through the extensive and too often avoided task of thinking about the materials of a speech before giving it. One purpose of writing reports on speeches that you hear is to give you additional exercises in mastering speech essentials. You learn from carefully observing the successes and failures of others, determining the causes of success or failure, and then either copying or avoiding that which you saw and heard done. Another purpose of these reports is that in them your training for listening is possibly best realized. Reading assignments, outlines, and reports of speeches are all geared to aid your growth as a public speaker and as a member of an audience. They are meant to coordinate with your speaking and listening so as to enrich your learning of those skills. That is why they are part of this course and also why they figure significantly in the determination of your grade. Should you neglect them, your instructor will have every right to assume that you have not made the progress you could and should have made in the course.

A FINAL WORD

We ask then, that you approach this course with an open mind as a new, exciting, and rewarding experience that will be greatly beneficial to you now and in your later life; that you ignore as well as you can whatever misconceptions you or others may have had about the study and practice of public speaking; that you realize at this time that you are adding to your knowledge of oral communication as a means of social control that you can master with diligent study and practice; and that you look forward to a strong beginning in gaining confidence in yourself and in the ideas with which you deal. By so doing, you can make your entire experience both pleasurable and challenging.

   This book is designed to aid you in your development as a speaker. Its major purpose is to save instructional time and avoid student confusion. Here in quick reference form are the basic materials you will need to guide you through the various assignments in the course.

   Included here you will find, for each unit of your course, background discussion of the various assignments, instructions for the preparation and presentation of speeches you are asked to give, and supplementary materials for evaluation of your speeches and speeches you report on. Together with what your instructor tells you and what is discussed in your class meetings, these materials can provide a well-coordinated learning experience.

This book and the course you are taking in public speaking have been constructed to help you become a more effective and persuasive speaker and a more conscientious and critical listener. Whatever the instructor and the class can do for you they will. But the rest, the most important part, is squarely up to you.

Optional Unit A

Introductory Practice

BACKGROUND

For most people the most difficult thing about any new project they attempt is to get started on it. The initial impetus needed to "get the ball rolling" is a scarce commodity; ordinarily, once the ball does get a push, it quickly gathers momentum and very soon is traveling entirely under its own power. Since the study of beginning public speaking is no exception to this general rule, the majority of those who teach it waste no time getting the student started in his learning. Within the first week of the course, sometimes even during the initial class meeting, they have their students up on their feet giving brief speeches.

This procedure can have its drawbacks as well as its advantages, the chief of these being the inability of the student to do a thorough job of speech preparation. To circumvent this difficulty, the assignment options in this unit are specifically designed to be manageable on short notice, or possibly on no notice at all. They have been made relatively simple and undemanding so that, even with minimal time for preparation, you should be able to do a quite satisfactory job on them.

We would not want to mislead you into thinking that any of the speeches of this unit, in and of themselves, are common in public speaking. Impromptu speaking, which to some degree you will almost certainly be doing, is not often called for in the everyday speech situations. True, there are times when you have to give a speech on very short notice, and more frequent occasions when you add impromptu remarks to a prepared speech; but for

17

the most part you are given ample time for preparation and are expected to use it.

Purposes of the Assignment

That is not to say, however, that the speech you give cannot have value for your public speaking training beyond that of "getting the ball rolling." You will notice that all of the assignment options are alike in one respect: the basic ingredient of your speaking effort is a story or anecdote from your own personal experience. One obvious advantage of such an assignment is that you can gain experience in using a type of speech material that you will often find helpful for developing points that you want to make in your speeches. Another, possibly even greater virtue, however, is that in giving your speech and hearing the speeches of others you may become alert to what we shall call the "personal equation" in public speaking.

The Personal Equation in Public Speaking

The personal equation is a unique distinguishing feature of oral as opposed to written communication. There is always impersonality in written forms of communication, and especially so in those designed for public consumption. Always the writer, whether he wishes to or not, wears a mask. The speaker can also wear a mask, of course, but it is much more difficult for him to do so and infinitely less desirable that he should. Public speaking is a direct personal relationship of one human being with others. There is no intervening agency of paper and ink. Most often the persons to whom the speaker is presenting the speech are in the same room with him; and even when they are not, as in radio or television speaking, his means of communicating his message are the same. Always the speaker conveys his message through his own person—his voice, his movement and gestures, and his personality as it is both consciously and unconsciously revealed. While it is very often neither possible, necessary, nor desirable for the writer to reveal himself as a person, it is almost universally possible, necessary, and desirable for the speaker to do so.

Most of your training in communication has been as a writer rather than as a speaker. For that reason you may be handicapped in your speaking by notions of what is proper and what is improper that, applicable as they might be to writing an essay, are completely inadvisable for giving a speech. If so, you will have to learn that not only is the speaker *allowed* to talk about himself and his activities, his thoughts and his feelings, his knowledge and his ignorance, his attitudes and beliefs, his loves and his hates; he is *impelled* to do so by the nature of the form of communication he is using.

One of the things you will have to learn is that the personal pronouns— "I," "me," "myself," "you," "yourself," "we," "us," and "ourselves"—that you so conscientiously learned to avoid in your writing will have to be put back into your speaking. In oral communication expressions of personal involvement are perfectly proper. Unless you say "I feel this way; and I want you to feel that way, too; and I think that together we can get the job done by doing thus and so," you are not really using oral communication. It must be done in even the most formal speeches. Right now go over what you remember of Lincoln's Gettysburg Address in your mind and listen for the numerous uses of "we," "you," and "us."

"Do you mean I should talk about myself?" The question is often asked of speech instructors by beginning public speakers, the incredulity in the voice almost equalling what would be there if the question were, "Do you mean I should be a sinner?" The answer is a resounding "Yes!" There are reservations and qualifications to be made on that "yes," certainly, but for most beginning public speakers, they are not nearly so important as the assurance that your audience is interested in you as a person, in what you have done, what you know, and what you stand for. They do not want the feeling that you are reciting an essay to them; they want the feeling that you, a unique individual, are conversing with them about a significant matter of mutual interest, giving them the benefit of your knowledge and views.

The audience, as well as the speaker, is part of the personal equation in public speaking. Not only must the speaker reveal himself as an individual; he must also think of his audience as individuals, and act accordingly. The writer can and most often does address a "general" audience. For the speaker the audience is always particular. You must learn that as a speaker you do not just broadcast for anybody who might be interested; that instead you design your message to convey that part of what you know, think, and believe which will be most applicable and beneficial to your particular group of listeners. They are there as persons, and they usually want to be and always need to be treated as such. If your listeners are wearing masks, try through the personal nature of your communication to have them very soon drop them. And if they are not wearing masks, do not in your own mind put them on them. If you see masks in your imagination, they will soon be there in actuality.

THE ASSIGNMENT

This unit is designed to do three things: to help you to feel at ease in front of a group, to alert you to the personal equation in public speaking, and to give you training in the use of the story or anecdote drawn from your own personal experience. The experience or experiences which you relate should be chosen for their ability to reveal your personality to your listeners. They should be presented in a way that gives your audience an insight into what you are like. You should, in short, "explain" yourself to your audience by narrating an incident or incidents in which your behavior was typical of your essential personality.

One or more of the following options may be given you for choice of a speech subject in this unit:

Option A: Free Choice.   You may choose to relate any personal story or anecdote so long as it fits the general requirements of the assignment outlined above.

✓ *Option B: The Speech of Self-Introduction.*   You will give a short introduction of yourself to the class, the principal component of which will be a revelatory story or anecdote from your own experience.

Option C: The Impromptu Speech on a Suggested Topic.   Your instructor will suggest topics for short, "spur-of-the-moment" speeches, or he will ask you to make such a talk on your pet peeve or your reaction to some phase of college life. No matter what the precise nature of the assignment may be, remember that once again you are being asked to relate a story or anecdote that tells something about you.

Option D: The Discussion.   Your instructor will assign a topic for discussion in class that will call mainly for contributions from your own personal experience, or he will ask you to devise such a topic. A single discussion may take place with the whole class as the discussion group, or there may be several shorter discussions by separate small groups. Your contributions to the discussion will be miniature speeches of an impromptu nature. You will endeavor to be completely frank in stating your thoughts and beliefs; and you will further try, whenever possible, to illustrate your points with pertinent stories and anecdotes from your own experience.

Option E: Instructor's Assignment.   In order that your assignment may better suit the needs of your particular class, your instructor may choose to modify one of the above assignment options, combine features of two or more of them into one assignment, or possibly give you an assignment entirely of his own devising.

PREPARING THE SPEECH

Choose an Experience to Relate

Your first impulse on being instructed to give a speech about a past personal experience will probably be to look to the most singular and exciting events of your life for your subject. This impulse should be stifled. Such experiences may provide excellent supporting material for other speeches you will give, but the special condition of this assignment is that the experience be one in which your essential personality is revealed. Most of us are not our ordinary selves in the extraordinary situations, but quite literally another person. The time you rescued the child from drowning, or earned a trophy, or won the football game in the last five seconds was a time when you were a more unselfish, attractive, capable, or courageous person than you habitually are. You were then *extraordinary;* what your audience wants to know about is the *ordinary* you.

But if I do not tell about such an event, you say, how can I make my speech interesting? Think a moment. In your everyday conversations with your friends and acquaintances, do you listen to what they have to say only when they are speaking about romantic adventures in faraway lands and thrilling last-minute escapes from impending disaster? Not at all. Their ordinary experiences are interesting to you just because they are so like your own. An audience listening to you speak is in no way different. Whether it should be so or not, a speaker will usually get completely undivided attention from his listeners only when he is telling them about the human interest details of his own life. Of course, more solid materials than that are essential for worthwhile public speaking, but that relative trivia (to use the very worst possible term for it) is usually also necessary if the public speaking is to be interesting and worthwhile.

You will want to make your speech, brief and hastily prepared as it might be, as worthwhile as you can. How can you talk about everyday matters and avoid complete triviality? Again we ask you to think a little bit. Is any knowledge you gain about the personality of another person really trivial? Does it not always tell you more about the world in which you live and sometimes also tell you something about yourself? Can you not provide a worthwhile service for your listeners by a conscientious effort dedicated to giving them insight into your personality? Choose not just any ordinary experience of your life, then, but one that can give illustration of you at your normal best or worst.

Decide on the Point to be Made

Your story or anecdote should have a point. Anything you say or do in a speech you give should have a point. Speakers are successful in spite of extraneous material they drag into their speeches, not because of it. Certainly the whole speaking effort should not be extraneous. You may or may not state the point of your story or anecdote to your audience—you may very well want them to get it themselves rather than be told it in so many words—but you should be clear in your own mind about what that point is. The time to start thinking about the point is not while you are giving the speech, but just as soon as you have decided on the experience that you are going to use as your speech subject.

Eliminate the Unimportant Details

Undoubtedly the most universal and quite possibly the most deadly fault of storytelling, oral or written, is lack of selectivity. Why do you avoid Mrs. Brown whenever you can? It is not that she always tells you about her latest visit to the doctor, but that she "bends your ear" for an hour telling you about every single, blessed, last detail of that visit.

No story you tell is ever as interesting to the listener as it is to you. To make it interesting to your audience, you should eliminate those details that bog down and confuse the story. If you are telling about a camping experience, it is not necessary to start with the ringing of the alarm clock on the day of departure and end with your return home, chronologically narrating every minor happening of the entire weekend. Pick out the big moment or moments to talk about.

Paradoxically, when you do that, details much more minor than the ones you have eliminated become very interesting and important to your story. An audience will listen avidly to your description of every sight, sound, aroma, taste or touch sensation, feeling, or thought connected with the big moment, while cursory narration of many minor moments along with the big one will be deadly dull to them.

Tell the Story in an Interesting Way

One way to make your speech interesting is to put as much of yourself into it as you possibly can. You cannot neglect to tell what others may have thought or said or done if they are essential to the story, but as much as possible make it *your* story, told from *your* point of view. Do not delay in using the personal pronouns "I," "me," and "myself." Since you are the one that is talking, it is you that the audience wants to know about.

Almost any anecdote or story is the better for a little suspense. If you can get your listeners to wonder until the very end about the outcome of the incident and to worry all along the way about what is going to happen next, you are on your way to becoming an excellent storyteller, for that is one of the essential techniques. The devices by which you will create suspense we will leave to your own ingenuity, but we will suggest that all such devices create questions that the listener worries about until they are resolved by the storyteller. Suspense is not an ingredient only of great tales of adventure; it is one of the inherent qualities of our life that makes that life as interesting as it is. Suspense, in the last analysis, conditions every breath we take. There may not be a next one.

Storytelling makes use of exposition, description, narration, and dramatization. Most writers of stories are sparing in their use of the first two, and use more dramatization than narration. The practice of avoiding exposition and description whenever possible is a good one for the oral storyteller to emulate, but he is ordinarily better off reversing the writer's practice in regard to dramatization and narration. It is extremely difficult in oral storytelling, unless one is a consummate actor, to sustain a dramatized development of any length. Too often the characters speaking get mixed up, or a seemingly endless number of "he said's" and "she said's" result. Dramatization, or acting out everything the persons did and said, should be reserved for the climactic moments of the story, with narration, or the detailing of the time progression of the major actions and impressions, being the primary means used to build up to the climaxes.

Exposition and description cannot be dispensed with entirely. You will have to make some explanation of why the event took place, or why some people acted as they did, or why it was impossible to solve your problem in the ordinary way. Not only make such exposition as brief as possible; make it as clear as possible. Some of these matters may be so obvious to you that you are offhand in your explanation; remember always that your listeners will not know anything that you do not tell them. As for description, you will have to satisfy them with the dominant impression. You cannot go into great detail, both because you do not have time and because your audience may lose interest and fail to take it all in.

Finally, all else will fail if you are not vitally interested in the story as you present it. Look at the audience; actually want to tell them about yourself; live the experience yourself and so make it come alive for them.

Review of Preparation

1. Choose not necessarily the most exciting event of your life to talk about, but the one that you feel best shows you as you really are.
2. Decide on the point you are going to make to your listeners with the story or anecdote you tell.
3. Eliminate the unimportant details and concentrate on the big moment or moments of the story.
4. Tell the story in an interesting way by making it *your* story, by creating suspense, by using narration as your principal means of storytelling, by presenting exposition clearly and limiting description to the dominant impression, and by delivering it to your audience in a vital manner.

Unit I

The Single-Unit Speech

BACKGROUND

Which is more important, what you say or how you say it? Does the speaker's greater obligation belong to his subject matter or to the speech techniques by which he communicates it? This question could probably be most easily answered by saying that both are equally important, and one cannot really be separated from the other.

Let us say at the start, then, that you share equally both of these obligations as a speaker: you want to speak effectively, and you also want to be a competent spokesman for sound and substantial subject matter. Were you to become a skillful speaker with little or nothing of merit to talk about, your education in public speaking would be sadly lacking. Yet were you to have brilliant and vital ideas to impart without the ability to express them in a manner that would interest and move your listeners, you would be no public speaker at all.

We can approach the matter of how you can begin to fulfill these obligations by first describing some tasks that derive from your relationship with your materials, then outlining other tasks resulting from your relationships with your listeners, and finally discussing still other tasks instigated by the relationship of your own personality to the particular speech situation. These tasks are not confined to the assignment in Unit I alone, but carry through in each speaking assignment of the course. Principally they are jobs of analysis.

Analysis of the Material

What do you analyze? For one thing the subject matter and materials with which you deal. Many centuries ago Aristotle said that the main requirement in speaking is to state a point, then prove it. This teaching still holds, and not only for the public speaker, but for anyone endeavoring to communicate. Just saying a thing is so does not make it so. The communicator must elaborate—he must have the willingness and the ability to present additional materials in support of every statement he makes that is not absolutely clear or completely worthy of belief. This is the process that William Norwood Brigance calls "amplifying an assertion." [1]

The speaker should not be speaking unless he is able to provide adequate support for each of the points he makes. If his audience is not likely to understand the point, the speaker must present explanation. If the audience has not seen the person or place or thing that the speaker is talking about—at least in the way that the speaker wants them to see it—he must describe it. If the listeners believe there is no problem contained in the subject matter of the speech, the speaker must cite either examples of its existence or an authoritative statement that the problem exists. And so it goes. Every statement of any importance that the speaker makes must be backed up in some way. Of such significance to good public speaking is this basic precept that the primary purpose of your first major assignment in beginning public speaking is to teach it to you.

Yet you have an additional obligation to your listeners. The problem of gaining and holding their friendly attention is one of the most persistent and troublesome ones you face as a public speaker. It is one of the most important ones, too, for it stands to reason that, if the audience does not listen, your speaking effort is wasted. While audiences are expected to and will make considerable effort to pay attention to what you are saying, they will not do all the work. It is your job to make your ideas as clear and interesting as you possibly can. That accomplished, the audience will take over. Alan H. Monroe calls the first in a "motivated sequence" of steps by which the speaker adapts to potential listeners' responses, the "attention step." [2]

So it is that from the very beginning of this course—in this very first assignment—we ask you to concentrate on analyzing what will serve to clarify your ideas and draw attention to your speech and to apply the knowledge you gain from this analysis. This teaching is a secondary purpose of Unit I.

[1] William Norwood Brigance, *Speech: Its Techniques and Disciplines in a Free Society* (New York: Appleton-Century-Crofts, Inc., 1961), pp. 49 ff.
[2] Alan H. Monroe, *Principles and Types of Speech* (Chicago: Scott, Foresman and Company, 1962), pp. 280 ff.

Analysis of the Audience

You should also analyze the audience and the occasion, of course. What do you do in the light of this analysis? Basically, you state your points in such a way that they will be clear, interesting, and memorable for the particular audience you are addressing; you choose the precise supporting materials to interest, inform, or convince them; you organize and word your speech in such a way that they can follow your thinking; and you deliver it in a manner that will be pleasing to them.

All audiences and all occasions are alike in some ways, and each is distinctive in others. The audience you have in this course will in one sense be unlike any other you will ever speak to. This audience is here mainly to learn along with you some of the basic principles and techniques of public speaking. Audiences you eventually will be speaking to will be in attendance mainly to hear what you or others on the program have to say, and will have different goals and interests from those of your "practice" audience. You need to learn both about audiences and occasions in general and about each audience and occasion in particular. We can make only suggestions for "handling" audiences and occasions in general; no one but the speaker can determine the adjustments that he will need to make for a particular audience and occasion. Your speech class audience will be a good one to work with. Remember that their interests and goals are practically the same as yours. Remember too that all audiences on all occasions tend to react favorably to:

1. Subjects that are shown to them to be significant and interesting.
2. Speeches that are organized and worded in such a way that they can be easily followed from point to point.
3. Speakers who give evidence of wanting to communicate with them. (This shows up in the way the speaker picks supporting materials that seem to be meant for them and gauges his language to their level of understanding and appreciation, his concentration on them during his speech, and the apparent sincerity and vitality he shows as he tries to communicate.)

Analysis of Yourself

Often surprising to the student of beginning public speaking is the knowledge that to function well as a speaker he needs to analyze himself as well as his subject matter and his audience. The wise speaker, realizing that he is the most important single element of the oral communication process, does a job of self-analysis as part of his preparation for every speech. He endeavors to discover exactly what is "going for him" and what is not. Among other things, he evaluates the extent of his interest in, knowledge of, and opportunity to learn more about his subject. He measures his present public speaking skills; his present physical, mental, and emotional capacities; and his present degree of self-confidence against the demands of the speech situation. On the basis of this analysis, he gauges the nature and amount of preparation that it will be necessary for him to make.

For this first major assignment, whether it should be or not, your greatest concern of self-analysis will probably be with your confidence, or rather, your seeming lack of it. Nearly every beginning speaker is concerned that the audience might react unfavorably toward him. An extensive study conducted at the University of Kansas indicated that beginning college speech students rate gaining self-confidence as one of their most important goals.[3] Certainly one of your earliest problems and the one that may seem most important to you right now is that of nervousness about the prospect of getting up before a group to speak. Nearly everyone feels a certain amount of "stage fright" as he nears the time to speak. Various studies have been made of this common phenomenon, many of which are reported by Milton Dickens.[4] These studies reveal some of the more constant aspects of what constitutes stage fright. Nervousness is your body's reaction to your knowledge that you are about to face an extraordinary situation. You experience a similar feeling on the first date with a special someone, when applying for an important job, waiting your turn in a contest, going to the dentist, or any time you are apprehensive about the unknown. Of course, once the dreaded event actually takes place, it loses much of its dreadful aspect, and can even be enjoyable. So it will be with this first speech. And the more speeches you give, the less frightening will the prospective one seem.

All of you are probably familiar with the physical symptoms of stage fright: the tensions, perspiration, shortness of breath, rapid heart beat, and odd feeling in the pit of the stomach. These are physiological reactions to a mental attitude that can be identified more easily than it can be overcome. Such nervousness is a natural, normal reaction, and the other first speakers in your class feel it as much or maybe even more than you do. Accept it as the first stage speakers go through in gaining self-confidence; realize that your first goal is not to eliminate it but to control it.

The attitude we referred to is more one made up of a complex of various fears and misgivings than one having a single, identifiable source. The speaker, even though he knows he has to be the center of attention for a

---

[3] E. C. Buehler and Wil A. Linkugel, *Speech: A First Course* (New York: Harper & Brothers, 1962), pp. 28 ff.
[4] Milton Dickens, *Speech: Dynamic Communication* (New York: Harcourt, Brace & World, Inc., 1963), pp. 25 ff.

time whether he likes it or not, does not want to be the center of unfavorable attention—no one does. And so he may fear, in varying degrees, failure, adverse criticism, forgetfulness, inadequacy, and the show of nervousness—fear of the evidences of his own fright. Whatever the cause, our concern is dealing with the immediate problem. It may be helpful to know that others have the same problem and are as sympathetic with you as you are with them, and that being keyed up is not only normal but useful to you in the circumstance of giving a speech. Successful speaking, after all, requires a great amount of mental, nervous, and physical energy. Yet the problems you have are highly individual ones—ones that concern you right now, that you must live with, deal with, and overcome. For these difficulties, experience is the best cure.

But you surely want more specific advice than that. Unfortunately we cannot presume to write out a prescription for you as a medical doctor might prescribe a nerve tonic to be taken thirty minutes before each speech. We can, though, make some observations that should be helpful, observations based upon experiences of other speakers who began just as you are beginning.

Adequate preparation helps. When you are confident of your material, you have greater chance of being confident of yourself. If you have chosen a worthwhile subject, found supporting materials of a high caliber and selected from them the very best, organized the speech into a meaningful pattern, worded it well, and rehearsed the speech aloud several times, you have a sure knowledge that you are as ready as possible to face the situation. You can then be free of distracting thoughts and concentrate on how well you are getting your ideas across to a friendly, attentive audience. Such concentration will help tensions disappear. Most experienced speakers agree that there is nothing like solid preparation to make them feel at ease on the platform.

Part of your preparation can be psychological, too. If you can work toward building a positive attitude about your task, it will compete with and help crowd out negative attitudes that could hamper your efforts. Brigance calls public speaking "enlarged conversation." [5] Thinking of your audience not as your enemy but as your friends, whom you will approach and speak directly to as you would in everyday conversation, will help put you in the right frame of mind. Yet there is something you should really be afraid of: the possibility of failure to communicate to your listeners. If you do not achieve the purpose of your speech, if the audience does not grasp the central idea and what you say to develop it, then you have a real cause for alarm. Worry about this possibility of failure rather than about yourself, and your energies will be directed toward constructive ends, your tensions will be put to proper use. Getting well acquainted with your classmates and

[5] Brigance, *op. cit.*, p. 76.

talking over your problems with them and with your instructor will be helpful, too, in psychologically preparing for the up-coming assignment.

On the day on which you are scheduled to speak, go to the front of the room with as much confidence as you can muster, breathing as deeply and regularly as you can, pause before beginning to speak, looking directly at your audience, smile, then start with your first sentence. Doing these things should help calm you down. While you are speaking, think of speaking to individuals rather than to a mass of blank faces blended together in a frightening confrontation. Then, as you concentrate on your subject and your listeners, you will find that the ordeal was not as bad as you imagined it would be.

Understanding and applying these techniques of psychological adjustment to the speaking situation as a first step in gaining self-confidence is the third thing we want you to achieve in this assignment.

Preparing the Speech

Every public speech is a work of art, the composing and delivering of which demands creative effort. Please do not misunderstand. Speech is not a decorative art that aims only to please the listeners, but rather a useful art that aims to influence their behavior. There is also another way in which speaking differs from the usual concept of artistic creation. A painter or sculptor exhibits his product as his own creation, but a speaker expressing his ideas is in a real sense both the creator and the creation. Not only is he identified with his message, but his whole being—his thoughts, attitudes, language, voice, and action—become essential parts of the communication of his message.

The ancient Roman teacher, Quintilian, said many centuries ago:

> That speech is an art may be proved in a very few words. If the definition be accepted that art is a power reaching its ends by a definite path, that is, by ordered methods, no one can doubt there is such method and order in good speaking.[6]

He went on to state that speech as an art serves a useful end. The necessity of using "ordered methods" is also borne out in modern teaching and practice.[7]

---

[6] Adapted from *The Institutes of Oratory*, Vol. II, p. 17.
[7] Waldo W. Braden and Mary Louise Gehring, *Speech Practices: A Resource Book for the Student of Public Speaking* (New York: Harper & Brothers, 1958) illustrates how contemporary speakers and those of the past century went about preparing their speeches. Details of their methods varied, but similar basic steps of preparation were used.

Similarities to the steps in planning works of art may be observed, although the creation of a public speech has distinctive requirements and qualifications of its own. A painter must plan his painting, starting with an idea and assembling materials, then execute the painting, which becomes something of an end in itself as a work of art. A builder of a public building begins with an idea and a reason to build, assembles materials, then, by following a blueprint, constructs a building which is to be used by others.

A speaker, too, needs to plan. Unlike the painter, a speaker uses himself as part of his creation and has an audience present to receive the benefits of his efforts immediately. The speaker's creation, like that of the builder, is essentially a useful art, not a creation to be admired for its aesthetic qualities alone. But unlike the builder, the speaker works entirely with resources of thought and feeling and gains a response from the "users" of his creation that includes the thinking and feeling of his listeners.

The speaker begins with an idea and a reason to communicate it to others. He draws upon resources from within and outside himself, then, after assembling these materials, composes his message, rehearses it, and finally delivers it to a group of listeners. Preparation is a necessity, and the quality of that preparation has direct bearing upon the quality of the end result. It holds that the speaker must concern himself with his message and also with his means of communicating it to a particular audience on a particular occasion. These concerns help govern the planning which goes into his preparation.

The specific steps of preparation you go through will vary somewhat with each speaking assignment. For the assignment in Unit I they will be comparatively simple, but they will become increasingly complex as the assignments become more difficult. We can say that the preparation involved for the Unit I speech, the speeches in later units, and, indeed, for any speech you give, involves certain basic stages of accomplishment. These are listed briefly as:

1. Becoming thoroughly acquainted with the subject matter and materials that will eventually be drawn upon in constructing a speech.
2. Analyzing the particular audience and occasion so that you can adapt specific subject matter to both audience and occasion in order to accomplish a specific purpose.
3. Constructing a speech by organizing and wording a message consistent with your knowledge and your analysis of audience and occasion.
4. Preparing yourself to speak by becoming thoroughly acquainted with the message you have constructed and by rehearsing it aloud in order to practice delivery.

Each of these stages must be accomplished if you are to be adequately prepared. For this and each succeeding unit of this course that includes a public speaking assignment, we shall give suggestions for your speech preparation, grouping the more specific steps of preparation for each particular assignment under four general headings and adding to their specifications additional ways of dealing with the increasingly complex kinds of speaking situations that you will be undertaking in subsequent assignments. These are the headings:

1. Subject and Materials
2. Application to Audience and Occasion
3. Construction of the Speech
4. Preparation for Delivery

In preparing the speech for this unit you will need to choose a subject, find and select materials for the speech, then analyze the subject matter and materials in light of what you have learned. Next, you will need to analyze the audience and occasion—a continuing and all-pervasive step that will influence the remainder of your preparation, since your analysis will condition every choice that you make from the time you understand the nature of the assignment until you have finished delivering the speech. The next task will be to compose a message, which means essentially organizing it and selecting and using the language that will best convey the ideas it contains. The final task will be to familiarize yourself with the message and rehearse aloud in order to aid your memory and to begin to acquire some of the skills of delivery to be used when you deliver the speech before your audience.

THE ASSIGNMENT

Make a Single Point

The speaking assignment for this unit is to prepare and present a brief single-unit speech which should gain and hold attention. The single-unit speech should accomplish the clear statement of a single point and its development. For this assignment you are free to choose any assertion of fact or opinion as the general statement of your speech, and to expand upon it by using supporting material. Whatever you do, however, you will want to give a speech that has a clear-cut pattern of organization, that is worded effectively, and that is designed to be interesting to the audience. Try in every way to make it a complete speech in its own right, not just a segment taken out of a longer speech.

SUBJECT AND MATERIALS

Subjects

A good speech conveys something worth communicating. In this assignment and all the others to come you should choose a subject that will be worthy of the time and attention of your audience. In saying this, we do not mean to contradict our previous statement that you are not expected to deal only with world-shaking ideas; rather, we mean to warn you away from subjects that are just too ordinary, too trivial, too unrewarding to merit the serious attention of your listeners. Very simple subjects can be deserving of an audience's interest, if they are not matters that the audience already understands thoroughly. If in your speech about commercial aviation your only point is that there are many people, including yourself, that enjoy flying, your talk will not be particularly rewarding to your listeners. However, if you reveal something about a flight plan that they did not know and perhaps should know, their time will be well spent in listening. If you tell the audience that there are annoying check-out regulations in the women's dormitories, you will be telling them something that they may know better and feel more deeply about than you. However, if you advocate a particular change in college disciplinary procedures that you can show to be sensible and sound, you may be able to stimulate some constructive thought on their part.

The choice of a particular subject area and a subject for your speech is your primary responsibility. No one will tell you what to say. But there are certain criteria to keep in mind about subjects that should guide you in preparing not only for the speaking you do in this assignment, but for any speech that you give in the future:

The Occasion.   The choice of subject and the manner in which you handle it must fill the assignment. This holds true for any occasion on which you speak. You have a wide range of possibilities for choice of subject in the beginning speech course, but when you enter your profession, your range will be somewhat limited by your own professional qualifications. You will most likely be asked to speak as a doctor, teacher, engineer, or whatever profession or specialization you represent. Even though you speak as a private citizen, there will be some degree of professional identification. In any event, the nature of the occasion largely dictates the subject of your speech. For the speaking you do in this course, you should always choose your subject so that your handling of it will contribute most meaningfully to your own learning experience. This criterion applies not so much to the general areas of subject matter you will investigate, but to the way in which you narrow them down to specific topics and to your determination of a specific purpose for your speech. This process will be discussed in connection with the assignment for this unit, and will be taken up in connection with each of the assignments to follow.

Your Qualifications.   The choice of subject area must be consistent with your qualifications as a speaker. This follows from what has been said above, and suggests further that in future years your qualifications will be determined largely by what you know, what you have experienced, and what you have accomplished. As a student in beginning speech your qualifications in this regard depend mainly on what you learn in preparing for the speaking assignment. This means that whatever subject area you choose—governed for the present only by the self-limitations of your own interests and curiosity—must be thoroughly investigated, and that you must learn as much as you can about it in order to earn the right to speak about it to your audience.

Your Audience.   The subject area must be adapted to the interests and needs of your audience. Choosing a subject is one of the most troublesome problems facing the student in beginning speech. Too many beginning speakers worry about choosing a subject that will interest the audience by its unusual nature. This is not the real issue. Actually, any subject area can be *made* interesting to your audience, and can be adapted to them so that they will benefit from your treatment of it. Your main problem, then, becomes one of adaptation. This means that you must handle whatever subject area you select in such a way that the audience will be impelled to listen to you and will gain something from what you say. That is why your steps of preparation for each speech assume such great importance for both you and your listeners. This, too, is an emphasis with which we want to deal more completely in connection with this assignment and the assignments to come.

The principal reason for assigning you the single-unit speech, we have said, is to teach you the principle of stating a point, then proving it. To accomplish this learning, you must select a rather modest subject out of a broader subject area. In this assignment you should make a relatively narrow, specific assertion of fact or opinion and develop it as fully as you can, using plentiful material, rather than make a wide general assertion that you can expand upon only skimpily, if at all. For your subject in this speech, then, choose some particular topic about which you can say a sufficient number of things to amplify your statement in a few minutes, not a topic that would take an hour or more to cover adequately. You cannot tell the whole story of

Napoleon's life in this speech, or even recount the Battle of Waterloo; the more proper subject would be something like how Napoleon came to make the fatal mistake that led to his defeat at Waterloo. It is probably better to underestimate than to overestimate what you can accomplish in the short space of time given you for this speech.

For this assignment you had probably better select a subject area about which you already know something and which is so interesting to you that you love to talk to others about it. This advice holds for almost any speech you give, but it is especially pertinent to this first assignment, where you want to reduce your problems of subject choice to a minimum.

Finding and Selecting Materials

As a consequence of the counsel given above, you will probably rely to some extent on your own present knowledge of the subject for the ideas and supporting materials you will use in this speech. By itself, however, such knowledge is not enough for this or any of the other speeches that you will be giving. For all of them, you will have to supplement with knowledge gained from research.

Although the necessity for research will continue in future years, it has special significance for you now. When you become established in your profession and gain a great deal of experience, much more of what you say may come out of your own knowledge and experience. At present whatever credibility and authority you have on the speaker's platform must largely derive from other sources. Whenever a speech shows evidence of research, an audience is flattered and favorably impressed. The most direct way to show evidence of research is, of course, to cite directly and accurately from a source, thereby crediting the origin of your information. Research sources include what you learn from reading, listening, and observation.

Reading.   Now that you are a student in an institution of higher learning, you will be doing more reading than you have ever done before. Part of your reading is assigned work for your classes. Another part is research done in the library to supplement the knowledge you are gaining. An additional portion may well be leisure-time reading of periodicals, books, and newspapers. Ideally part of your general education should be reading a daily newspaper and a weekly magazine to keep up with what is going on in the world.

As a college student, too, you have an opportunity to improve the quality of your reading habits. You can include editorials, writings of news analysts, and significant news items along with the sports page and the comic section.

You can learn to appreciate the various competent and well-written news magazines. You can become acquainted with high-quality periodicals and journals, some of which you may not have known existed before. Certainly in your search for material to use in a speech you will need to rely on the "better" sources. Your instructor and many of your classmates would, and rightly so, take a dim view of the worth of material gleaned from books or periodicals written mainly for entertainment or sensational impact rather than for the enlightenment of more select and intelligent readers. Material that you gather and use from your reading should be accurately recorded and documented so that you can communicate it accurately and give proper recognition to the source from which it comes. This involves recording an accurate statement of the item of information, quoted either directly or paraphrased, the exact source, and a topical heading or title to identify what the statement is about.

Listening. You gain information that you may later communicate from speeches and lectures that you hear and from interviews and conferences in which you take part. Public information programs on radio or television are also good sources of information. As a college student, you now have the distinct advantage of taking courses in a variety of subjects where each day you are exposed to new ideas. The concentrated learning that you are now doing can provide you with a wealth of information. Again, the quality of your source needs to be considered. No one source is completely infallible, but there are distinct differences between what you may hear in casual conversation or may report from rumor and what comes from an identifiable individual who is in a position to know. Just as in your reading research, material that you get from your listening and use in your speech must be communicated accurately and documented to show the exact source. This means that you should record this material as carefully as you do material gained from reading.

Observation. Purposeful observation of events around you can also be a source for materials used in a speech. If you are going to give a speech about the condition and capacity of the gymnasium, your best source of information might well be to go there and make some accurate observations of your own rather than trying to learn about it from a book or by listening to what someone else has to say about it. Observations must be made accurately if they are to be of any value as supporting material for your speech, and reported accordingly just as you would document materials gained from sources other than yourself.

These are possible ways of getting materials; now we can turn to a discussion of their uses in speechmaking.

Uses of Materials

Materials in a speech are used to develop points that the speaker wants the audience to understand. Speech materials and their uses are frequently referred to as *proofs*. If you consult a standard dictionary you will find a number of definitions of the word *prove*. Among these are: trying out or testing, showing or demonstrating, attempting to establish the genuineness of an event or statement by argument or evidence. The use of materials in a speech can accomplish any one or several of these functions. Another way of putting it is to say that you can use materials as proofs in any one of three ways or by combinations of the following:

1. *To clarify.* When materials are used to clarify, they make understandable to the listener something that he might not otherwise understand. This may involve knowledge or belief that is entirely new to him, or different aspects of a topic about which he previously had only partial understanding.
2. *To reinforce.* When materials are used to reinforce, they give further support or strength to knowledge or beliefs which the listener already possesses. Repetition and restatement of points are the most obvious means of reinforcement of an idea.
3. *To establish.* When materials are used to establish an idea or belief, they are used to demonstrate the greatest likelihood of the truth or value of a point of view which the speaker holds and which he wants his listeners to accept.

Kinds of Materials

We have told you about the sources of materials and the general ways in which they are used. Now you may be asking, "What kinds of materials can I find to incorporate into the content of my speeches?" Let us examine three general categories of materials through which we gain understanding or which we use in communication in order to give understanding to others.

Physical Materials. We learn through our senses. Materials that are presented to the view or hearing of an audience can be used to inform or persuade them. The more common use is for the presentation of information. Visual aids are actual objects or their representation by such things as models, drawings, pictures, or graphs. Speakers also use audio aids, such as recordings of live performances of music and other sounds. Physical materials, then, are audio-visual aids that the speaker uses to illustrate or prove what he says with words.

Authority Materials.   Materials gained from reading or listening that depend primarily upon the expressed opinion of others or that are based upon knowledge that others have acquired compose the greatest part of the speaker's material, especially in informational speaking. They consist of direct or indirect quotations, or reference to knowledge that has been learned, recorded, and transmitted from sources other than the speaker himself. Such materials generally constitute the "authority" by which the speaker backs up the statements that he makes. Sometimes the speaker will bring into his speech facts that he himself has observed, and on occasion he may even quote his own statements from some previous speech or writing. All such facts and opinions gathered by the speaker through reading, listening, and observing can be classified as authority materials. The various kinds of authority materials will be discussed shortly.

Reasoning Materials.   All materials used in a speech need some interpretation and application by a speaker. Just quoting an authority and then going on to another point does not complete the development of an idea. The speaker must make a connection between what he is quoting and the idea he is trying to establish. Along with materials found and selected from research, much of what a speaker says represents his evaluations of the materials, the inferences he draws from them, the connections he makes between them and his points, and the general conclusions he propounds. These statements we call reasoning materials. They result from the speaker's thought about the implications of his other materials. Whenever a speaker makes statements like "These figures show conclusively that the problem exists in every large city in the United States," or "Thus we have seen that, with only one or two exceptions, the critics praised the movie's good intentions but panned it as an artistic monstrosity," or "My own observations over a number of years have led me to believe that college students are really interested in learning," he is using reasoning materials. They represent the *application* of his physical and authority materials in developing points and in accomplishing his specific purpose. The expression of the speaker's own thinking, feeling, points of view, and interpretations is a part of the substance of what he says; we would even go so far as to say the most important part. You will remember that our definition of public speaking is "one particular speaker communicating purposefully a particular message to a particular group of listeners." The speaker's reasoning materials are the means by which he gives his message purpose, particularity, and applicability to his audience. They are what make his message a speech rather than a mere research report.

Coordinating Uses and Kinds of Materials

Perhaps we can clarify these general categories by showing how they are used in an imaginary circumstance, which we shall make the prosecutor's presentation during a murder trial.

Part of the evidence in the trial consists of physical objects (material evidence). The revolver used as a murder weapon, letters and other documents, and the bloodstained coat found in the trash can are submitted by the prosecutor as People's Exhibits A, B, C, and so forth. These are what we have spoken of as physical materials or audio-visual aids.

A larger part of the evidence presented consists of testimony by witnesses. The witnesses represent authority materials. The prosecutor puts on the stand the doctor who testifies that the death was caused by a gunshot wound and probably happened around the time that the defendant was known to have been quarreling with the deceased; the ballistics expert who reports his findings about tests conducted with the revolver and markings on bullets he has fired, which demonstrate that it was the defendant's gun which fired the fatal shot; and the fingerprint expert who reports on his findings, which are that the only fingerprints found on the gun were those of the defendant. Other witnesses that the prosecutor presents are not experts, but ordinary people who testify that the defendant is known to have quarreled with the deceased and to have threatened his life. They report as "eye witnesses" that they saw the defendant at the scene of the crime, and also give information about other circumstances related to the crime. While it is not likely that the prosecutor would present his own observations as part of these authority materials, the speaker can sometimes be his own witness.

Our prosecutor has the job of presenting the material evidence and questioning and cross-questioning the witnesses. However, his job does not end there. He must develop his primary point (the guilt of the accused), and accomplish his specific purpose (to get the jury—his audience—to vote "guilty"). He must tie together all the evidence he has presented, interpret it, apply it, and sum up his case at the end. He not only has physical and authority materials to present, he must organize them and use reasoning in order to develop his point and to gain his objective. The statements that would result are what we have classified as reasoning materials. They might run something like this:

> It has been demonstrated to you that the gun which was found in the defendant's possession and which we have presented as Exhibit A is indeed the one which fired the shot that killed Jonathan Jones. Further, it has been shown that the only fingerprints found on it are those of the defendant. Exhibit C, the defendant's bloodstained coat, was found stuffed in an ash can in an alley

behind his apartment building. The blood on the coat, our experts have told you, is human blood of the same type as that of the deceased and of a different type from that of the defendant. Witnesses have testified that the defendant was at the scene of the crime at a time very close to that which the coroner has set as the time of death. Other witnesses have told you that he was not only on bad terms with Jonathan Jones, but that on at least one occasion he threatened his life. The documents which we have presented as Exhibit B clearly show that Jonathan Jones had information which he was intending to present to the bank examiners that proved the defendant to be an embezzler. We have shown that the defendant had the motive, the opportunity, and the means to do willful murder to Jonathan Jones. That he did so is clearly proven by the facts that the murder weapon was his, that his fingerprints are the only ones on it, that his bloodstained coat was found the next morning, and that he is known to have been at the scene of the crime. The defendant's claim that he is the victim of a "frame-up" we have shown to be a patent fabrication. Ladies and Gentlemen of the jury, this man is guilty beyond any reasonable doubt. He sits before you convicted by this evidence, guilty of the most despicable act one man can commit against another and against society— the deliberate and willful taking of another man's life. There is only one conclusion you can draw: the defendant, Anthony Smith, did willfully and with malice aforethought shoot and kill Jonathan Jones. You must return a finding of "guilty of murder in the first degree."

Reasoning materials, it can be seen, are not new or separate from the other kinds of materials: they are derived from them. They are a very necessary part of the speaker's argument, however, as they are the direct means by which he makes his point with the audience.

The prosecutor's job and that of the defense attorney opposing him is to persuade. Your job in speaking may be either to inform or to persuade, but your central idea is on trial in either case, and your use of materials to present your case will largely determine the verdict of your jury. Please do not take this advice too literally. We do not want you to attempt to play the role of Perry Mason every time you give a speech! The important thing, as we have said before and will say again, is to back up what you say. When you present your points, you must develop them with carefully selected, sound materials. Then when the verdict of the audience is in, you hope they will have learned something from your speech, or have been persuaded to accept your point of view.

Physical materials, or audio-visual aids, will be required in the speeches you give in Unit II. A further discussion of reasoning materials as they apply to persuasive speaking is included in Unit IV. We shall now enlarge upon the nature of authority materials as they apply to your speech in Unit I and to all other speeches you will be giving.

Authority materials are things you say in your speech that enlarge upon or amplify a particular point you want to make. They may be details that clarify or further explain what you mean; they may be statements or stories that reinforce your point of view; they may be statements of fact or authoritative opinion used as proof of your point.

Types of Authority Materials

Various lists of the "types" of authority materials can be found. The listing given here is an abbreviated one. The most important thing for you to consider, however, is not whether an item is of one type or another, but how the materials may be used to develop the thought in your speech and to arouse the reactions in your audience that you desire.

We shall identify for you some of the more common types of materials that you will probably be using and that are referred to in other units following this one. We do this mainly to guide you in looking for and selecting materials, and then in making judgments of their worth and effectiveness in planning your speeches. The information should also be helpful in making critical judgments of the speaking of others. In either case, however, the emphasis must always be on the *use* of the materials—what they accomplish—rather than on the labelling of them just for the sake of identification. It is most important to consider their use in relation to the thought development of the speech, and the structure of its organization. The judgment of the worth of the materials goes beyond considering merely their usefulness, however. As we have said, both speaker and listener must assume responsibility for accepting the truthfulness, the accuracy and validity of each statement that is made or listened to.

In finding and selecting materials for your speech, you should keep in mind that a variety of materials will be more likely to interest, inform, or persuade a listener. A speech composed of nothing but quotations, nothing but examples, or nothing but statistics would probably not impress your listeners very favorably. Often more than one type of approach is needed in a speech to reach any one or all members of your audience.

Quotations. Perhaps the most common kind of authority material is the quotation. Quotations may be in the form of testimony, or they may be literary quotations. *Testimony* is a direct or indirect quotation from a single person or from a reference source that usually constitutes an endorsement of a point of view. A *literary quotation* is always a direct quotation from prose or poetic literature, and is used most often to reinforce or to illustrate an idea or feeling.

Literary quotations are used frequently in an introduction or in a conclusion, if the point of the quotation leads into or reinforces the central idea of the speech. Sometimes they are also used in the body of the speech to enlarge upon or to illustrate a particular point. A speech may begin with a literary quotation such as:

> "Speak the speech, I pray you, as I pronounced it to you, trippingly on the tongue. But if you mouth it as many of your players do, I had as lief the town crier spoke my lines." This advice that Shakespeare had Hamlet give to actors could also apply to public speakers. Use of careful diction is important to the art of speaking.

You can see how the same quotation might be used to illustrate a point in the body of the speech, or might even serve as a concluding statement in a speech on the use of diction in public speaking.

Let us cite examples of direct and indirect quotations used as testimony in the development of a point:

> The art of speaking requires great effort. As the great Roman rhetorician, Quintilian, wrote in the first century in his *Institutes of Oratory*, "The art of speaking depends on great labor, constant study, varied exercise, repeated trials, the deepest sagacity, and the readiest judgment."

This could also be stated as an indirect quotation:

> Quintilian said that the art of speaking requires effort, study, exercise, practice, wisdom, and judgment.

This quotation is attributed to a writer considered to be one of the great authorities in the field. The kind of *testimony* it represents is "expert testimony."

Quotations may also be given from "inexpert" sources:

> Mr. Smith, a neighbor of mine, said, "It seems to me that the ability to speak requires a great deal of knowledge as well as training and practice in speechmaking."

"Inexpert" sources can, taken together, constitute authority, as illustrated by this example:

> A survey taken of 100 business men in St. Louis asked what they considered most important for excellence in a public speaker. The item that was checked most frequently was that the speaker should have thorough knowledge of the subject area.

Results of surveys or interviews, whether given in a general statement or reported statistically, resemble multiple indirect quotations. Their effect is often that of the authority of a majority opinion. This kind of reporting can be considered as authoritative opinion, but comes closer to the type of material commonly called *the example*.

Example.   An example is a detail used to illustrate a more general point. You have very probably heard statements in a speech introduced by "for example," or "for instance." What follows these phrases is intended mainly to sharpen the awareness and understanding of the listener by calling his attention to a more particular detail or group of details which relate to a more inclusive statement the speaker has just made.

The term *instance* is sometimes used synonymously with *example*. When a differentiation between the two is made, the instance is considered to be a brief example. An extended example is sometimes referred to as an *illustration,* or, when presented in a narrative form, may be designated as a *story* or *anecdote*. Examples, then, may be either brief or long. They may also be either real or imaginary. When the speaker wishes to illustrate something that is typical of the experience of many persons or places, he uses the imaginary example of "Mr. X" or "the typical college freshman" or "a mythical European country." Imaginary examples are not untrue. They merely use fictitious names, dates, and places to better illustrate a general truth.

Let us suppose that you are giving a speech about a new Student Union that has been built on your campus. You might use brief examples, or *instances,* to make a point:

> The new Student Union provides a wide variety of recreational facilities. For example: it has a music listening room, three separate game rooms, a ballroom, and conference and meeting rooms.

The statement could be turned around:

> The inclusion of such facilities as a music listening room, game rooms, a ballroom, and conference and meeting rooms, leads one to conclude that the new Student Union was planned to accommodate a wide variety of activities.

Whether the statement of your point comes before or after the citation of instances, it is always well to have a rather large number of them. Their authoritative weight to some extent derives from the effect of accumulation. One of these instances could be expanded into an illustration. You might, for example, give an entire speech describing the music listening room as illustrative of an unusual activity now accommodated in the new building. Stories or anecdotes might be used to illustrate the reactions of students and faculty to the new building. Still another way of dealing with the topic might be to use an extended imaginary example, or illustration, telling about the things which the typical visitor might see or do on a tour of the premises.

Statistics are also really a form of examples. That is, individual examples are codified in figures represented as percentages or ratios in a neat and objective manner that lends authority to what is being said. Some additional discussion of the use of examples and statistics in relation to reasoned argument is included in Unit IV.

As we have said, more extended examples frequently take the form of stories or anecdotes, real or imaginary. While a purist might insist that these should be considered only under the topic of examples, we feel that it might be helpful to consider them separately.

Stories or Anecdotes.   The great interest value of well-told stories is obvious enough. You have certainly been entranced by them from your earliest years and have doubtless appreciated their use in speeches that you have heard. Some speeches are built completely around one or more stories. The effect of such speeches is usually that of entertainment alone, yet often very important points can be made or illustrated by use of an anecdote. Consider how many of the teachings of Jesus recorded in the New Testament are in the form of a parable or story. How better could the idea of loving forgiveness be illustrated than by the parable of the Prodigal Son?

The last thing you would want to do is to introduce a story by saying, "This reminds me of a funny story that will prove my point. . . ." Just begin the story; the usefulness and point of it should be evident to the audience if you tell it well. Each story you use should have a point, and the point of the story, if tied in with the point you are making in the speech, is proof enough of its usefulness.

A story used in the introduction is an excellent means of gaining audience attention and leading pleasantly into the central idea of the speech. Likewise, a story used as a conclusion may contain a point that can effectively reinforce the central idea.

As you gain more experience in public speaking, you will be compiling a storehouse of anecdotes that you will want to use. Start now using brief stories that you have read or been told, or possibly true incidents from your own experience that will introduce or reinforce the central idea of your speech or illustrate a point which you are making.

Analogies.   You may have heard *analogy* used and defined as a "figure of speech." As a term applied to authority material for a speech, it might better be understood as being the use of comparisons and contrasts. An analogy is actually an extended comparison of two examples.

Figurative analogies are imaginative comparisons of two classes of things that in actuality are totally unlike one another. This kind of comparison and contrast can be used to reinforce a point and as a means of making your language more vivid. That is, if you were to say that going to college is like discovering and exploring a strange new land, you would not be proving anything by the implied comparison itself. The similarities and contrasts that you would point out in developing the comparison would probably contain the more direct proofs. Along with them you would be attempting to stimulate the imaginations of your listeners so that a more meaningful point would be made clear.

A *literal analogy,* on the other hand, is a more direct comparison of things in the same general class or category. If you compare your college with X college to see similarities and differences in the courses of study, you come much closer to offering direct proof for a point you are trying to make. If you are giving a speech about the advantage of going to a large university over a small college, some direct and particular comparisons between the two should be made.

The analogy we used earlier showing points of similarities between a public speaker's use of reasoning materials and a prosecuting attorney presenting his case is essentially a figurative analogy, although some of the particulars involved in actual oral presentation could be literally applied.

Analogies are useful forms of support and relate quite closely to ways of reasoning. This relationship you will find discussed in Unit IV. Try using analogies in your early speeches as a way of testing out their effectiveness and their soundness in clarifying, reinforcing, or establishing a point you wish to make.

Process of Selecting Materials

After you have completed research for a speech, you should have much more material than you can use. This is not so much a waste as you might think. Research is done as much to educate the speaker about the subject as it is to discover usable ideas and supporting materials. A speaker is on very uncertain ground if he knows no more about his subject than what he is presenting in his speech. If you have ever given a speech of that type, you know what a sorry thing it is and how unsatisfying, if not downright painful, it is to give. You have certainly heard enough speeches of the type to know how unhappy an audience is about them.

From the mass of ideas and supporting materials that you have compiled, you will want to select only the best to use in your speech. Do not try to overwhelm your audience with a mountain of proof. One superior example, well amplified and presented, is preferable to three or four fair examples hurriedly thrown at the audience. You will want sufficient supporting material for every one of your important points, of course, but remember that quality as well as quantity can create that sufficiency.

Let us go through with you the possible development of a short, one-unit speech to see how your preparation would have progressed up to this point, then go on to show how your preparation could be completed.

Let us say that in your sociology class you heard reference to Thomas Malthus' famous essay published about 150 years ago, "A Summary View of the Principle of Population," and discussed the Malthusian theory of population growth. Further, you were impressed by a recent article in a current news magazine which stated that more than half the world's population is perpetually hungry.[8] The relationships of hunger, food supply, and the population explosion you believed to be a most significant area to explore, one that suggested problems that could be discussed at some length.

You had also noticed reference to the writings of Frederick Osborn in your sociology textbook, and your professor had suggested articles by Julian Huxley that discussed modern problems of population growth as supplementary reading. Guided by these references, by class discussion, and by questions that had been asked in your class, you did some further investigation in the library. Examining the *Reader's Guide To Periodical Literature* showed you that a great deal had been written in recent years about this subject. You looked into some of the articles available in the periodical room of the library.

In taking notes on what you were learning, you came across startling and disturbing statements, such as that nearly 290,000 babies are born each day and more than 100,000,000 each year, that the rate of increase of population is rapidly increasing, and that one could predict that in time there will not be room enough for people even to stand on the earth's surface, much less area enough to grow food to feed them.

Here is material enough not just for one speech, but many speeches. Your problem now is to narrow down to one significant statement that you can develop in a few minutes, then select the materials that will best prove this statement. You decide that you would not have time enough to argue a particular solution, nor would your research place you at this time in a position of knowing yourself what the possible answer may be. Therefore, you decide just to make your audience aware of the existence of the problem of increasing population and to try to impress it forcefully upon their minds so that they will be aware of its significance. You decide tentatively upon the statement, "One of the greatest problems facing the world today is the

[8] "Hunger Around the World," *Newsweek*, 61:43–51 (June 17, 1963).

population explosion." We say "tentatively," because you may want to alter that statement for the sake of further clarity or limitation by the time you are through composing the message of your speech.

APPLICATION TO AUDIENCE
AND OCCASION

At this stage, however, you are now able to begin selecting the materials from the research that you have done so that you can organize them into a message to communicate orally to your classmates. Since this is to be given to your classmates, you need to consider some things about them. Some of them are taking the same course in sociology you are, some of them are not. A variety of majors is represented in your class, but you can assume that not only are they alert to new ideas in nearly every field, but that they are as conscious of their need to meet problems of the world after graduation as you are. They are no more trained sociologists or economists than you, but could be made as interested in your subject as you have become. This interest can be aroused best by use of forceful statements, possibly some examples, analogies, and authoritative testimony, that will help show them the magnitude of the issue with which you are dealing. Therefore, what you are going to say, the manner in which you arrange it, and the language that you use, should be adapted to them. The occasion is rather easy to identify. This is a regular speaking assignment of the beginning speech course. Your classmates are present to learn about speaking and listening from their own performance and yours, but they are also quite willing to learn through their listening about a wide range of subjects that will stretch their mental horizons.

Let us suggest a possible way in which you could compose your speech into outline form as the next step in your preparation, first by stating some things about this step in general.

✓ CONSTRUCTION OF THE SPEECH

Although your instructor may not ask you to hand in an outline, we strongly advise you to make one as part of your advance preparation. It will be a simple one, of course, since the single-unit speech calls for nothing very elaborate in the way of organization; but even this early in the game you should think in terms of a speech that has a beginning, a middle, and an end.

Make your introduction and conclusion brief and simple; but do have an introduction and conclusion. Also endeavor to make the pattern of your thought clear to your audience by use of transitional words, phrases, and sentences.

Accomplishing a Specific Purpose

In planning the organization for this speech, think through exactly what you want to accomplish. In other words, figure out a specific purpose. After your speech is over, your audience should have a clear idea of what you were attempting to do to their thinking. For that to happen, you need to have a clear idea of your specific purpose as you are presenting the speech. Do you want your audience to learn that a Genetics Institute exists on your campus? Do you want them to favor increasing the minimum age for granting driver's licenses from 16 to 18? Do you want them to be concerned about the population explosion? Do you want them alerted to the danger of shortage of food supply? Or do you want them to join a national organization that promotes information about planned parenthood? Whatever your subject, the audience should understand completely the point of view from which you are presenting it.

Organizing the Speech

The introduction of this speech should gain favorable attention for you and your subject and give the audience a clear idea of the speech. The development should contain identifiable supporting material related to and elaborating on the general statement. The conclusion should reinforce the general statement. One idea stated, developed, and restated: that is the single-unit speech.

Here is an example of what might constitute the end result of your outline on the subject of the population explosion.

Subject: Population explosion.
Specific Purpose: To get my audience to realize that there is an alarming increase in the world's population.
Introduction: Would it startle you if someone told you that population might some day be as much a threat to your life as the hydrogen bomb is today? Is it possible that population can become a threat to the world? Demographers, who study population, are saying that if the present trend in population increase continues, the world will be in serious trouble. They call this trend the population explosion.

Transition: (The one idea with which I want to impress you today is:)

Statement: The population of the world is increasing at an alarming rate.

Development: A. We need to realize that world population has been growing rapidly for the past three centuries.

    1. Before the 1700s, birth rates were approximately balanced by high death rates.

    2. After the 1700s, the rate of births accelerated greatly; the present growth rate being estimated by the United Nations at 44 million a year.

    3. We can see, for example, the impact of this growth in our own country.

        a. The U.S. Bureau of Census reported in 1960 that a baby is born every $7\frac{1}{2}$ seconds.

        b. Every 20 seconds, someone dies.

        c. Balancing this with immigration and emigration, the prediction is that our population should double in 40 years.

        d. Joseph L. Fisher, President of the Resources for the Future, predicts a redoubling shortly thereafter.

Transition: (Making the problem more significant still is the fact that,)

    4. As Frederick Osborn has pointed out, population is increasing even more rapidly in underdeveloped nations where about 75 percent of the world's population now lives.

        a. Java now has over 800 persons per square mile.

        b. Portions of India are even more heavily populated.

Transition: (Can we project the possibilities even further?)

    B. An article in the *U. N. Review* makes the prediction that at the present rate, in 600 years each human being will have one square yard of the earth's surface to stand on.

Transition: (Whether this happens or not, we can be sure that more and more people will have to be fed.)

    C. The population explosion is already creating problems of food supply that will certainly become greater.

Transition: (This can lead us to conclude that)

Restatement: It is important for us as future leaders in this country to become aware that the population explosion is becoming one of the great issues of our time. More and more people, whether they are meek or not, are inheriting the earth.

References: 1. *Advanced Reports of U. S. Bureau of Census,* November 15, 1960.

    2. Cook, R. C., "Population Pressure and World Peace," *Foreign Policy Bulletin,* August 1, 1959.

    3. "Hunger Around the World," *Newsweek,* June 17, 1963.

    4. Osborn, Frederick, *Population: An International Dilemma,* Princeton University Press, 1958.

    5. "Standing Room Only," *U. N. Review,* February, 1959.

This is the outline of a speech that a student actually prepared for a three-minute presentation. You can see that he made efforts to narrow his field, to specify his purpose, and to use a variety of proofs that included an analogy in the introduction, authoritative testimony, and a form of an example used in the development. Only the anecdote as a form of support was not included.

Another student speaking about the same subject area, presented a three-minute speech outlined in this manner:

Subject: Population explosion.

Specific Purpose: To make my audience aware that the population explosion is creating great problems for the nations of the world.

Introduction: Almost all of you in this class will be graduating from college in a few years, will be married, and probably will be raising a family. Have you ever considered how the problem of overpopulation may affect generations to come?

Statement: The problems presented by the population explosion are more serious than most of us realize.

   A. Thomas Malthus predicted over one hundred years ago that man would geometrically reproduce himself to starvation.

   B. His theory is being borne out in the light of the present population explosion.

   C. Medical science and better living conditions are helping to create a great imbalance between birth rates and death rates.

   D. In Asia, Africa, and other underdeveloped areas of the world, people are actually starving because of too many people and too little food.

   E. Many authorities say that either world food supply must be increased or some means must be found to restrict the population growth.

      1. New and more efficient methods of agriculture are now being experimented with in order to find new sources of food supply.

      2. Some nations and many individuals are becoming conscious of the need for family planning if the explosion is to be curtailed.

Transition: (So we can see that)

Restatement: The problems presented by the population explosion are mainly those of feeding more people and must be solved either by getting more food or planning for some kind of population control.

The difficulties encountered by this student can be easily seen. The main one was that he was trying to do far too much in too short a time. Each of the statements was in itself rather general and deserving of some kind of detailed development. Whether he had the resources available or not to include some specific proofs, he did not have time to use them. He succeeded in making several statements, but did not really accomplish the assignment of making a one-unit speech.

PREPARATION FOR DELIVERY

If you have a willing roommate or a member of your family to listen to your speech, you may find his reactions a helpful indication of how your audience is likely to react. But even if you must rehearse aloud by yourself, by all means do it and do it repeatedly. This is the means of fixing your ideas well enough in mind so that you will be confident of them—and of yourself—when you speak before your audience. Although you are not memorizing the speech, you are significantly reducing the possibility that you will be at a loss for words on the platform, and consequently so dependent on your notes that you fail to make adequate contact with the audience.

The Language of a Speech

We shall now take up some aspects of language in relation to oral communication, since the wording of the speech is a process that takes place both in composing the message and in preparing yourself for the speaking situation. Further, language is the vehicle by which your ideas are conveyed to your listeners.

When you read something from the printed page, ideas and experiences come to life in your conscious mind; the message in print becomes a part of your own experience. When you listen to someone speak, messages are comprehended in a similar way, but the speaker's own personality and manner of delivery influence the kind of reception he and his message will receive. More subtle shades and variations of meaning can be conveyed by the spoken word; language comes alive.

A vital part of a speaker's task in composing his speech is planning the wording of the speech. This means he must not only think about and practice using language to express his thoughts, but also give attention to correct usage of language and choice of particular words and phrases. Wording the extemporaneous speech does not mean writing the speech out word for word, and then either memorizing or reading it before an audience. It does mean a careful consideration of the language used in expressing the message of the speech as it is to be delivered.

After you have completed the steps of preparing the message and analyzing the audience and the occasion, you are ready to begin the step of composing the message by organizing it into outline form. The wording you use in composing your outline is the first stage in aiming for an effective use of language. Remember that not only are the words you put down on paper for your own use in speech composition, but they also express a part of the content of the speech you will eventually give. Therefore, choose words that are in an "oral style" rather than in a "written style," wording that is for the ears rather than the eyes of the audience you will be addressing. What we mean by this is using a style of language appropriate for a live audience, one that is physically present, rather than a style more appropriate for the unseen reader of a written communication. An excellent description of what constitutes "oral language" used in speech is given by Gladys L. Borchers and Claude M. Wise, two authorities in the field of speech, who emphasize how the personal approach used in speaking relates to the actual composition of phrases and sentences.[9]

The next step in preparation is to prepare yourself by rehearsing the speech aloud, as though you were extending conversation with real persons to a larger group of individuals. Using your outline in your first rehearsal will help you remember the content and organization of your message. However, a vital part of your practice is not only to help your memory and exercise your use of voice and action, but also to practice expressing the message in words. This means rehearsing your use of language as the medium of your oral expression.

The language you use in rehearsal and will probably draw upon when you deliver the speech will largely reflect your habitual use of language. You do not learn a new language when you learn about public speaking, but you can learn and practice some new things about usage that should improve the entire pattern of your communication.

We mentioned that an "oral style" can be somewhat different from "written style." Now let us draw upon your present knowledge of language to direct your attention to the various qualities you need to be conscious of and use well in your public speaking. The most general things we can say are that the language of your speech should be clear, interesting, and correct.

Spoken language must be clear. It should convey understandably and accurately the idea you want to express. It should be interesting, conveying a vitality of expression not found in trite, ordinary phrases and figures of speech. It must be correct. Poor use of language detracts considerably from the effectiveness of any speech. In this unit we want you to be more conscious of the correct use of language and to continue that consciousness throughout the other speaking assignments. Other aspects of language will be considered in connection with each of the succeeding units, since language is an integral part of all communication. In Optional Unit B we consider language from the points of view of voice production, articulation, and pronunciation. In Unit II use of language is emphasized from the point of view of its denotative func-

[9] Gladys L. Borchers and Claude M. Wise, *Modern Speech: An Introduction to Speaking and Understanding* (New York: Harcourt, Brace and Company, 1947), pp. 191–212.

tion, the use of words to symbolize most accurate identifications. In Unit III its connotative functions are examined, the significances of word meanings and their relationship to ideas and concepts. In Unit IV language is considered in relationship to reasoning processes, and in Unit V in its relationship to attitudes and feelings.

The beginning speaker's speech is often unclear to his audience because of faulty language habits. Even persons who write quite acceptably are sometimes guilty of gross language errors in the oral communication of their ideas. It is not too early to start ridding yourself of such errors if they do occur in your speaking. Bad habits are hard to break. Becoming conscious of unconscious errors is the first and most important step in making sure that you use language well in public speaking and in everyday speech. Your classmates and your instructor will be listening for errors in order to help you become conscious of them, just as you will be helping your classmates by recognizing their errors.

Grammar may be a nuisance, but it is a necessary one; it is nothing more or less than that organized system of language rules which men have devised to make more precise communication of ideas possible. As a university graduate you will be expected to understand the use of the English language, as well as your field of specialization. Begin now to become aware of good language usage. You can note errors in the speech of others, not (except in this class) to correct their errors, but to help make yourself more conscious of ones you might make and should avoid. More important, give careful attention to language usage in speeches that you give. Your audience and especially your instructor certainly will. Endeavor to make their reaction a favorable one.

Rehearsing Aloud

Another part of preparing yourself for the speech is to plan and practice techniques of delivery. A question is frequently raised about the use of notes. Most speech instructors will allow you to use notes, if you use them well. You can usually speak better when you dispense with them entirely, but that is not always feasible, at least at the start. If and when you do use notes, remember that your audience should hardly be aware of the fact that you are referring to them. The outline which you use in planning your speech is something quite different from what we are now calling notes. We have said that you will find it helpful to use your outline in your first rehearsal, but after you have gained sufficient familiarity with the content and organization of your speech, you can dispose of it so that you can free yourself from it during the actual delivery of your speech.

We advise you to make separate notes for the delivery of your speech. Most speakers find it more convenient to record them on small cards—3 × 5 is a convenient size to handle and is not obtrusive. Few things are more distracting than taking large sheets of paper to the platform and awkwardly leafing through them. Yet using cards like a card player shuffling a deck before he deals can be equally distracting.

What do you put in these notes? Notes are frequently used to record statistical information that the speaker may find difficult to recall unaided or that he wants to be sure to quote accurately. The same would hold true for quotations from authorities. For other than these purposes, however, notations should be as brief as possible. If you have rehearsed aloud enough times and with enough concentration of purpose, single-word reminders of your points and transitions should be sufficient. By all means rehearse aloud with these notes before using them in public. The speaker should know what is on his notes as well as what should develop from them.

You should also learn to be free from the speaker's stand or lectern. It is designed as a place on which you can conveniently place your notes, not as a support for your sagging body. Undue dependence on the speaker's stand can inhibit any kind of effective bodily action. Remember too that often in the years to come you will have to work without such a prop.

REVIEW OF PREPARATION

Let us now review briefly the steps of preparation to follow for this speaking assignment.

1. Choose a subject area.
2. Investigate the subject area by gathering materials.
3. Consider your audience and occasion and the purposes of this assignment in determining the delimitation of your subject.
4. Determine a specific purpose for your speech in terms of how you want the audience to respond.
5. Determine the statement that you want to develop and select the materials that will best develop that statement and accomplish your specific purpose.
6. Plan a brief introduction for the statement so that you can gain attention of your listeners and alert them to what you are to say.
7. Plan the wording of a restatement that can serve as a conclusion.
8. Familiarize yourself thoroughly with the message you have now composed.

9. Practice the wording to be used in your extemporaneous delivery.
10. Continue to rehearse the speech a number of times in order to aid your memory and to gain confidence in your ability to deliver the speech.

If you complete these steps of preparation and do them well, your chances of giving a successful speech will be enhanced. You will then be most able to fulfill your two fundamental obligations as a speaker: being a sound representative of your message, and effectively winning a desired response from your particular audience.

Now you should be ready for your first major speech. In many ways it will be the hardest one to give, but you should find much satisfaction in what you accomplish if you have prepared it well.

Optional Unit B

Voice and Diction

BACKGROUND

It may seem a bit odd to speak of the human voice as a natural resource, but in a number of respects the implied comparison is an apt one. Your voice is one of your greatest natural gifts. Moreover, as with most natural resources, the gift is more often abused than correctly used, more often neglected than given proper care. The reason for this maltreatment is the same as for the misuse of our earth's natural resources: people take their voices too much for granted.

Arguments for the conservation of natural resources are rather self-evident. Those for the proper understanding and care of the voice possibly are not. But it is shameful that people often treat carelessly the principal agency through which they make known to others their thoughts and feelings and on the basis of which others make judgments about their intelligence; their social, economic, educational, and cultural backgrounds; and their personalities.

To gain complete understanding of the voice and how it relates to the entire communication process is a complex and extensive task. In an introductory public speaking course you are not expected to learn the entire anatomy, physiology, neurology, or psychology of voice production. But as a public speaker you do need to be aware that your voice is the primary instrument by which you make your thoughts known. Moreover, you need to realize that the kind of voice you have and the way you use it can be either an asset or a liability to you in any kind of oral communication. Actors, radio and television performers, ministers, and teachers must give special attention to the study and development of pleasing vocal qualities. Those entering such professions should certainly emphasize special course work, exercise, and training in use of their voices. For them what we have to say will be merely introductory, for we shall discuss only those aspects of voice and diction that should be of most direct and practical use to the majority of you in the kind of public speaking you will be doing.

The premise with which to start is that you have a distinctive voice, one that distinguishes you from others as much as your fingerprints do, and that your goal is to work with nature, not fight it or try to change it completely. The way in which you say words, the element of diction, also needs some consideration.

First let us define the terms *voice* and *diction*. Strictly speaking, *voice* refers to the sounds of speech, and *diction* to the distinctness with which the sounds are produced. More often than not, however, the term *voice* is used as an inclusive term embracing the meanings of both terms. A good voice has adequate loudness, a pleasing quality, and the requisite variety of loudness, pitch, and rate for the communication of the speaker's meanings. It is also characterized by clear and accurate diction.

As we have said before, in public speaking the audience is present and their reception of what is said is an immediate one. This means that if you as a speaker hope to transmit a message to your listeners, you must first of all speak loudly enough to be heard and distinctly enough to be understood. If your voice fails to accomplish these tasks, you fail to communicate well what the message intends.

When you write something, you can help the reader to understand by proper spelling, capitalization, and punctuation. You do not have these aids in speaking, but you do have a means of communicating meanings to far greater advantage. You have ability to vary your voice into an almost infinite number of different patterns by which any imaginable shade of meaning can be made clear. You can change the loudness of sounds and words in order to emphasize some and de-emphasize others; you can change the rate at which you speak in order to communicate the mood of the moment; you can change the pitch of your voice in order to express how deeply you believe what you are saying, or possibly that you do not believe it at all; you can do all this and much more by varying loudness, rate and pitch. Further, by varying the sound of your voice, you add to the pleasantness of the reception. Few things are more irritating than a voice that is monotonous, that seemingly never changes in its levels of loudness, rate, or pitch.

All this does not mean that you as a public speaker should think of your voice as a musical instrument and that you should learn the techniques of playing upon it in order to create deliberately and mechanically different shades of meaning in your speech. The important thing to remember is that the meaning of what you are saying is foremost; that it comes first in accomplishing your communication. You should use your voice in a way that adds and gives greater impact to the meaning of what you are saying.

In general, we can say that you should use your voice in such a way that:

1. You can be heard.
2. You can be understood.
3. You can be pleasing to your listeners.
4. You can add to the meaning of what you are saying by vocal variety.

Suggestions of how this might be done at this stage of your learning experience will be discussed in this unit under the headings of *Characteristics of Voice,* and *Vocal Variety.*

THE ASSIGNMENT

The main purpose of this unit is to give you some understanding of what voice is, how it is produced, and how it may be best used so that it will be an asset to your speaking rather than a drawback. You will be working to improve both voice and diction. This is a task that is not accomplished by study of this unit alone, but should be an additional concern in the rest of the speeches you give. Your instructor will continue to evaluate your use of voice and give constructive suggestions for continuing improvement. In Unit I some emphasis was placed on the correct use of words and their pronunciation; in this unit a similar type of emphasis is placed on clarity of diction, the accurate articulation of speech sounds.

Each one of you will want to make a voice analysis, and in so doing will learn where your strengths and weaknesses lie so that you can plan continuous voice improvement. The Inventory Page for this unit will be an aid to you in making that analysis, and your instructor may give you some assistance in filling it out. Some members of your class may need additional help in analyzing and eliminating particular difficulties in use of voice and diction. In that event your instructor will work with them individually.

Should you have a marked defect that interferes with your normal communication, your instructor may refer you to a speech clinic for professional help. Fortunately, such handicaps affect only a few. More often any difficulty you might have will be one that can be overcome by your own effort and concentrated practice. Your instructor may arrange a conference with you for individual work and analysis, including a recording of your voice and recommended drill material to correct vocal faults or to improve your diction. Work with a tape recorder is especially helpful both for your own work and for an instructor to give you individual analysis and advice. The opportunity and ability to hear yourself as others hear you will do more to sharpen your awareness of effective use of the voice than any amount of reading or hearing others talk about it.

The assignment your instructor gives you, then, may include recording sessions combined with conferences. Or he may assign the class a round of oral readings designed mainly to illustrate use of vocal qualities and to give you practice in communicating effectively the ideas and feelings contained in the selections you read.

Oral reading can be most valuable practice for a public speaker. Although the regular speeches you give in this class are not written out and read from manuscript, some public speakers, especially those in positions of prominence, find it necessary to employ this mode of preparation and delivery. Unfortunately, many of them are not able to read well aloud and could benefit from instruction and practice in oral reading. In selecting, practicing, and reading material aloud to a class, you need to realize that although the ideas being communicated are not your own you must understand them fully as well as your own and employ the best techniques of vocal delivery in order to help your audience understand them also.

We recommend that the selection you choose be either poetry or "literary," as distinguished from "factual," prose, in order to give you better opportunity to exercise the uses of vocal expression and variety required to communicate wider ranges and shades of meanings. Choose a selection that you can respond to yourself, one that has meaning for you and gives you inspiration. Practice it by reading it aloud a number of times—to someone else if possible—then read it aloud before the class, concentrating mainly on conveying the meanings of the selection, and on the elements of vocal expression.

In the evaluation of your performance, your instructor and the class will discuss with you mainly how well you were able through your use of voice to create the proper mood and to convey the ideas in the selection.

Whatever the nature of the specific assignment you are given, it will certainly be to your advantage to make your voice an effective means of communication and pleasant to your listeners. This takes some time and effort, but it is worth every minute you spend on it.

SUPPLEMENTARY MATERIALS

We call the materials that follow supplementary, not because they are of less importance to your learning and use, but because reading them carefully should supplement your awareness of use of voice and diction and aid you in accomplishing the purposes of whatever form the assignment in this unit takes.

Voice Production

Basic to knowledge of use of the voice in public speaking is some understanding of the speech mechanism and the major processes which produce speech. The major processes by which speech is produced may be described in four steps. *Breathing,* or more specifically, exhalation of breath, supplies the raw material for the production of vocal sounds. *Phonation,* or the vibration of the vocal folds, is the second step. The third step is *resonation,* the giving of added dimension to the vocal sounds. The final step is *articulation,* the forming of the separate, distinct sounds that compose the spoken language. We shall take up each of these steps in order, so that you may be able to identify just what takes place.

Breathing.   Inhalation is the taking of air into the lungs to supply oneself with oxygen. It is accomplished by expanding the chest wall and lowering the diaphragm, the large muscle separating the chest cavity from the abdominal cavity. This action creates a partial vacuum in the chest cavity, and outside air pressure forces the air into the lungs. When the chest wall is contracted, the air is forced out of the lungs and escapes through the nose or mouth. It is this waste product, the exhaled air, that supplies the raw material for producing speech sounds.

Parts of the Breathing Mechanism

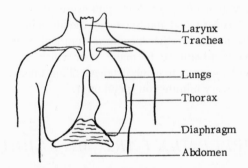

Larynx
Trachea
Lungs
Thorax
Diaphragm
Abdomen

Phonation and Vibration.   The second step in voice production is that of making the vocal sound. Vocal sounds are produced in two ways. The first way is called *phonation*. In phonation, exhaled air makes its passage from the lungs through the bronchial tubes, then through the trachea, or windpipe. At the upper end of the trachea is a cartilaginous structure called the larynx. As the air passes through the trachea it vibrates the vocal folds contained in the larynx. This small pair of muscular tissues, commonly called the vocal cords, is stretched across the opening of the tubelike structure, and when one makes vocal sounds, it closes off the opening. The force of the exhaled air pushes through the inner lips of the vocal folds setting them into rapid vibration. This action is much like the vibration of the lips when one is playing a brass instrument. The sound that results from this vibration is called *vocalized* or *phonated* sound.

Not all speech sounds are phonated. Consonant sounds such as the *h, k, s, sh, t, f, p, ch,* and the voiceless *th,* are not made by the vocal folds, but by direct vibration of the air stream as it passes through or across the articulators. These sounds are called *voiceless* speech sounds. The sounds are actually made by the friction of the air stream as it comes in contact with the particular organs of articulation.

Resonation. The third step in voice production is that of resonation. This step applies only to the speech sounds that are phonated or voiced—those sounds produced by vibration of the vocal folds. This part of the process is really that of amplifying the sounds, giving them an added dimension, principally by a reverberation of the sounds in the cavities of the pharynx, or throat, the mouth, and the nasal chamber. The quality of the sound is further influenced by other bone and tissue structures of the head and neck. It is during this step of voice production that most of the particular quality of the voice is determined. A full resonant voice is one more pleasing to listen to, whereas tension, or constriction of the main resonating areas may result in a voice that is "flat," harsh, or otherwise unpleasant to listen to.

Articulation. The final step is articulation. This is the process in which the distinct, separate sounds that make up our spoken language are shaped. In it the articulators take separate positions or make distinct movements that give the unique character to each sound which makes it different from the other sounds.

The main articulators are the tongue, the lips, and the soft palate, all of which are mobile during speech. Their position at any given moment of utterance of a sound, and their movement in making continuous sounds, determine most of the differences among sounds. The movement of the lower jaw also affects articulation, and the teeth and the hard palate, or roof of the mouth, are often considered articulators because they influence the kinds of sounds made. Finally, the glottis, or opening between the vocal folds, is considered an articulator for the *h* sound.

Parts of the Vocal Mechanism

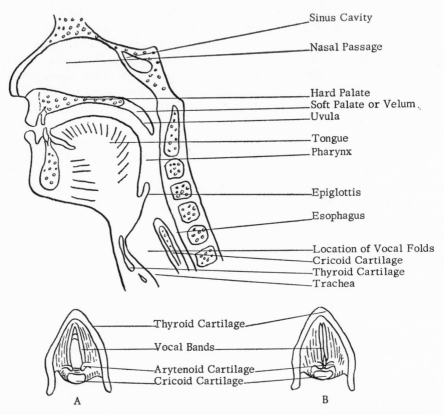

The vocal folds: A, in position for breathing; B, in position for vocalization.

The position, movement, or relative position of the articulators against or near another alter the sound waves in such a way as to give them a distinctive character. This is *articulation*. When you speak, you make separate, distinct sounds that are combined and blended together in continuous speech to make up the words and sentences used in speaking. This larger process is what is contained in the term *diction*. When your articulation of the separate speech sounds is indistinct, or when you do not have flexible movement of the articulators, blurred, indistinct speech may result.

Attempts to codify the separate, distinct speech sounds have been made and an "alphabet" produced which is composed of phonetic symbols. A work such as Kenyon and Knott's *A Pronouncing Dictionary of American*

English uses phonetic symbols as a guide for accepted pronunciations.[1] A list of phonetic symbols generally used in American English is included on page 72. This listing will probably have limited uses for you in this course, but can serve as reference for diction and pronunciation aids. Using pronunciation guides given in the standard dictionaries will also be helpful.

These, then, are the four steps in the production of voice:

1. *Breathing.* Exhaled breath supplies the raw material for production of all speech sounds.
2. *Phonation.* Vibration of the vocal folds produces voiced sounds.
3. *Resonation.* Voiced sounds are amplified.
4. *Articulation.* Separate, distinct sounds are formed.

Characteristics of Voice

All sound is vibration, and all sound has characteristics of intensity, frequency, quality, and duration. By *intensity* is meant the strength of the vibration, by *frequency* the rapidity of the vibration, by *quality* the peculiar, identifiable nature of the dimension of the sound, and by *duration* the length of time the sound lasts.

For description of the human voice, the characteristic of intensity usually goes by the name of *loudness,* that of frequency is most often called *pitch,* and that of duration also has the more common designation of *rate.* Only *quality* is a term that we ordinarily apply both to all sounds and to voice. There is a reason for the separate terminology. The human voice cannot be adequately explained in terms of the characteristics of all sound. It defies the relatively precise measurements called for, and it embraces greater complexity than they suggest. The characteristics of the human voice cannot be isolated one from the other, for they all affect and are affected by one another. Moreover, the voice is made up of a complex of sounds. Terms which might have meaning for one of the sounds have none for considerations of the whole complex. Certainly while you are delivering a speech you cannot separate nor concentrate on use of any one of the characteristics at any one point. The total effect is what will register in the consciousness of your listeners. It may be instructive to note that quality, the one characteristic which has a common designation, is the one in the human voice which is considered to be the most constant, the least subject to any kind of variation in public speaking.

It is not enough that your voice be loud enough to be heard; it must

[1] John Samuel Kenyon and Thomas Albert Knott, *A Pronouncing Dictionary of American English* (Springfield, Massachusetts: G. & C. Merriam Company, 1953).

be loud enough to command your listener's attention. After all, a member of an audience hears many sounds during any one given moment. Your voice is one sound among many; the sounds of the audience or those from outside the room also simultaneously register in his hearing mechanism. He gives conscious attention to the most prominent sound, which should be your voice, and becomes oblivious to other sounds he hears. The loudness of your voice is determined mainly by the force of your exhalation. The most common reasons for insufficient loudness are either an inadequate breath supply or inability to control exhalation to give strength to the sounds produced. Exercises for improving loudness concentrate on improvement of breathing habits, and especially on acquiring an adequate supply of air, maintaining it, and controlling its exhalation. Many beginning speakers lack sufficient loudness. Gaining it is a must.

Do you know if you are speaking loudly enough while giving your speech? One way to find out is that your instructor will tell you. But do not wait for his comments to find out for yourself. Realizing that you need enough loudness to keep your listeners alert and focusing their attention on your message, you can watch them while you are speaking and try to judge their reactions. If those in the back of the room, especially, appear less attentive than you want, try increasing your loudness to win their complete attention. This is not done by shouting, but by a controlled increase in the force of your exhaled air to produce a louder sound.

The natural pitch of your voice is influenced mainly by the length and thickness of your vocal folds. These factors limit both the basic pitch of the voice and its range. They are unchangeable. But the vocal folds are elastic, enabling you to vary your pitch over a considerable range. You literally stretch the vocal folds tighter as you go up the scale. The trained singer, actor, or speaker has developed a pitch range for his voice of several octaves. The wider the pitch range, and the more skill with which it is used, the more varied and accurate can be the meanings communicated. Most beginning public speakers need to learn how to make better use of this attribute of voice. Exercises in this area usually call for the speaker to expand his pitch range by putting unusual demands of communication upon it, and to gain conscious control over the changes and variations of pitch while he is speaking or reading aloud.

Do you know whether the pitch of your voice is in the best range while you are speaking? This is not as easy to determine as the loudness of your voice. Again, your instructor can tell you and the use of a recording that gives you a chance to hear your own range will give you part of the answer. You should concentrate on getting adequate variations in pitch chiefly during the time you rehearse the speech aloud. Some additional comments about pitch variation are made under the heading of *Vocal Variety*.

The quality of your voice is what distinguishes it from all other voices. It is influenced greatly by the degree and quality of its resonance. If the vocal sounds are fully and adequately resonated, the quality is most likely to be pleasing. When voice production and amplification are faulty, unpleasant qualities of harshness, hoarseness, shrillness, or nasality may result. Basic exercises for improvement in this area stress relaxation of the vocal apparatus, so that the initial sound produced at the vocal folds may be undistorted and the amplifying chambers may be fully and efficiently used. Here is the area of voice improvement probably most readily recognized and deeply appreciated by your listeners.

Your evaluation of the quality of your voice while speaking has obvious limitations. You must rely mainly upon your own voice analysis aided by your instructor and by recording sessions. Little conscious control can be achieved while speaking, other than to avoid as well as you can unbalanced tensions of the muscles of the neck and throat that may interfere with your potential quality.

The rate of speech can be measured grossly by the count of the approximate number of words spoken per minute. Rate includes both the sounds and the silences. Speech that is too rapid tires the listener and often leaves him behind in his effort to follow the thought. Speech that is drawled, hesitant, or frequently interrupted by "ah's" or other vocalized pauses is equally distracting. It is estimated that the average number of words per minute which can be easily understood by your listeners is 120–180. This advice should not be taken to mean that you can use a stop watch and word counter while giving a speech, but it does suggest that if you habitually speak much faster or slower than that, you may be putting an unnecessary burden on your listeners. Exercises for improvement of rate involve either prolonging or shortening individual speech sounds, or practicing speaking with more or fewer pauses.

The experience of many beginning speakers is that, although they time a five-minute speech well enough during the rehearsal, for some reason when they give the speech in class it comes out about one minute short. Some of the material may have been left out, but more likely, as a result of nervousness, the rate is speeded up so that it is much too rapid. You need to use pause, especially at the end of section or unit of thought, to give the listeners a chance to let the idea sink in. If during your talk you become conscious, as you probably will, of stumbling over some words, forgetting a key phrase, or letting your words get ahead of your thinking, realize that this is a likely symptom of too rapid speaking. Slow down. You will find it much easier to communicate, and your listeners will appreciate it.

Practicing to improve these vocal characteristics is not accomplished by concentrating on each in isolation. Each can and should complement the others.

Vocal Variety

Loudness, pitch, rate, and quality have been discussed as vocal character-istics. *Vocal variety* means the changing of patterns of loudness, pitch, and rate, and to some extent quality. In other words, it is avoiding monotony. Changes or variations should be governed first of all by the meaning of what is said. Secondarily, the variation of speaking pattern should help create some interest in what is being said. Few things are less pleasant than a monotonous voice. A monotonous vocal pattern may occur because you have insufficient control over your vocal mechanism, but more often the cause is the speaker's lack of responsiveness to his own ideas and feelings, to the responses of his listeners, and to the sounds he himself is making. If your audience appears to be bored, it may be that your voice is monotonous. Further variety in loudness, rate, and pitch may make them more alert.

The voice frequently reflects the person. A dull voice often reveals a dull person; a monotone can reveal a person who lacks vitality of mind and body. In public speaking, however, these faults often occur not because of inherent personality characteristics, but because the speaker is quite literally a duller person on the platform than he is in real life. The first step in gaining vocal variety, if this is your problem, is to attain full responsiveness to your own purpose and message and to your listeners, thus producing in yourself a strong, enthusiastic desire to communicate. The second step is to concentrate on specific points of emphasis and variation while rehearsing aloud. The third is to develop an awareness of vocal range being used while speaking in public.

Variation of loudness adds emphasis, and when combined with pitch and rate, directly influences both pronunciation and diction. Emphasis is gained not only by increasing loudness, as is commonly supposed, but through any change in loudness. Either increased loudness or a marked decrease in loud-ness can make the delivery different enough to attract attention to a word or phrase. Stress and accent, which must be correct if your pronunciation is to be correct, are partially achieved through changes in loudness. Proper variation in loudness also to some extent determines the clarity of your dic-tion. "Mumbling" is one of the most common diction faults. Unvaried loud-ness, pitch, and rate patterns usually accompany what we call mumbling.

Let us take a few sentences from a student's speech to illustrate how emphasis can aid both meaning and the gaining of audience attention.

There are four traditional theories of play which I shall review in turn. These are the surplus energy theory, the recreation theory, the instinct theory, and the recapitulation theory.

The underlined words are the ones most important to gaining understanding of the entire statement. If the entire statement were spoken rapidly with little or no variation in loudness or rate, chances are that the entire meaning and intention of the speaker would be lost. "Four traditional theories of play" needs some emphasis as the key part of the total statement. These words require more stress by a slight increase of loudness and a slightly slower rate than is used in speaking the rest of the words in the sentence. Likewise, each of the separate theories requires emphasis if it is to be registered in the listener's consciousness as being important in the context of the speech.

Making marked changes in pitch is called *inflection*. In speaking there is an almost continual variation of pitch up and down the scale. These changes are made either at step intervals, which are changes in pitch between syllables or words; or with slides, which are changes of pitch upward or downward during the continuous utterance of the syllable.

Again, we can illustrate possible pitch variations in the following statement taken from a student's speech:

> If some malicious enemy wanted to hurt us greatly, he could deal us no greater blow, short of utter destruction, than to blight the beauty of our woodlands and pollute our streams.

By using some simple markings, we might indicate ways of altering pitch consistent with the meaning and intensity of feeling being expressed. The straight lines indicate steps upward or downward in pitch level; the arrows represent "slides." If the first part were spoken monotonously with little pitch variation, it might go along something like this:

```
                                              ‾‾‾‾
                                              deal  __ __
If some malicious enemy wanted to hurt us great↘ he could   us no
                                            ly
```

A speaker who is expressing indignation and intending to arouse his listeners would possibly say these words more in this pattern:

```
‾‾                          ‾‾‾‾‾‾  ‾‾‾‾
If ____      icious ene     wanted  hurt
    some ↗            ↘                                       ‾‾‾‾
                                                             deal
     mal             my          to     __ us great↘
                                              ly __ ____       ‾‾  us __
                                            he could          no
```

Emphasis can also be achieved through pitch change. Probably the most helpful task which inflectional variety can perform for the speaker, however, is to let the listener know his attitude toward what he is saying. Upward changes of pitch usually indicate that the speaker is either to some degree doubtful about what he is saying or in extremely high spirits about it; downward changes show either certainty or low spirits; mixed upward and downward changes, exaggerated, demonstrate that he does not really mean what he is saying, that he is being cynical or sarcastic.

Changes in rate are used to give emphasis more to larger portions of a speech than to individual words and phrases. The climactic paragraph of a speech of persuasion, for instance, is usually spoken with a slower, more deliberate rate in order to give greater importance to it. Rate changes can also be an excellent means of creating a mood. A fast rate can help create a tense, expectant mood; a slower rate a calm, deliberate atmosphere; an even slower one a solemn feeling. Rate change is related to pronunciation, since it is created by prolonging the utterance that is usually given an accented syllable.

A student speaker who was advocating joining the Peace Corps said this as part of his conclusion:

> The Peace Corps gives the United States its greatest opportunity to take constructive action to promote the welfare of all men and to improve understanding among all nations.

The speaker may have been impelled more by the desire to get through and return to his seat than to impress this climactic statement on the minds of his listeners, but in any event, it came out something like this:

> ThePeaceCorpsgivesthe   UnitedStates's'greatsopportunity—ah—ah—t'take constructiveaction—ah—t'p'motewelfare fallmen 'nmprove unstandn mongllnations.

Better use of rate would have aided his meaning and intention, and would certainly have gained more favorable attention from his audience.

> The <u>Peace</u> <u>Corps</u> (short pause) gives the United States (short pause) its <u>greatest</u> <u>opportunity</u> (short pause) to take <u>constructive</u> <u>action</u> (pause) to promote the <u>welfare</u> of <u>all</u> <u>men</u> (pause) and to <u>improve</u> <u>understanding</u>—among—<u>all</u>—<u>nations</u>.

Appropriate emphasis needs to be given this statement, if it is intended to climax his appeal.

Variations of quality are the most effective means the speaker has for revealing his own emotional states and the emotional intent of his message. Changes in quality result most directly from changes in muscle tone and tensions in the vocal mechanism. These changes are so difficult to isolate that, even if you should want to, it would be practically impossible to put them under conscious control. Fortunately, you do not have to. If you feel the message strongly enough, your vocal mechanism will automatically respond with the appropriate quality for the emotion. Training for the achievement of variations of quality, therefore, is training in developing greater sensitivity to feelings and freeing yourself from the inhibitions that would prevent their public demonstration.

About all that we can do in a book on public speaking is to identify variations that do and should take place in your pattern of speaking. We cannot prescribe a program of advice that will fit you individually. Your instructor can help you do that. He may possibly suggest literary selections for you to read aloud, or prescribe exercises for you to work on. Following a program designed to increase and improve your vocal variety should add immeasurably to the effectiveness of your speech delivery.

Identifying the means by which the voice is produced and the characteristics of voice should help you gain better understanding of your own voice and better enable you to analyze the way that you are using it. Your analysis of your voice can be helped by your instructor's comments and suggestions, but his ability to aid you in using your voice in public speaking ends there. No one can alter or improve your voice but you, and you can do it only through continuing practice and conscious effort; it is your responsibility.

Diction

A speaker who habitually mumbles or slurs his words reveals his own carelessness and offends his listeners. When sounds are omitted or slurred to the point of indistinctness, listeners will have a hard time figuring out what is being said. Moreover, their estimate of the worth of what is being said will go down; their opinion of the speaker as a qualified, educated person will be diminished. Bad diction is usually the result of carelessness. "Lazy" speech suggests a lazy person. The kind of speaking you do does not call for overly precise diction that borders on affectation, yet you need to be understood.

Distinct speaking is not turned on during a public speech and forgotten thereafter. The kind of diction you habitually use in everyday conversation is the kind you will be using in your public speeches. Therefore, the necessity of listening to others speak and noting their use of diction and of listening to yourself to note your own degree of distinctness becomes an everyday matter. Many speakers find it a useful exercise to whisper their speeches as loudly as they can during one of their rehearsals of a speech. This practice often helps establish a habit of distinctness.

Pronunciation

The pronunciation of words is closely related to diction; however, it is not the same thing. Correct pronunciation is governed by standards set by the more "educated" persons of a society, the sounds and syllable accents being codified in dictionaries. The distortion, blurring, or slurring of sounds is usually called a fault in diction. Mispronunciations may be distinct, but they are not in accepted usage. The more common errors of pronunciation are:

> *Omission:*   pro'ly (probably)
> *Insertion:*   athaletic (athletic)
> *Substitution:*   git goin' (get going)
> *Accent:*   com par' able (com' parable)

The dictionary is an excellent source for checking correctness of pronunciation, but oral practice of the words is the best means of insuring habitually correct pronunciations. Read through aloud the sample list of words most commonly mispronounced on page 71. Check each word in the dictionary if you have any doubt about it. Let us take the first word on the list and suggest a means of working with it. Suppose you have mispronounced it so that it sounds more like "assessry." The pronunciation guide in a standard dictionary shows: ak-ses'ə ri. A phonetic guide such as Kenyon and Knott, *A Pronouncing Dictionary of American English,* lists the word as: æk ˋsɛsərɪ. These guides are just a start for you in assimilating habitually correct pronunciation of the word. Listen to others use it, and repeat several times the word in a context, such as, "He was an accessory to the deed."

The words most commonly mispronounced, incidentally, are mainly those words we use every day, not the more difficult ones that are seldom a part of our working oral vocabulary.

For improvement of your diction and pronunciation, you should observe the following advice:

1. *Make use of all available help.* This means taking and applying suggestions given you by your instructor to build better habits not only in the speeches you give before the class, but in your everyday speech. Make frequent use of your dictionary to check any pronunciations of words that may be doubtful.
2. *Listen carefully.* Listen to the speech of others. Notice examples of indistinctness and slurring in the everyday speech of those around you. This will make you more conscious of the distinctness of your own speech.

Listen especially to the speeches of your classmates. Check their diction and pronunciation in the speeches they give and be ready with suggestions for their improvement. Listen also to the speech of your instructors and radio and television announcers. Notice that they, for the most part, serve as models for others to follow. Most of all, listen to your own speech. Give most attention to your diction and pronunciation in your everyday speech and when you are rehearsing your classroom speeches aloud. That is the time for you to be most conscious of your correct diction, not while you are giving the speech before an audience.

3. *React to what you say.* Whenever you speak to others, especially when giving a classroom speech, develop a strong sensitivity to the ideas that you are communicating. A strong sense of conviction and enthusiasm for the worth of what you are saying will do most in helping you to be distinct and to get the force and vocal variety that you need in successful communication. The complexity of the act of speaking is something that you will want to appreciate. Forceful and accurate speech requires a tremendous expenditure of effort that must be exerted if you wish to be an effective speaker. Such effort you will naturally give to matters that you care deeply about.

Words Commonly Mispronounced

accessory	except	literature	pretty
accurate	experiment	manufacture	prevent
again	family	many	probably
aggravate	February	memory	quiet
always	fellow	metal	second
and	figure	miracle	somewhere
arctic	film	nearest	status
asked	for	news	stomach
athlete	forehead	nuclear	strength
because	garage	or	surprise
can	genius	parade	temperature
cavalry	get	perform	tomorrow
chic	government	perhaps	understand
data	guarantee	perspiration	university
deaf	harass	picture	veterinary
definite	hundred	poem	where
different	instead	police	wonderful
diphtheria	introduce	poor	wrestle
drown	larynx	popular	you
education	length	potato	your
escape	library	practically	–ing endings

Phonetic Symbols Generally Used in American English
The symbols are followed by key words containing the equivalent sound value

Consonants

p	pit	ŋ	sing	ʃ	shoe	tʃ	chew
b	bit	θ	thin	ʒ	azure	dʒ	cage
m	man	ð	then	h	hat	j	you
t	to	f	fan	w	we		
d	do	v	van	hw	what		
n	new	s	sit	r	ran (called a semi-vowel)		
k	can	z	zoo	l	let (called a semi-vowel)		
g	get						

Vowels

i	he	**	o	notation
ɪ	hit		ʊ	put
* e	ate		u	cool
ɛ	set		ʌ	up
æ	cat		ə	sofa (unstressed)
ɑ	far		ɜ	bird (in parts of eastern and southern United States)
a	ask (Eastern speech between æ and ɑ)		ɝ	bird (in most of United States in stressed syllables)
ɔ	jaw			
ɒ	watch (midway between ɑ and ɔ)		ɚ	better (unstressed, as used in most of United States)

Diphthongs

aɪ	bite		ɪu	cute, or
aʊ	cow		ju	use (usually with j as initial element of the sound)
ɔɪ	boy			
			*eɪ	say (often used if sound is stressed)
			**ou	go (often used if sound is stressed)

References for Optional Unit B

1. Anderson, Virgil A., *Training the Speaking Voice* (New York: Oxford University Press, 1961).

    An excellent discussion of each of the voice characteristics combined with useful exercise material that can be applied to general speaking, public speaking, and reading aloud.

2. Eisenson, Jon, *The Improvement of Voice and Diction* (New York: The Macmillan Company, 1958).

    As the title states, both voice and diction are covered. Especially useful is the practice material for improvement of diction.

3. Hahn, Elise, Charles W. Lomas, Donald E. Hargis, and Daniel Vandraegen, *Basic Voice Training for Speech* (New York: McGraw-Hill Book Company, Inc., 1957).

    Although this work is somewhat more technical than the beginning public speaker may require, the coverage of the steps of voice production and the vocal processes is both thorough and authoritative.

Unit II

Information and Physical Materials

BACKGROUND

Man does not live by facts alone, but man must learn to live with facts. Sooner or later everyone has to face up to some of the realities in his environment. His environment forces him to if his fellowman does not. Enlightened, civilized people make efforts to find the best answers available to them about the nature of the world in which they live. And so, collective knowledge has been accumulated over tens of thousands of centuries as a result of efforts of men to explain themselves and their surroundings. Of such accumulations are our civilizations and cultures composed. Yet the more that man learns, the more he becomes impressed with the truth of the statement that his search for knowledge has scarcely begun.

Whatever a person is able to learn directly about his immediate environment he learns through his senses. Whatever he is able to see, hear, taste, smell, or feel becomes known to him and underlies his understanding or interpretation of it. Yet most of what one learns today, especially in formal education, is based upon observations made by others, not by the person himself, and has been systematized into bodies of information that are transmitted to him to accept as part of his education. A great part of what is transmitted consists of what we call factual information.

Facts

What constitutes a fact or a statement of fact is often misunderstood. Many of the occurrences or even suppositions that are labelled "facts" are not really facts at all, and many ostensible statements of fact are not really based upon facts as they can be determined.

A fact is an admitted reality, and a statement of fact is an effort to report as accurately and completely as possible what has been carefully observed. This means that facts are occurrences or phenomena that can be weighed, tested, measured, or, in other words, verified. Statements of fact are statements that can be verified by checking them against known facts. To say, for example, that all blue-eyed persons have superior intelligence and to call that statement a statement of fact is erroneous. Systematic, controlled observations and experimentation have not supplied evidence to bear out such a conclusion. It would, therefore, have to be called a supposition rather than a factual statement.

Statements of fact have certain qualifications or limitations. First of all, a statement of fact must be based either upon one's direct observation or upon competent observations made by other persons. These observations must be accurate, as complete as possible, and capable of being subjected to further verification and testing. Therefore, the statement of fact can be verified either by direct observation or by checking with a reliable source.

In addition, the statement must be restricted to what has been observed, and cannot go beyond it. Let us say, for example, that someone makes the following report: "Mr. X ran his automobile into a tree; he doesn't know how to drive very well." Is this a statement of fact? The first half may be; the second half obviously is not, because it adds an interpretation to what has been observed. The factual part of the statement merely reports what happened. Additional statements could be made about the accident of Mr. X, and an infinite number of interpretations and conclusions could be drawn. It follows from this limitation that statements of fact are relatively few in number when compared with inferences drawn from observations. Inferences can pile up one after another, ranging all the way from statements representing sound judgments to comments based entirely on the imagination, or even including deliberate falsehoods.

Finally, we must realize that facts exist whether we talk about them or not. All language, on the other hand, is inferential. It is not reality, but a means of representing reality. This is true when it represents physical reality as well as when it presents concepts derived from pure thought. What is called factual language is that which attempts to present physical reality as accurately as possible, and to report information that will reconstruct an understanding of the physical reality in the minds of those who receive the communication.

One definition of fact is that it is a demonstrable truth. But fact is not what more direct and perhaps relatively easy ways of presenting a truth or a to be so easily equated with truth, for although statements of fact are some-

portion of a truth, and even though they may tell us nothing but the truth, they do not always tell us the whole truth. The whole truth is probably not entirely understood by any one person. Moreover, his understanding of any portion of it derives not only from observations of physical events, but also from reflective thought, from human experiences and interpretations of experiences, and perhaps from inspiration as well. But he does *not* make it up to suit his own convenience.

We have been describing some of the characteristics of statements of fact because much of what is communicated in informational speaking consists of factual information. One of the primary qualifications for good informational speaking is the kind of objectivity that requires the speaker to confine himself to materials of a factual nature in order to help his audience understand the information.

Kinds of Speeches

In your study of English composition, you probably became acquainted with the standard types of discourse that are usually labelled exposition, argumentation, narration, and description. Narration and description appeal mainly to the imaginations of the readers. Telling stories or recreating a picture by use of language may be means of enlightening readers, or even, possibly, of influencing their attitudes and behavior. Their parallel use in oral discourse may also have such effects, but they are more frequently used to add interest to the communication. If the entire material of the discourse consists of this kind of material, it usually serves to entertain rather than to enlighten the listeners. While it is true that the use of anecdotes or, if you will, the method of narration, can be used most effectively in influencing belief or action of a listening audience, we do not call a speech that makes use of this device a speech of narration.

Exposition in written discourse, as Cleanth Brooks and Robert Penn Warren point out,[1] is used mainly to inform the reader. This means that a subject is set forth in order to add to the knowledge and understanding of the reader. Argumentation is used in an effort to get the reader to change his mind, attitudes, or actions.

We have made the point that public speaking is primarily a useful art rather than a decorative art; its main use is for practical rather than aesthetic ends; the speaker is concerned more with the immediate reception and the immediate responses of his listeners than he is with the kind of leisurely con-

---

[1] Cleanth Brooks and Robert Penn Warren, *Modern Rhetoric* (New York: Harcourt, Brace and Company, 1958), pp. 37–40.

templation that readers can give to a written message. In describing general "types" of speeches, we can draw closer parallels between exposition and argumentation in writing and information and persuasion in speaking.

The effort to classify types of speeches according to their general ends and to call them speeches *to inform, to entertain, to activate, to convince, to stimulate,* or *to inspire* is more of an academic exercise on the part of the speaker or critic than a recognition on the part of a listener of what the speaker is trying to do with him or to him. Such classifications come closer to representing degrees of emphasis in the speaker's general intent than to describing rigid, unalterable categories of oral discourse. A speaker can and should use information in order to persuade. The results of his persuasion may be belief, direct action, or a changing of someone's mind, but not always and not for everybody. One member of his audience may be inspired by the speech, another may change his mind, still another may remember only certain details of information used to develop a main point. Reactions to the same speech are not necessarily uniform ones on the part of every listener. A single speech may elicit a variety of responses; often the so-called general ends or functions overlap.

We have tried and shall continue to try to make clear that the essential part of a speaker's planning in getting an audience to respond to his speech in a particular way requires his determining a specific purpose—his statement of what his particular intention is in giving his speech. Yet students of speech have found it useful—and you should, too, as part of your learning about public speaking—to make some general distinctions or categories of types of speeches. In real situations these distinctions derive mainly from the nature of the speech situation and the over-all function that your speaking is expected to perform in satisfying the requirements of the occasion and the expectations of the audience. It should be recognized that some occasions call for informative speaking, others call for persuasive speaking.

We are, therefore, dealing with the two most general "kinds" of speeches in this and in subsequent units: speeches of information and speeches of persuasion. Speeches of information are intended mainly to add to the knowledge and understanding of an audience. Members of the audience are not expected to make any particular decisions about what is said, other than whether they will listen to it and make an effort to understand and remember it, even though they may later use that information in their own communication or even allow it to influence their behavior. Speeches of persuasion, on the other hand, are intended mainly to influence the attitudes, actions, and beliefs of the audience. Their ultimate intent is directed toward getting action, as we shall explain in Unit IV. Members of the audience are expected, as a result of hearing the speech, to make decisions about accepting (or possibly rejecting) what is being proposed by the speaker.

In informational speaking, the speaker wants the audience to learn something, whether they act upon the knowledge they have gained or not. In persuasive speaking, the speaker wants the audience to act upon what he is proposing. He may teach them something they did not know, but that teaching is done for the purpose of getting them to do something or believe something as a result of what he says.

The Need for Informational Speaking

This unit introduces you to what is called informational speaking. The emphasis of the assignment is on instruction. You will be expected to present a specific area of knowledge to your listeners by telling them facts and reporting reliable information representing what reputable authorities have discovered; and thereby inform them about some particular aspect of their environment.

You are doubtless well acquainted with speaking of this sort. Let us say that your physics professor has in his hands two metal objects of equal weight, width, and diameter. One is a solid disc, the other is a wheel open in the center. He wants to illustrate physical principles of mass, friction, and centers of gravity. He asks you the question, "If I roll these two objects down an inclined plane at the same time, which one will roll faster?" Possibly you do not know. You might discuss the answer, or look it up in a book, but you can learn better and more quickly if he performs a simple experiment before your eyes. He rolls them down a board propped up at one end. It is the disc that rolls faster. You have learned something that you will probably not forget.

Psychologists who study patterns of learning and recall conclude that if a person sees something and hears about it at the same time, his learning is greater than if he just hears about it or reads it in a book. But you do not need psychologists to tell you that. You undoubtedly have learned and are learning the efficacy of this method of instruction in your own educational experiences.

Information and Education

The essence of the educational process is giving and receiving information. The education that takes place in the schools comes first to mind. There the young are taught the history and nature of the society of which they are a part, the arts and skills by which they can survive and participate in that society, and the appreciations that will enable them to live full and happy lives in it. Then there is the education that is centered in the home, where those same young people are taught the acts and processes necessary for taking care of themselves and the manners and morals necessary for getting along with others. And, of course, there is the education that takes place in the churches and synagogues, where the moral teachings of the home are reinforced and amplified and the backgrounds and implications of the young person's particular religious faith are taught.

Educational activity is not limited to the home, the school, and the church, nor is it all directed entirely to the young. In every job or occupation there is considerably more time devoted to education than might be imagined. Apprenticeships, internships, and "on-the-job" and "in-service" training programs are as old as human civilization and are becoming more numerous as time goes on. Skilled workmen and technicians newly employed in an industry are often put into training classes where demonstrations of their tasks are presented to them. They see how various jobs are done so that they can eventually perform these tasks with greater skill. Junior executives frequently are put into orientation or training programs and are taught the various problems of administration by acting out imaginary situations involving the use of the problem-solving techniques that they need to learn. This training is given them so that they may be better equipped to meet similar situations in the performance of their duties.

Conventions, in which business and professional men and women hear about new ideas and advances in their fields, keep our major hotel chains solvent. More importantly however, they provide opportunities for the professional man to learn from the many speeches of information given as part of the convention program. Organizations spend immeasurable amounts of time and effort and a great deal of money educating their members about the nature and organizational structure of their group, its aims and purposes, and the means by which it should accomplish those aims and purposes.

In most human activity, public or private, there is something to be taught by someone and to be learned by someone else. Many of you are acquainted with public information programs presented on television; some of you are acquainted with the instruction given by home demonstration agents, agricultural experts, or representatives of various businesses and professions in adult education programs. All of you are undoubtedly acquainted with the informational demonstrations used in advertising, ranging all the way from television commercials showing how aspirins dissolve in the stomach, to the demonstrations of the road performance of the latest model automobile. There must even be instructions for the use of a new boxtop, lest the box be damaged and the product in it rendered unusable. Detailed instructions for the assembly and use of all kinds of equipment or gadgets are enclosed in packages and boxes brought home by the consumer.

Not all of this educating is done orally, of course, but a considerable portion of it is. Books, magazines, and newspapers; pamphlets, bulletins, handbooks, outlines, and syllabuses; maps and charts—all of these are wonderful aids to education, but they are none of them the indispensable agent. That honor must still be accorded to the teacher. He may have another name— the parent, the preacher, the professor, the coach, the foreman, the executive, the chairman, the lecturer—but whatever the name, he is the one who through oral discourse conveys his understanding to another person or persons who lack that understanding. His job is one of instruction. He is not ever likely to be superseded.

A course in beginning speech would be derelict in its duty if it did not teach you something about a kind of speaking as important as this. Many of you will not go into teaching, but all of you will be doing some kinds of teaching. You will need to know how to convey information to the minds of others. Your success in whatever occupation you go into may depend upon it. Your success as a parent may depend upon it. The measurement of success of your entire education may depend upon your ability to communicate what you have learned.

Purposes of the Assignment

This unit and Unit III are designed to help you learn some basic things about informational speaking. In this unit we shall emphasize the aspects of oral instruction concerned with so-called "material" matters, or actual physical events and phenomena, along with uses of physical materials designed to aid your information-giving. In Unit III we shall emphasize the kind of informational speaking that deals with more abstract ideas, concepts, and principles.

One thing that you should accomplish in this unit is an understanding of what makes a successful speech to inform. The most obvious requirement, of course, is that you must add to the knowledge of your audience. Your information, therefore, must be *new* to the audience either because they have not heard it before, or because the information presents them with a different facet of understanding or a fuller understanding of what is already familiar to them.

A second requirement is that the information must be made *understandable;* you only antagonize your listener if you fail to present information clearly enough so that he can learn it well. Since you cannot assume a lot of detailed technical knowledge on the part of the average college student, you will probably have to limit yourself to relatively simple subjects and basic materials for explanation. Materials are used in informational speaking mainly to clarify. The choice of words is mainly for clear and accurate explanation.

A third requirement is that the information must be limited to the essential points and reinforced in a way that the audience can *remember*. In a short speech you cannot expect to give very many items of entirely new information, for they will not be retained if you do. Two or three main points containing fresh but not extraordinarily difficult information, each developed by two or three kinds of supporting material, and all arranged in a clear and orderly sequence, will provide a basis for a successful speech in this unit.

Preparation for your speech should be checked at all junctures to see to it that these criteria are being met. Although success or failure cannot be judged until the speech is history, it is too late then for you to worry about its being a success. As you are preparing your speech, and as you are giving it, ask yourself whether your speech materials are adding to your listeners' knowledge, whether they are fresh and interesting, and whether you are presenting them in a way that will make them understandable and memorable.

In this world of technological advance, physical materials or, as they are more commonly called, audio-visual aids, have more and more become a necessity of public speaking rather than a frill or furbelow. People are impatient with drawn-out explanations of matters that would be clear if only they were demonstrated in some graphic form. Even if the audiences were not so impatient, it would behoove the public speaker to use any means by which he can make his point clearer to his audience, or more emphatic, or present it in a time-saving way. Speakers often tend to avoid using audiovisual aids because they take time to prepare. More often than not, the time could not be spent in a better way.

As a beginning public speaker, you can begin to learn how to use audiovisual aids. Although these physical materials are useful for all types of speaking, they are most commonly used in speeches of information. We believe it to be wise, therefore, to couple your learning of the speech to inform with one of the primary agencies by which you can make your information more understandable and memorable for your listeners. The proper selection, preparation, and use of physical materials is another major learning that should be accomplished in Unit II.

Of course you should continue building on what you have previously learned and put into practice in Unit I. We expect you to review carefully the discussion in that unit about kinds and uses of materials, and the basic steps in organizing the single-unit speech. The speech that you give in this unit will be longer and more complex in its structure, but much of what you accomplished in the construction of a single-unit speech applies directly here. Further, we expect you to review the Speech Inventory that you completed for Unit I, along with the comments and criticisms you received in class. In this unit we shall discuss some aspects of using action in connection with your preparation, but what you learned and experienced in your first major performance should be continued and improved upon in the practice and delivery of the speech you are about to prepare.

THE ASSIGNMENT

The speaking assignment is to give a speech of information in which you use one or more physical materials as partial support. Quite appropriately, therefore, you will be dealing with subject matter of a factual nature, based upon physical existence. The speech should concern itself with actual objects, events, processes, or phenomena that exist as part of your environment. Your main object is to clarify this "existence" for your audience. In order for you to accomplish this, additional planning for the speech beyond what you did in Unit I, and a more involved process of organizing materials will be required, as we shall explain in a later section.

SUBJECT AND MATERIALS

The starting point in selecting a subject area for this speech, as it is for beginning preparation of any speech, is to examine what you already know. You may begin by drawing upon your own knowledge and experience to examine an aspect of your environment and ask yourself some pertinent questions about it. All of us take many of these aspects for granted, having either no real knowledge at all about them, or having a hazy and often incorrect understanding of what is really going on.

It is raining today; everyone knows that. Dark clouds are in the sky, thunder is heard, and drops of water are falling to the earth. What more do we need to know? Much more, if we are really to understand what is happening. How many of us have any knowledge of what takes place in the process of the precipitation of a single drop of rain?

All of us know that, when we get into an automobile and turn the starter switch, the motor begins running. But do we really know what makes the automobile start?

We have all seen reproductions of the famous painting, the "Mona Lisa." Some privileged few have seen the original. We admire it as a great painting. Do any of us know how da Vinci mixed pigments in order to produce that particular shade of blue we like?

Some of the questions you can ask yourself about what you have observed are: What is it? When does it occur? How is it put together? How does it work? What is it intended for? What does it mean? What is its use, significance, or worth? Finding answers to such questions will require you to examine your present understanding; further, it may require you to make additional observations, ask questions of those who have additional knowledge, or to do some reading on the subject.

Criteria for Subject Choice

You may find a variety of answers to any one question, even differences in points of view, but for this speech and the one you prepare for Unit III, you should avoid subjects of an entirely controversial nature. You want to confine yourself mainly to an examination of information of a factual nature. While it is true that a speaker can give an acceptable speech of information on a controversial subject, it is considerably more difficult than if the subject were not controversial. No matter how much he may attempt to be objective and impartial, he will constantly run the danger of reflecting his own attitude on the subject through slips of the tongue revealing his own feelings, inadvertent use of emotionally loaded words prejudicial to his stand, or unconsciously slanted treatment of the subject through greater attention to arguments favorable to his own point of view than to those opposed. Therefore, you should emphasize in this speech what *is* rather than what ought to be. Your job here is essentially that of reporting rather than "editorializing."

Another criterion to keep in mind for choice of subject is whether or not it can be illustrated adequately by the use of physical materials. Essentially you will be explaining a process or demonstrating the construction or nature of material things. You will be attempting to do this in such a way that the audience can visualize the workings of the process or the form and structure of the object. You will employ visual aids to help your explanation by supplementing what you have to say. The visual aids might tempt you to unfamiliar subjects and inadequate knowledge. While admittedly they are helpful to the speaker as well as to the audience, there has not yet been one designed that will completely speak for itself. If anything, physical materials impose a greater task of understanding upon the speaker. They must not only be fitted in with other explanatory material in a necessary and unobtrusive way, which is in itself no small task; but they also must themselves be explained and interpreted.

Therefore, you need to keep in mind when selecting your subject your ability to find or make and then to use physical materials to illustrate it.

An exaggerated example of a subject that did not fit the criterion of adaptability to the use of physical materials was one that was given on the basic tenets of the Christian faith. The only visual aids that the speaker could think of to use were three cards on each of which one of the words "Faith," "Hope," and "Charity" was written. It is obvious that these words could have and should have been merely spoken by the speaker. The best subjects for this assignment, as we have said above, are likely to be those dealing with a physical process or with physical objects. Such subjects do not so much invite the use of physical materials as demand it.

We stress again that your subject should have value for your audience. A demonstration of how to shine shoes or apply lipstick can be illustrated and can be well organized and skillfully presented. But it is questionable whether such explanations would add much to the kind of learning your audience should expect or deserve. Your listeners should go away from your speech feeling rewarded by the experience of listening to it.

Among other things, this means that it must be interesting to them. We are not suggesting that you burn the midnight oil trying to dream up an "interesting" subject. That would probably be fruitless as well as time-consuming. As we said in Unit I, almost any subject can be made interesting if you will only take the time to figure out how to do it. Further, the kind of explanation you give and the use of illustrative materials will help insure that the audience will want to listen to you.

Choosing colorful speech materials related to the previous experience of your listeners is one way to hold their interest. Visual aids, if carefully worked out, are especially good at creating audience interest in the subject.

Limiting the Subject

One of the greatest dangers in preparing this type of speech is the error of trying to say too little about too much. The subject area must be limited if you are going to accomplish anything at all. You do not have time enough to explain the entire area of photography. In the time available for giving your speech, you might be able to deal with the process of enlarging prints. Attempting to explain such broad areas as tennis, golf, archery, or bowling might give the audience some vague general notions about them, but would not contain enough concrete, useful information to make the speech worthwhile. An attempt to cover the history of the printing press from its invention through the development of early kinds of presses down to the complicated machinery used in producing a newspaper is just too large a task to undertake. A more thorough explanation of one of the functions involved in typography would lend itself to more successful handling. It is better to take a limited area and explain it fully than to skim over the surface of a larger area. To borrow from the terminology of photography, do a close-up, not a panoramic shot.

Finding and Selecting Materials

Physical materials, of course, are the ones most applicable to this speech, although they are not the only ones. You must also have authority materials both separate from and related to the physical materials, and reasoning materials must be used to tie them all together for the accomplishment of your central idea. We will limit our suggestions to the use of physical materials and advise you to review what you learned in Unit I about the use of the others.

When you were introduced to the three major categories of speech materials in Unit I, a sharp distinction was made between physical and authority materials. At that time such a differentiation was necessary in order to make you understand the total concept. But the distinction is more an academic one than a real one. The two categories have more similarities than they have differences, the only essential difference being that physical materials are tangible and concrete things while authority materials are verbalizations. Otherwise the two types of materials have essentially the same nature and purposes.

Both physical materials and authority materials are used by the speaker to develop a point by clarifying it, reinforcing it, or establishing it. Most physical materials are analogous in kind and use to examples. When use of them or reference to them is extended, they serve as illustrations of the ideas you are developing. Actual physical objects are merely examples which we can see, hear, touch, taste, or smell. Representational aids, such as models, drawings, charts, maps, and graphs, are also usually examples of one kind or another, and their extensive use in the speech serves the purpose of illustration. Then too, examples presented as statistics are very often put on a chart or graph rather than presented verbally. Examples of bird sounds or human voices or musical compositions may issue from a phonograph or tape recorder rather than from the speaker's mouth, but they are examples or illustrations nonetheless. When two objects or other physical materials are compared for their likenesses and differences, we are analogizing as surely as when we do it with words alone. The counterparts in physical materials of stories and anecdotes are, of course, live or motion picture dramatizations of events. As for quotation, it is not often presented by means of audio-visual aids, but when it is it does not change in nature or use. Do not think, then, of physical materials as a special kind of decoration for a speech. They are "proofs" for your points as surely as authority materials are, and should be treated as such.

One of the attitudes necessary for success in any endeavor is the feeling that if you are going to do something at all, you should do it well. This attitude should certainly prevail in your searching for and selecting audio-visual aids for this or any other speech.

Kinds of Aids

We suggest for this speech that you plan to use certain types of audio-visual aids and delay using other kinds, which we shall mention briefly, until you have gained some proficiency.

For one thing, we suggest that you use a blackboard sparingly, perhaps only for printing a term or a formula or for drawing a few lines to supplement what you say about the other visual devices you are using. Of course the blackboard is convenient and can be used effectively. Your teachers make much use of it, but the frequency with which they or others use it is not a tribute to its uniform excellence. Instructors use it as much as they do because only rarely do they have the time to find or make a better aid. More often than not the blackboard is not the best device to use. If you have any doubt, you should avoid it. Chalk-talking is an extremely difficult art, and proficiency in it usually comes only after long practice.

Audio aids consist mainly of phonographic equipment, tape recorders, or sound motion pictures. These devices may be excellent physical materials to use in a longer speech, but are difficult to use in a short one. The time needed to set them up and take them down, not to mention the time which must be spent when something goes wrong with the equipment, makes them inadvisable for the speech in this unit.

Visual devices such as slide projectors, overhead projectors, flannel boards, or magnetic boards are also excellent aids for those who have had some experience in operating them. Even more complex devices are frequently used in televised demonstration programs. We would warn you away from use of any of these complicated devices. Use of handout materials, either printed or consisting of objects, can get you into some difficulties that we shall mention in the latter part of this unit.

What is left? As visual aids for this speech, we suggest that you plan to use either actual objects or models if they serve your purpose best, or that you use borrowed pictures or drawings that you yourself prepare. Should you have some other visual materials in mind, and believe that you could handle them well, you should consult with your instructor about the advisability of using them. If you are planning to use the actual physical object you are explaining as your aid, be sure that it is large enough so that it— and more important, its component parts—can be easily seen by everyone in the audience. A student speaker explaining the skeletal structure of a human being used a life-sized skeleton as his visual aid. He was able to disassemble it in order to show how the various bones fit together. Another speaker attempted to explain the structure and use of contact lenses which he held up to show the audience. They could not be seen even by those in the front rows and his explanation was much less effective.

Models, which are usually too difficult to construct but which you may be able to borrow, show either enlargement or a reduction of the size of an actual object. Some of them may be taken apart and reassembled or are cut away to show the working parts. One speaker was able to illustrate rather well the workings of an internal combustion engine by using a cut-away model of an automobile cylinder. Another speaker explaining the parts of the hearing mechanism in the middle and inner ear used a large plaster model of the entire ear. He was able to remove the bones and other organs in order to show their relative size, structure, and function.

Drawings that you make on stiff sheets of cardboard or drawing paper are probably the aids which most of you will call upon to help clarify your subject for your audience. The principal piece of advice about the use of these is that you must make sure that they do clarify, not confuse. Usually the speaker has to make these himself, since those put out by organizations and manufacturing companies are ordinarily designed to be read and studied at close hand, not explained from the speaker's platform. They tend to be too cluttered, too full of detail, and too difficult to read from a distance to serve a speaker's purpose. In preparing your own drawings, avoid the qualities which make the commercially prepared ones unsuitable. Make them neat, simple, and easy to read from the back row of the room. Keep in mind the principle of economy; use only a minimum of lines and labels to picture most clearly and directly the object, process, or idea that you are explaining. Also do everything you can to make them attractive and appealing to your audience. You are not expected to be an accomplished graphic artist, but you can use bold, heavy lines and bright, contrasting colors whenever possible. Beware of light lines and pastel colors. Avoid extraneous detail and unnecessary labeling. Keep printed words on the charts at a minimum. These aids must not only help the job of explanation, but carry their own interest value and be clearly seen and understood by your entire audience.

APPLICATION TO AUDIENCE AND OCCASION

In a speech of information, you need not know as much about your audience's feelings, attitudes, prejudices, and beliefs as you would need to know for a speech of persuasion. What is crucial is that you determine as well as you can the audience's present level of knowledge about your subject, their ability to comprehend what you are presenting, and their present interest in it. Generally speaking, you should never overestimate the amount of knowledge your listeners have about your subject; conversely, you should never underestimate their capacity to learn about it, even in the relatively very brief time you have to make your presentation.

How can you be sure about how much knowledge they already have? You cannot be absolutely sure, but your job of making an educated guess about it is not as difficult as it may seem. First of all, you have already had some opportunity to get acquainted with most of your classmates and know what they are majoring in and what classes many of them are taking. This should give you some clues about their level of education, clues that you would have a much harder time discovering about another audience. Further, your present accumulation of knowledge and experience has been much the same as theirs, and what is new to you will probably be new to them. However, for this audience or for any audience to whom you give an informative speech, you can make some estimates of their present level of knowledge about your particular subject on the basis of an analysis of your materials. The recency of your sources, the indications by authorities of the newness of the discovery, or the degree of knowledge that most people have about it will give you a basis for assuming what your audience is most likely to know or not to know at the time of your speech. If there are some members of your audience that you suspect may know as much or even more about your information than what you are going to tell them, do not let that discourage your efforts. They too can benefit greatly from your particular handling of it. Further, they probably have a lively interest in a subject that touches upon their particular area of specialization, since they are better acquainted with its significance than those who have little or no direct use for the information that you are giving. However, the main effort should be made to inform the uninformed, to give understanding to the greater number of your listeners who have had little or no acquaintance with your subject matter.

The ability of college-level audiences to comprehend information given to them is great, greater perhaps than that of any other kind of audience. That gives you a special advantage in making your information understandable. You and your classmates are by now rather experienced in learning about a wide variety of subjects in the classes you have taken and are now taking. Yet beware of the pitfall of assuming that because they are subjected to informative lectures four or five hours of each day that they attend classes, your listeners are automatically going to comprehend everything that you present. The motivations that can influence their learning should be taken into account.

Psychologists who delve deeply into matters of learning motivation conclude that people are impelled to learn for reasons of reward or of punishment. Any number of their experiments have illustrated the greater power of reward in impelling a person to learn and to learn well. People do want to learn things if they believe that what they learn will benefit them directly. This is a point to keep in mind, especially if what you are telling them can either help them now or will have indirect benefits for them in the future. If such is the case, tell them so. This is a good way of getting them to attend more carefully to what you have to say. You and your classmates are spending a great deal of time, money, and effort in getting a college education. You are motivated largely by your desire to better yourselves, to make yourselves well educated, competent in your profession, and possessed of greater potential earning power. These are examples of anticipated rewards, which are probably used more by the public speaker than immediate rewards.

Another part of a person's motivation can be the avoidance of penalty or punishment. You work hard at your studies not only for the reasons mentioned above, but also because you do not want to fail and bring disgrace upon yourself and your family. People are also impelled to learn if they believe that failure to learn will bring harm to them. For instance, a very good reason for learning how to apply the brakes in your automobile the right way while travelling on an icy road is to avoid being injured or killed in an accident. You seldom would want to introduce an informative speech by: "You had better learn this, or else," but a more subtle suggestion of the harmful results of misinformation about your subject is another means of reinforcing an audience's incentive for learning.

Another and very strong reason why your audience should want to learn from you is simply that of curiosity. A healthy intellectual curiosity about the world and the universe is one of the greatest assets that anyone can possess. There may be no direct reason at all in terms of reward or punishment why your audience should learn about your subject, other than it adds something to their storehouse of knowledge. This is reason enough.

You will be helped greatly in giving this speech by the assurance that just using visual aids will help create interest and arouse the natural curiosity of your listeners, but do not rely upon them alone. The points that you make, the clarity of your explanation, and the liveliness of your delivery are all required to help insure that your speech is a success. The fundamental measurement of your success is how much the audience has learned and how well they have learned it. To achieve that success, all the elements we have discussed and shall continue to discuss in the next section must be brought into meaningful focus at the moment of your delivery.

CONSTRUCTION OF THE SPEECH

You learned in Unit I that a speech unit consists of a general statement that is enlarged upon or developed by means of supporting material. Your brief, single-unit speech consisted of a statement, development, and restatement, which illustrated a basic organizational and developmental principle. A longer speech consists of a number of speech units, introduced by the speech introduction, presented and developed in the body, and re-emphasized in the conclusion. These units are unified by the over-all theme of the entire speech. The theme is called the *central idea*. The central idea of any speech is the entire content of the speech expressed in a single, inclusive statement. The introduction introduces the central idea; the body develops it through a patterned series of speech units; the conclusion reinforces or re-emphasizes it.

You determine the *specific purpose* of the speech—your reason for speaking to your particular audience expressed in terms of how you want them to respond—as a guide to lead you through the succeeding steps of speech preparation. The central idea on the other hand, is the starting point for the composition and organization of the speech itself. In short, the specific purpose tells you what you intend to do, the central idea gives you a general statement of what the end result is to be—what main idea you want implanted in the minds of your audience. Determining the specific purpose guides you in the total preparation of your speech; determining the central idea starts you out in the process of organizing the speech.

Let us say that you are planning a speech of information about the properties of protein. Your statements of specific purpose and central idea may take these forms:

> *Specific Purpose:*   To get my audience to understand the place of protein in the structure of body tissue.
> *Central Idea:*   Protein is the most important component of the body tissue since it contributes most to tissue structure, growth, and healing.

As you see, the specific purpose is constructed as a prepositional phrase—to do something. The central idea is constructed as a single, complete sentence, expressing a complete thought.

Constructing your entire speech is best accomplished by outlining the speech and being guided by the limitations of what you want to accomplish by giving the speech. After determining the subject area, completing your research, and determining a particular treatment of the subject in light of your analysis of the audience and the occasion, you should be able to write out a specific purpose. The next step is to write out a tentative statement of the central idea (one that may have to be revised after you have completed the entire outline).

With the central idea before you, plan the body of the speech, which develops the central idea and makes use of a number of main points coordinated with each other and each developing the central idea. Each main point is, in turn, developed by subordinate points which consist of the physical, authority, and reasoning materials of the speech. The content of the speech consists mainly of this supporting material. The next step is to determine the way in which you want to introduce the speech and to conclude it. The final step is to compose the outline in final form. This you can use in further preparing yourself for the speaking assignment by continuing to plan the actual wording of the speech and by rehearsing it in order to become thoroughly acquainted with the ideas in it, to learn the sequence of the arrangement, and to practice your delivery.

Main divisions of your outline will be: Specific Purpose, Central Idea, Introduction, Body, and Conclusion.

Let us illustrate this procedure further by using a subject that might be used for the speaking assignment in this unit. The subject area you have selected is a seemingly simple one, "falling leaves." In order to learn about and be able to explain why leaves fall in the autumn, you have drawn upon some of the information learned in your class in botany. You did some further investigation in other botany textbooks, the *Encyclopaedia Britannica*, and articles found in *Scientific American* and *Science News Letter*. Further, you were sure that you could illustrate the subject by making large drawings of the leaf and stem structure.

You have studied your audience and have learned that none of them is majoring in the plant sciences, and that those few who are taking the introductory course in botany along with you have probably read no more about this particular subject than the brief paragraph in your textbook. Most of them, therefore, should be able to learn something about which they know little. You are sure that you could give a concise, clear explanation in the five minutes (or whatever the exact time limit may be) your instructor has allotted for each speech in this unit.

Your statement of the specific purpose has come out in this form: "To enable my audience to learn the chemical process which causes the shedding of leaves."

Having assembled your materials from notes taken from your readings, and having clearly in mind the visual aids you will be using, you are now ready to begin organizing the speech. You plan to use this as your statement of the central idea: "The plant hormone, auxin, and the relationship of the amounts of this hormone contained in the plant stem and the leaf are responsible for the falling of leaves."

Now, how might you word two, three, or four main points that would best explain or develop this statement? If you were explaining the structure of some object, you would probably decide upon its major parts, the explanation of each of which would constitute a main point, and group explanatory details under each of these. You would also probably arrange the points in some kind of "space" order; that is, going from top to bottom, bottom to top, left to right, inside to outside, or outside to inside.

If you were explaining a process or ways of constructing an object, you probably would choose the major steps as your main points: what is done first, second, and third, and would arrange them in a "time" sequence according to the order of their occurrence.

The statement of our sample central idea should suggest to you a causal relationship: here is something that happens, what causes it to happen? In order to answer that question, you would want to tell what led up to the discovery of a cause, what the discovery was, and how the cause applies in producing the particular phenomenon. The next step would be to compose the wording of three main points that express these ideas, then to group your materials of explanation, including visual aids, under each of these headings. Then you would be able to compose a conclusion that summarized the content of the speech, and in so doing, would re-emphasize the central idea. An introduction could then be planned that would arouse the curiosity and command the attention of your audience, and lead into your subject by posing a question to be answered.

The following represents an abbreviated form that your final outline might take:

Introduction

Undoubtedly at some time or another in our childhood, each of us has asked the question, "Daddy, what makes the leaves fall?" He probably answered with something about how Jack Frost paints the leaves with a brush in the autumn and then makes them fall. Today, this explanation may make you smile. But let me ask you the same question, "Just what does make the leaves fall?"

Body

I. Botonists have been trying to find a scientific explanation for falling leaves for over a century.
    (The point is developed by examples and quotations used to show how temperature change and deterioration of plant tissue were eliminated as possible factors.)
II. Botanists discovered clues to the problem in the early 1950s.

(The point is developed by explanation along with a drawing of leaf and leaf stalk to illustrate that experiments showed that if leaf blades were cut off, stalks then dropped off. Additional explanation tells how continuing experiments led to discovery of auxin, a plant hormone influencing growth factors. Definition of the term is given, and it is printed on the blackboard.)

III. Their continuing experiments showed that leaves do not function separately, but are interdependent, leading to the conclusion that a common element in the plant was responsible for the falling.

(The point is illustrated with drawings showing how the rate of fall is affected by deblading separate leaves of a plant, and how this relates to the proportion of auxin in the stalks and leaves.)

Conclusion

This tells you why leaves fall. The discovery of auxin gave botanists the answer. Jack Frost may be a magical character, but he is less magical than nature's chemistry and the wonderful ways of nature in eliminating the old to make way for the new.

Although the example we have used for development of a subject was drawn from the biological sciences, you do not have to restrict your subject matter to that field. You may want to draw from the social sciences or the arts for your subject choice and may do so, as long as you confine yourself, in this unit, to actual occurrences or things that can be explained by the use of factual materials.

You may be asked to hand in a detailed written outline for this speech. If not, we suggest as your minimum preparation the Outline Page for this unit on which you should indicate your steps of preparation and list the major parts of what constitutes your outline structure: subject, specific purpose, central idea, and main points of the body written out as complete sentences.

PREPARATION FOR DELIVERY

Although this section focuses on action, that does not mean that the element of language and the wording used for the speech are less important. Some observations about the wording of the speech should be made.

Use of Language

You want your audience to understand the meaning of what you say. Meanings are conveyed by the words that you use. In one sense, separate words are symbols in that they represent things, events, or ideas that have existence apart from the word that symbolizes it. As Wendell Johnson says, there is a world of words (language) and a world of "not-words" that language represents.[2] One of your main considerations in wording your speech is to make sure that the words you use convey as accurately as possible the things that they represent. The greater part of the meaning that you want listeners to understand is conveyed through language. You need to avoid using technical words that may mean nothing to your listeners. Specialists have a tendency to use jargon; they often speak a language all their own, using technical terms in special senses that are understood only by members of their own profession. If you find you must use technical terms not likely to be understood by your listeners, you should define them as soon as they are introduced.

This unit emphasizes the *denotative* function of words. This is a term that you have probably encountered in your studies in English composition. Generally speaking, denotation concerns more exact or "dictionary definitions" of separate words rather than the suggested meanings or implications that the words may have. Exactness as well as clarity in use of language will help insure greater exactness and clarity in your explanations of informative material.

Principles of Action

Optional Unit B introduced you to use of voice and diction as the primary instrument of oral communication. However, a public speaker is seen as well as heard. What the audience sees of the speaker may in general be called the speaker's action. This includes his appearance, posture, movement, facial expression, and gesture. You will be expected to learn the general principles that should govern use of action at this time.

Speakers communicate through language, but they often communicate as much, if not more, with their bodies. This is not easy to understand, but its truth becomes apparent if you think about it for a moment or two. If a speaker urges you to immediate action on a problem of tremendous importance while he himself is lounging on the speaker's stand with a cigarette dangling from his limp hand, you are going to believe what his body says rather than the words he is speaking. If your favorite date says, "I love you" while looking longingly at someone else walking by, you are not going to be thoroughly convinced. The speaker's body must say everything that he

[2] Wendell Johnson, *People in Quandaries* (New York: Harper & Brothers, 1946), Chaps. 5, 6.

says with words; it must reinforce his meanings. In addition, it must be capable of saying many things that cannot be said as well with words. What words can say what a smile says, or a frown, or the outthrust jaw of determination? What words can create the emotional effect of a fist banged upon the desk, or an accusing finger in the listener's face, or eyes meeting eyes to beseech or implore? A vital part of the speaker's communication equipment is his body. The student in this course should learn something about its potential and make some initial strides toward accomplishing at least a small portion of that potential.

We ask you to start working on improving your bodily communication at this point in the course because such work fits well with the speech using visual aids. Most beginning speakers feel more at ease using their bodies in such a speech. Probably this is because the visual aids give the speaker objects to which he can move and from which he can move away, to which and about which he can gesture, and which excite his interest as well as that of the audience. They give him reasons for using action.

Action reveals to the audience the speaker's personality and contributes to whatever general impressions they form of him as a person and as a speaker. What the audience sees may reveal some things about the speaker's attitudes toward himself, the audience, his message, and his task of speaking. As we shall soon illustrate, what they sense about his attitudes affects the meaning of what is conveyed. Yet fundamentally the use of action is to give meaning to a message, just as the use of voice is to express meanings conveyed through the medium of the spoken language. Action, then, should be most closely related to the meaning of what is being said, and if it is, will be more likely to add to whatever favorable general impressions the speaker makes on his audience. Working on this premise, we can say that these general principles about the nature of a speaker's action apply:

1. A speaker communicates by nonverbal as well as verbal means.
2. Action supplements voice in oral communication.
3. What is seen by the audience should be coordinate with what is heard by them.

The nonverbal communication of a speaker consists mainly of his bodily action. Visual aids consisting of objects, pictures, or drawings are also devices of nonverbal communication, which supplement verbal communication. As we have said, voice is the primary instrument of delivery; action has a secondary role. Do not take this to mean that action is unimportant; action, like visual aids, should add to the effectiveness of your speaking, not detract from it.

These general principles in and of themselves may not have great significance for you at this stage, unless you can learn some ways by which they can be applied. Here are some applications we can suggest at this time.

Uses of Action. We do not expect you to show complete poise and effectiveness in bodily communication or action this early in the course, but we do expect that your delivery will be spontaneous, communicative, and relatively free from distracting mannerisms. This means that the first step toward effective use of action is getting rid of mannerisms that distract the audience. Some common distractions are slouching, standing on one foot, shifting weight, swaying, foot shuffling, leaning on the speaker's stand, and looking anywhere but at the audience. These mannerisms indicate that you are ill at ease and not quite sure how to stand up in front of the audience. Is this part of your message, related to the subject matter of your speech? Of course not. Such distractions may tell a true story of your attitudes and misgivings of the moment, but they negate the role that the speaker must assume each time he gets up before an audience—that of being an effective spokesman for a sound cause. Failure to look at the audience tells them something, too. It tells them that you are concentrating more on yourself or on your notes than on them. This too, may be an accurate communication of your feelings at the time, but again it negates the role that you are expected to and must perform: that of speaking directly to your listeners in order to gain a response favorable to the specific purpose of your speech. Therefore, to be true to yourself and to the real meaning of the role you are playing, your first effort should be to avoid mannerisms that are not a part of your main task or the proper performance of that task.

Once you have accomplished the first step of reducing distracting mannerisms, the next step is to practice standing with very little movement, looking directly at the audience. At least by doing this you will be telling them not only that have you something worth listening to, but that you are confidently assuming the responsibility of speaking, and further, that you recognize them as the most important ingredient in the speaking situation.

The next step is to practice using movement and gesture. It will probably seem awkward to you at first, and may also seem so to your audience, but you are making progress. Remember that overt action can be learned best only through practice. Remember, too, it is at this stage of development that action becomes coordinated with the meanings contained in the message you are delivering.

The final step in achieving good use of action is attaining skill through continuing practice in speaking. When you have that skill, your action blends into the total impression made by your delivery. The audience is aware of the force and vitality of your speaking pattern, but not especially conscious of the specific gestures or movements you are making.

You are not expected to try to master all the techniques of use of action immediately, but to do what you can now and to continue improvement in each of your speeches. Most of what you learn will come from practicing and delivering your speeches and from following suggestions given by your instructor and your classmates. As we have said, the speech that you give in this unit provides you with an excellent opportunity to use action as a vital part of your communication. The action you will use in handling your audio-visual aids and referring your audience to them should give you valuable first lessons in timing, coordination, and spontaneity.

Here is some more specific advice designed to help you in both your rehearsing and in your performance.

General Appearance.   While you are not expected to dress formally for classroom speeches, you should remember that neatness of dress and careful grooming are ways of showing respect and consideration for your audience, and are appreciated as such.

Posture.   Related to your general appearance is the way you stand. It takes physical and nervous energy to deliver a speech well. A speaker who slouches, leans heavily on a table or stand, or does not keep his weight evenly and comfortably distributed on both feet, usually not only looks like a "sad sack" but operates like one before his audience. Conversely, a speaker who stands stiffly and rigidly as though frozen in position does not show constructive release of energy at all. Remember that you as the speaker become a focal point of the audience's attention, just as they should become a focal point of your attention. Standing "at attention" is good advice if in doing so you are reasonably erect, ready to release the physical and nervous energy required for your best performance.

Movement.   By movement we mean changing position or stance, going from one place to another. Most beginning speakers plant themselves firmly behind a speaker's stand and stay there throughout the speech. Such a single spot should instead be a convenient point of departure and of return. In a longer speech especially, you will want to change your position, rather than being anchored to one spot throughout. Short steps to one side or the other and slightly forward will be sufficient. Most movement should be executed from a position facing the audience, not away from them or to the side. The time to do this is during a transition between one main point and another, or for strong emphasis of a key phrase or sentence.

Eye Contact.   This term literally means looking directly at your audience, not at your notes, the wall behind you, your visual aids, or out the window.

You can look mainly toward the center part of your audience, but do not fix on any one person or row of listeners for an extended period. Take in as much of your audience as you can with your gaze, but do not neglect at least an occasional glance at those seated in the outer edges of the assembled group. If you look at them, they will look at you, and they must if they are to follow what you are saying.

One of the best compliments you could hope to receive from a listener would be that you seemed to be speaking directly to him, almost as though he were there alone rather than being part of a large group of listeners. Such an impression is one that results from what we have called maintaining a lively sense of communication. This is a phrase described by Professor James Winans in terms of speaking directly to persons rather than just speaking in their presence.[3] By looking at your audience, you can better judge their degree of attentiveness and can exert maximum effort to keep them listening to you rather than being distracted by private thoughts of their own.

Gesture.   Gesture is specific movement made with any part of the body, but we usually think of gesture as being movement of the arms and hands. "Making gestures" is a problem that very frequently worries and confounds beginning speakers and inhibits their entire performance. If you observe someone engaged in an animated conversation, you will probably see him gesturing freely and extensively without being aware of what he is doing. What he is doing appears to be a natural and normal part of his total communication. Were you to do this kind of gesturing in your public speaking, we could say that you have an ideal beginning in using this aspect of action. Some speakers attempt to learn gestures and practice them. This is a mistake. Gestures should not "stick out" as mechanical or contrived devices. They should be a perfectly blended, practically unobstrusive part of your total pattern of action.

The late Irving J. Lee of Northwestern University once stated emphatically in a classroom lecture that there is no such thing as an awkward gesture while talking, and that no one gesture should be classified as being out of place if related to some imaginable context of meaning; it can only seem awkward to an audience if it calls attention to itself rather than giving emphasis to an idea. If we credit this assumption, we can say that effective gestures might be described but cannot be prescribed. Some textbooks in "elocution" of the last century went to great lengths in diagraming various kinds of gestures in the assumption that they could and should be taught, that every little movement had a meaning all its own. Modern teaching

[3] James Winans, *Speech Making* (New York: Appleton-Century, 1938), Chaps. 20, 21.

tends to hold that gesturing, particularly individual kinds of gestures, cannot be taught in a manner that can help the public speaker. If gestures do indeed reinforce what the speaker is saying, their effectiveness can only be described in terms of *motivation, timing,* and *coordination.*

We can say that a gesture is *motivated* if there is good and sufficient reason for making it. Gestures are used frequently to point out, locate, or show size, dimensions, or direction. They can also emphasize, in a manner similar to underlining a key word or phrase in writing. They can also show feeling or attitude on the part of a speaker. Few things are more eloquent than a shrug of the shoulders expressing doubt; a forceful downward movement of the hand indicating certainty; or hand and arm movements conveying ideas and attitudes of urgency, acceptance, or rejection. However, such gestures appear artificial and contrived if they are not motivated by the attitude and meaning conveyed both by the words and the tone of voice.

Gestures further appear to be artificial if the *timing* is off. A well-timed gesture accompanies what is being said, not coming before or after it. The action should slightly precede what is being said and go along with the words that are spoken.

In addition, the action of gesturing is *coordinated* if the entire body is involved in the total action. The hand or arm should not move independently as though the gesture were "tacked on" with no apparent connection with the physical attitude of the speaker's entire body.

We do not want you to learn particular gestures, but we do urge you strongly to practice using them both in rehearsal and in performance so that you can begin to acquire the animation, strength, coordination, and variety of action that will contribute to the sense of the spoken word, the proper attitude the speaker should assume, and the total effectiveness of your bodily communication. If the gesture appears inappropriate, or if you are using the same action too much, your instructor will help you by pointing it out. Skill in using gesture, or any of the kinds of actions we have been describing, may be gained through continuing practice aided by constructive advice.

Facial Expression. In many ways your facial expressions can be considered a part of, or certainly closely related to, your gestures. The inclination of your head, the raising and lowering of your eyebrows, and the expressions of your mouth can add to the meaning of what you are saying. Franklin Delano Roosevelt, deprived by paralysis of other means of gesturing, did amazing things with facial gesture. Incidentally, animated facial expression will also tend to improve the clarity of your diction. A frozen face, with immobile lips and lower jaw, usually muffles diction. A smiling, pleasant expression indicates the friendliness that you should show to your listeners under most circumstances; a grim or pained expression does not. Conceivably, if what you are saying represents grim or painful subject matter, the smile would be out of place. Again, as with all action, the expression should be consistent with the meaning of the message you are attempting to convey.

Working with Visual Aids

Since the visual aids you will be using—unless they contain some printed or spoken words—constitute a form of nonverbal communication, much of what we have said about the role of action in public speaking can generally be applied to the handling of the aids while speaking. The general principles listed earlier can be reworded to describe the functions and uses of the equipment, for aids also tell a story or communicate ideas, supplement your oral presentation, and must be coordinated with what you are saying. In a previous section of this unit we described the nature and uses of these aids as physical materials in planning your speech. Now we shall take up some of the problems connected with their direct uses in rehearsing and delivering your speech.

As we advised you in Unit I, use your outline for the first few rehearsals until you have the organization and wording of the speech well in mind, up through the stage where you might compose notes for delivery. You may want also to rehearse with the notes, but try if possible to free yourself from them in the final rehearsals and in delivering the speech. You will have too many things to do while speaking to be bothered by having to consult your notes frequently in order to find out what you are supposed to be saying and doing next. Your final rehearsals should be with the visual aids. This will not only help insure a degree of proficiency in handling them and reduce the possibility of mishaps, but will give you a chance to time your speech and to rehearse action that you will be using in your delivery. The following suggestions about handling visual aids should help you both in your rehearsing and in your delivery:

Position.   Place the aids in a position where they can be seen clearly and easily by all members of the audience. Remember that the aids have been prepared for their benefit, not for yours. If you have assembled or composed them according to the qualifications of size, color, and distinctness of line that we discussed earlier, the audience should be able to begin to see the portion of the message that they convey. It will be helpful if you are able to mount larger charts or pictures on an easel or stand, or fasten them to a wall so that you will not have to hold them. If your table top is too low to be within the sight lines of all members of the audience, objects or models will have to be held up so that everyone can see them. Your position is important too. You will need to stand to one side of a mounted picture or chart so that you do not obstruct the view. If you are using the blackboard, the writing or printing must be large enough and placed where it can be seen.

Use.   As a general rule, show the aids only when they are needed; remove them from sight when you are through with them. When you go on to a topic where reference to one particular aid is not necessary, you had better get it out of the way so that it will not distract or confuse your listeners. If you have followed our previous advice about economy and simplicity in preparing visual materials so that they are not cluttered up with extraneous lines, words, or details, the idea illustrated should be quickly and readily grasped by the viewers.

Audience Contact.   Even while the aids are in view, keep contact with your audience. Their main focus of attention should be on you and diverted to the aid only as you direct their attention to it. When their eyes should be on the visual aid, your eyes should be on them. If you begin talking to your chart, an object, or the blackboard, instead of talking directly to your audience, you will be losing the contact necessary in any kind of speech. If you are using a chart or picture and move to one side so as not to obstruct the view, you may want to use a pointer to refer to various details being explained at that moment. There is no harm in quickly glancing at those details out of the corner of your eye to see that you are pointing to the right thing, but keep looking at your audience. By doing this, you can judge their degrees of responsiveness to what you are saying and what you are showing.

Handling the Aids.   Another sound general rule to follow is to keep the visual aids in your own possession. Some speakers have successfully used hand-out materials to be used according to instructions given as part of the speech. This can work provided that everyone in the audience has the same material at the same time, and that whatever work they do with it is coordinated with the speaker's instructions. But this use of visual aids is rather tricky. Until you have gained some experience in handling visual materials, we suggest that you defer using handouts. We recall one student speaker who handed out a coin collection to the audience while giving a speech. You can imagine the difficulties he got into. What he was trying to say about various coins was lost because the audience was involved in passing the coins back and forth, examining them, and giving their attention to almost everything else except what the speaker was trying to say.

So we repeat, rehearse with the visual aids. Observe our advice during rehearsal so that it may better be carried out in delivering the speech. The experiences you have in handling visual materials will help you in developing good use of action not only in this speech but in other speeches you will be giving.

There is a built-in reason for the main movements and gestures you make in such a speech; they almost always are motivated. The qualities of animated, coordinated, and motivated movement and gesture are ones to incorporate into your delivery of any type of speech, whether these movements and gestures involve handling of materials or not. They are perfectly proper in any speech that can benefit from their use, not just in a speech of demonstration.

As a final word, let us say that audio-visual materials can be used in almost any kind of speaking. Do not assume that use of physical materials is to be confined to the speeches in Unit II alone; if you find it appropriate to prepare and use them in other speeches you give, whether they be informative or persuasive speeches, by all means use them. Most accomplished public speakers do.

REVIEW OF PREPARATION

1. Choose a subject from a subject area that you now know something about, a subject that deals with some specific aspect of your environment and that can be illustrated by use of visual aids.
2. Do some research that includes gathering authoritative information and assembling materials appropriate for visual illustration.
3. Making sure that your treatment of the subject fits the assignment and will conform to your analysis of the audience's present knowledge, their current interests, and their capacity to learn, decide on a specific purpose for your speech.
4. Organize the speech into outline form by determining the central idea, the main points to be covered, and the introduction and conclusion most appropriate for handling your subject and informing your audience.
5. Prepare in final form the visual materials to be used so that they coordinate with the structure of your speech and illustrate major points rather than peripheral details.
6. Rehearse the speech with special attention to wording and practice in the use of the visual aids and action.

References for Unit II

The following references my serve as sources of information about the construction and uses of audio-visual materials:

1. Chandler, A. C., and Irene F. Cypher, *Audio-Visual Techniques for the Enrichment of the Curriculum* (New York: Barnes & Noble, 1953).
2. Dale, Edgar, *Audio-Visual Methods in Teaching* (New York: The Dryden Press, Inc., 1954).
3. Haas, Kenneth B., and Harry Q. Packer, *Preparation and Use of Audio-Visual Aids* (New York: Prentice-Hall, Inc., 1950).
4. Kinder, James S., *Audio-Visual Materials and Techniques* (New York: American Book Company, 1950).
5. McKeown, Harry, and Alvin B. Roberts, *Audio-Visual Aids to Instruction* (New York: McGraw-Hill Book Company, Inc., 1949).
6. Weaver, Gilbert G., and Elroy W. Bollinger, *Visual Aids* (New York: D. Van Nostrand Company, Inc., 1949).

Unit III

Information and Abstract Materials

BACKGROUND

The tree of knowledge has many branches. You have only to look into your own college catalogue to discover a bewildering and perplexing maze of departments and courses. Possibly you have thought, leafing through it, "All this learning available, and I will never be able to get even a small fraction of it."

There was a day, not so long ago, when a man could still be a universal genius, gaining distinction of a high order in many and diverse fields of endeavor. Today the odds against such an accomplishment are formidable. The tree of knowledge, discernible in its entirety a hundred years ago, has grown to the point where most people give up in despair of seeing even the complete dimensions of the colossus, much less examining closely any large number of its branches.

Nonetheless, each of us still wants to be and needs to be, in his own small way, something of a universal genius. That is to say, while all of us may be specialists of one kind and another, we all wish for and can use to great advantage information from other branches of study besides our own.

Your present study of public speaking is a case in point. Some of the information that you are learning from this textbook and from lectures and discussions is derived from the study of public speaking proper, but a considerable portion of it is not. A partial listing of some of the more significant contributing fields of study would include grammar, literature, linguistics, phonetics, physiology, psychology, sociology, philosophy, the arts, communications, and semantics. No branch of the tree of knowledge exists independently. It grows out of and into other branches and sprouts new branches of its own, and all eventually draw nurture from the same soil by way of the same roots and trunk.

As a result of the mushrooming of specialties and specialized courses, today's college student faces the danger of diminishing opportunities for diversity of learning. Fortunately, however, on college campuses everywhere far-sighted men and women are fighting to preserve the values of a general, or, as it is more often called, a liberal arts education. C. P. Snow, the eminent British physicist and novelist, writes and speaks continually of the necessity for better communication between the sciences and the humanities, so that both may grow stronger and more beneficial to mankind. It would be tragic if we were ever to forget that we are all looking for the same answers to the same questions, only in different places and different ways.

Fundamentally, all of man's investigations and thinking are directed to answers to, at the most, three questions: What is man? What is the world? What is man's proper function in and relationship to the world? An answer of any kind to any one of these questions is interesting and possibly useful to all men, not just to the specialists who have discovered it. One purpose of this course, we have said, is to aid you in conversing with your fellow-specialists; and another is to aid you in speaking about your specialty to non-specialists. Special attention was paid to the first of those purposes in Unit II; in this unit, it will be paid to the second one.

Speaking to a General Audience

When speaking to those in the same field as yourself, or about some relatively simple matter to those who are not in your field, you may deal almost entirely with facts. Specialists will know the larger concepts to which the facts relate; and when you are describing simpler matters for the lay audience, the conceptual context can be quickly given. When speaking about your specialty to general audiences, however, you only very rarely speak about the small matters. What the nonspecialist is interested in, and rightly so, is some rudimentary understanding of the large answer to the large question. With all that he needs to learn about his own study, he does not have time for the minutiae of yours. But, we repeat, he wants to and needs to know about the really significant terms, concepts, ideas, and principles connected with your branch of knowledge. What you will usually talk about in talking to him, then, are interpretations of facts rather than facts themselves; theories about rather than demonstrations of mechanisms; abstractions rather than concrete things. You will be *informing* him more than you will be *instructing* him.

How do you go about making clear to your listeners the meaning of an abstract term? It can be a most difficult task, but it is by no means an impossible one. There are available to the speaker many methods of definition and means of clarification. Moreover, he has within himself resources of intelligence and imagination that can help him greatly. No one has yet devised an idea whose basic premise cannot be reduced to relatively simple terms and transmitted to a lay audience. The failure of so many communications of this kind lies not in the message, but in the means used by the speaker to convey the message.

Purposes of the Assignment

The basic learning of this assignment should be the means by which you can clarify relatively abstract matters to an audience not conversant with the branch of human knowledge from which they derive.

One of these means is good organization of your speech materials. Any speech is the better for being well organized, but the speech of this unit is almost certain to fail without a very carefully conceived pattern. The hardest seas of understanding to sail are those of abstract thought. Unless you have a well-charted course to follow and are steady at the wheel for the whole journey, it will be easy for your listeners to fall overboard midway in the voyage or possibly even to be left behind at the dock. Therefore, asking you to prepare a detailed outline at this juncture appears to be advisable. Your instructor will inform you about what exact form it should take, and when and for what purposes you will turn it in to him to be checked. The necessity for careful outlining begins with this unit and continues through the rest of the course.

When listening to the speeches of others, do not neglect the benefits of general education that you can get out of them by being too eager to look for faults of speech content, organization, and delivery. Listen to learn, not to criticize. Rather than hurting your ability to offer helpful comments to your classmates, this procedure should actually help it. If you are really trying to learn, the important strengths and weaknesses of the speech will be many times more apparent, simply because they are then more gratifying or more annoying to you.

THE ASSIGNMENT

You are to give another speech of information, but of a different kind from the one given in Unit II. Rather than explaining the component parts of an object or the workings of some process as you did last time, you will be clarifying a term, concept, idea, or principle. You will, in brief, be talking about an abstraction (something which cannot be apprehended by the five senses; something which, as a synthesis and explanation of the facts of the physical world, exists only in the mind of man) rather than about any tangible, concrete thing. Not only must the term which you choose to define be of an abstract nature, but it must also meet these further qualifications: (1) it must be a term of such general significance that any reasonably well-educated person, regardless of his occupation or field of specialization, would be expected to know and understand it; and (2) it must be either completely new to or else not thoroughly understood by the majority of your audience. For instance, educated people ought to know what an Oedipus Complex is, or what Stoicism means, but most college students probably do not, or at least they do not have a clear and firm understanding of these terms. The same is probably true of the concept of Natural Selection, the ideas in *The Social Contract* of Rousseau, and Newton's First Law of Motion. You are to find a term, concept, idea, or principle that, like these examples, is of general significance and yet not well enough understood by your audience, and by well-chosen means of clarification bring your audience to understand it.

One or more of the following options may be given you for choice of a speech subject in this unit:

Option A: Free Choice. You may choose to explain any term, concept, idea, or principle you please so long as it fits the general requirements of the assignment outlined above.

Option B: The Great Ideas. You will be limited in your choice of subject to only those terms, concepts, ideas, or principles that might be studied in a "Great Books" or "Great Ideas That Have Shaped Our Civilization" course. You will be expected not only to tell about the man responsible for the idea and explain it, but also to do something by way of discussing its significance for the modern day.

Option C: The Latest Thing. It is getting to the point in many fields where textbooks are already out of date on the day they come off the presses. In all fields new ideas and sometimes whole new branches of study have come into being within the last few decades. Not too many years back such terms as *cybernetics, group dynamics, radiobiology, quantum theory, geriatrics,* and *existentialism* were totally unknown, yet today they are of significance to everyone. Your task is to find such an abstract term and explain it and its significance to your listeners.

Option D: The "Taken-for-Granted" Subject.   There are many seemingly simple abstractions about which we feel we know absolutely everything there is to know, but which actually are still mysteries to us. "Light" might be one such subject; "stress" another; and "wavelength," "realism," and "jazz" still others. Such an abstraction can be the subject of your speech.

Option E: Instructor's Assignment.   In order that your assignment may better suit the speech needs of your particular class, your instructor may choose to modify one of the above assignment options, combine features of two or more of them into one assignment, or possibly give you an assignment entirely of his own devising.

SUBJECT AND MATERIALS

Choose a Subject Area

One of the most perplexing questions in choosing a subject for this unit is how abstract the abstraction that you are clarifying should be. If you have inferred that the term, concept, idea, or principle should be somewhere beyond the reaches of everyday knowledge, you are right. However, it should not be so exalted that it is virtually indefinable or requires three volumes to clarify it. Avoid the great, boundless abstractions like "truth," "faith," "love," "honor," and "democracy." In the time that you will have to speak, you could not even begin to skim the surface of such subjects. But aside from that injunction, it is entirely up to you to make the distinction as to how abstract the term should be. There are no hard-and-fast rules to go by, no absolute yardsticks of measurement, no infallible tests. What advice we have to give on this matter, then, must be taken to be suggestive rather than prescriptive.

Abstractions

General semanticists (those whose study is the meanings of words, and the problems of communication resulting from improper transmission and reception of word meanings) make much of what one of their number calls an "abstraction ladder." [1] They would group all items in any general subject area

[1] The term "abstraction ladder" is that of S. I. Hayakawa, *Language in Thought and Action* (New York: Harcourt, Brace & World, Inc., 1964). Although the concept for which the term stands is common to all general semanticists, the term itself is not. Among other terms used are "vertical index" and "vertical levels of abstraction." We chose the term "abstraction ladder" for use here because we felt it was the one that would be most meaningful to the beginning student.

on such a ladder, with the lowest rung being the most discrete, tangible example of the species; the topmost rung the highest level of verbal abstraction; and an indeterminate number of intermediate rungs placed in an ascending progression between. The term, it can be seen, is a trifle misleading. Not all of the items on an abstraction ladder are abstractions, or even words; some of the lower ones belong to the world of concrete facts rather than the world of abstract thought.

Since it is necessary that your thinking be clear on this before we proceed, let us construct such an abstraction ladder showing the various levels of abstraction at which you could tell somebody about a bicycle:

Personal possession
Mode of transportation
Self-propelled vehicle
Bicycle
Red bicycle
Red lightweight bicycle
Cardinal red 26″ English lightweight bicycle with chrome wheels, leather saddle, headlight, tire pump, and luggage rack
Picture of that particular bicycle
Model of that particular bicycle
Showing the bicycle itself

This is a purposely simple ladder designed to demonstrate that the bottom rungs of an abstraction ladder may have very little that is abstract about them.

In a moment we shall be moving down an abstraction ladder more like the kind you will be dealing with in your speech. Before we do, let us generalize by saying that the term, concept, idea, or principle that you will be dealing with will probably not be found on either the very bottom or the very top rung of the ladder, but on one of the intermediate rungs. The precise rung will vary with the general subject area, the speaker, the audience, and the occasion. Some subject areas have fewer rungs than others, or do not rise as high; some speakers are capable of speaking effectively at higher levels of abstraction than others; some audiences can climb higher peaks than others; and their ability to climb varies considerably with time of day, mood of the moment, and what has preceded or is to follow.

A Sample Subject Area

We are now ready to take a sample subject area and see how this advice would work out in practice. We will suppose that you are vitally interested in the theater and somewhat knowledgeable about it; you are a member of the campus theater group; you have appeared in a number of plays and have worked backstage on others; you have taken several courses in theater and dramatic literature; and you intend to pursue this interest for the rest of your life. Such a high level of interest in your subject and knowledge about it we should like to see as a necessary qualification for speaking on any subject; certainly it is desirable for this speech, where you need to be several jumps ahead of your audience all the way. Only a person who knows a great deal about a subject can see its essentials, the simple ideas that form its basis, the foundations upon which the elaborate superstructure is built. The abstraction which you will be attempting to clarify is usually unknown to or misunderstood by your listeners because the superstructure has frightened or confused them. In the few minutes you have you are going to have to obliterate the superstructure from the minds of your hearers and show them the foundations. That, as we have said, you cannot do unless you are equipped with the mental X-ray machine of comprehensive knowledge.

You probably know that you cannot talk about "the arts," or "the fine arts," or even "the performing arts" in the time you have. What about "the theater"? No, that is still too high on the ladder. It might not take three volumes to make clear, but you would need at least one volume. You will have to narrow down your subject matter considerably more than that. You have an infinite number of choices, for the theater is a subject that reaches as far back in history as the beginnings of human civilization itself; that has a separate history for every country, and, for that matter, every town; that, as an amalgam of many arts and an art form in its own right, has a multitude of special subject areas contained within it. Will you talk about the Greek theater, the Shakespearean theater, the Restoration theater, the modern theater? Or about dramatic tragedy? Or the religious origins of the drama? Or the great scenic artistry of the Renaissance? Or the importance of the director in the modern theater? Or the art of acting?

Let us say that it is the art of acting that you choose to talk about. This, remember, is not yet your term; it is still a larger subject area from which you will choose the narrower subject area embodied by your term. You are still too high on the abstraction ladder. Now you will need to ask yourself what abstract term that is common in discussions of the art of acting is of general significance and is presently unknown to your audience or misunderstood by them. The obvious choice, of course, is "The Method," or, as it is also called, "The Stanislavski Method." Your listeners should know the meaning of this term. They cannot understand even the amusement pages of their newspapers or many of the jokes they hear on television if they do not know what is being referred to when someone like Marlon Brando, Paul Newman, Anne Bancroft, or Shelley Winters is spoken of as being a "Method" actor. Further, it is a term that many members of the acting profession, let alone the general public, misunderstand. You could not teach your listeners "The Method" in a few minutes, of course, nor would you want to; but you could give them enough basic understanding so that this would no longer be a completely dark, cobwebby corner of their general education. You have probably found the right rung of this particular abstraction ladder. To go lower into specific techniques of "The Method" such as "memory of emotions" or "relaxation through justification" would not be especially useful for a lay audience, and therefore they would lose their interest.

Other qualifications to keep in mind in choosing your subject area are those we discussed in connection with the previous unit. The successful speech to inform, we said then, is one which contains information that is new to your audience, that you can make understandable to them, and which is presented in such a way that it is memorable. Think of these criteria as you settle upon your subject area. Remember also that we warned you away from subjects of a controversial nature. In the speech to inform you are not trying to make your audience believe or do anything; you are merely trying to make some matter clear to them. The conditions of this assignment help insure that your subject will be worthwhile for your listeners. It may not be inherently interesting, however; and interest, we have said previously, is necessary to make your speech a rewarding experience for your listeners. There might be a few subject areas that you would have to rule out on this criterion, but do not be too hasty about your rejection. Interest lies more in the way the subject is presented than in the subject itself. "Fascinating" subjects can be made boring and "boring" subjects can be made fascinating.

Investigate the Subject Area

In your search for materials for this speech, you are urged to draw upon your past knowledge and experience as you have done before and as, indeed, you should do for every speech you give. Materials derived from that source, however, are not likely to go as far as they have previously. More of your material for this speech will probably have to come from research that you do as a part of your preparation.

You might want to start with your present knowledge as a basis, then consult general reference works, such as college-level encyclopedias, in order to gain additional background knowledge. Your third step, then, would be to consult the more specialized writings found in texts, professional journals, or the more "learned" periodicals. You might also wish to check up on popularized discussions of your subject area, if there are such, in the mass-circulation magazines and newspapers. Some of these will undoubtedly be too superficial to be of any use to you, but others might prove helpful. It is conceivable that complete books have been written on your subject area, and if you are interested enough and have the time to read them in their entirety, we would be the last to stop you; but there is often no need to go that far. A bit of judicious skimming and consultation of the index should be enough to provide you with the information most pertinent to your present task.

One thing to avoid is giving only a dictionary definition of your subject. A statement that begins, "According to Webster . . ." has its values, but they are limited. For one thing, the dictionary attempts to give only a concise denotation of the most commonly accepted and the most general uses of any term. Even though your task of informing is essentially one of defining, it should not be limited to the confines of a dictionary exercise. The objective is to give your listeners a more complete understanding of the term, concept, idea, or principle, not merely to add a new word to their vocabularies.

Materials for Definition

Obviously, the materials which you will be using in this speech will have definition as either their direct or indirect purpose. In this discussion we will not concern ourselves with those which only indirectly lead to definition; we will talk only about those which make the direct, frontal attack. Sometimes definition is accomplished with the same materials you have been using for other purposes in your previous speeches; at other times special methods are the better ones to use. We will look at both means.

The *example* could well be said to be the workhorse of speech materials. It can be used effectively for more purposes than any of the other materials. Definition is no exception to the rule. The example is useful for this purpose in almost any of its forms.

If a number of short examples, all demonstrating similar attributes, are presented to an audience, their composite effect will be to clarify to the audience the attributes of the term, idea, concept, or principle which is being defined. Since the extended example, or *illustration,* is likely to do this more expeditiously than multiple shorter ones, it is ordinarily used. Normally, too, it is the fictitious illustration rather than the real one which the speaker chooses. If one is trying to define the Oedipus Complex, for instance, referring to the fictitious "Mr. X," a typical example of one who has never outgrown this stage of his personality development and is suffering psychological problems as a consequence, is a most useful device.

Examples in the form of *statistics* are sometimes used by the speaker for definition, although their use is somewhat limited. Subjects selected from the field of statistics, or from other fields that make extensive use of statistics, would almost necessarily have to be defined in part by the use of statistical information. Subjects from fields not making much use of statistics, on the other hand, would probably need them little or not at all.

Analogy, or the comparison of two examples, is probably the most useful kind of authority material for definition. It, even more than the example, makes use of reference to the experience of the listener, of relating the unknown to the known. One could hardly explain the English game of cricket, for instance, without making analogy to the American game of baseball, pointing out the similarities of the two games and their differences. You will notice that analogy is used several times in the Sample Student Outline included on page 140, most notably in defining the term "cosmic static" by comparing it with the static you hear on your radio receiver. Nothing helps a listener understand an abstract idea better than when the speaker likens it to some simpler idea that he already understands.

Stories and anecdotes have their uses for the purpose of definition, but they are probably not as helpful as either the analogy or the example. If well told, of course, they can rivet your audience's attention to you as no other supporting material can, but they are usually a trifle roundabout and unspecific in making a point. Definition always calls for some measure of precision. When a term is taken from literature to apply to another field, however, a brief retelling of the story from which it derived may be the very best way of defining it. Let us cite the term "Oedipus Complex" again. Sigmund Freud took the name for the particular kind of behavior he was describing, a male child's abnormal hatred of his father and love for his mother, from a Greek legend of a king whose fate it was to kill his father and marry his mother. In defining the term, you might very well want to recount the ancient legend.

Literary quotations are ordinarily useful for definition only when the term is so high on the abstraction ladder that small reference to the more concrete types of material can be made. In that case, you may have no recourse but to define—as best any such term can be defined—by using a literary quotation. However, quoting directly a concise, thorough definition of a particular term from a recognized authority in the field could be an appropriate starting point from which you could expand an explanation in greater detail.

Although you are not talking about a concrete subject in the Unit III speech, you may find it necessary to define subsidiary terms that refer to a physical object or that are best represented by some sort of graphic means. The speaker of the Sample Student Outline, for example, found it necessary to tell his audience what a radio telescope was. Wisely, he chose to apply the learnings of Unit II and used a visual aid to define the term. Some terms, concepts, ideas, and principles belonging to the more scientific realms of thought might call for considerable use of pictorial representation. How could you define a principle of chemistry, for instance, without at least some resort to formula notations? Frequently, nonscientific terms are, for a given audience, explained in terms of equations and formulas, charts and graphs and drawings. Do not rule physical materials out as a real possibility for the speech of Unit III. As we have maintained before, they are essentially authority materials in another form.

Special Means of Definition

Definition is so constantly a problem in education that a number of special means of accomplishing it have been devised. Again these are, in the last analysis, nothing but authority materials in another guise. Here the difference is not between physical and verbal forms, but in a special kind of structuring which is given the authority materials. Some of these means relate to common patterns of organizing main points, and will be discussed in connection with them. At this point we shall talk about five other means so specialized that their use is restricted almost entirely to definition.

One of these means is definition by *context*. There are many terms difficult to define by any specific reference. It may prove helpful to put such a term into a context, those sentences or phrases in which it is customarily found. A standard device for teaching vocabulary, you will recall, is to have the student use the new word correctly in a sentence. But for your public speaking, unlike your vocabulary drills, not just any sentence or sentences will do. The context or contexts you give the word should have maximum meaning for your listeners. If, for example, you wanted to define "platonic love" by context, a sentence like "Hers is a platonic love" would not be the least bit helpful. More helpful would be a sentence like "Platonic love is seldom possible when the two persons are of the opposite sex." Usually definition by context will use not one, but several, phrases or sentences. When a term has changed its meaning several times over a span of years, selected sentences from authors representative of different periods may be used to show the changing contexts and meanings of the word. Such a specialized use of definition by context is a standard device of the *Oxford English Dictionary*.

Definition by *etymology,* or the history of the linguistic development of the word, is another special means you can use. In the original meanings of roots, prefixes, and suffixes there can often be found interesting and illuminating clues to the basic meaning of the term, as well as implications which may tend to unify anything else that you will want to say about it. Let us suppose that you wanted to define the term "agnostic." [2] It would be very fascinating to your hearers to learn that Thomas Huxley, the great English biologist (you

[2] The information about the history and derivation of this term was derived from Wilfred Funk, *Word Origins and Their Romantic Meanings* (New York: Wilfred Funk, Inc., 1950), p. 267.

may have read his famous lecture "On a Piece of Chalk") and himself an agnostic, proposed the term by which his religious position could be described at a party given in 1869, and that he used as the root word the Greek *agnostos*, which means "unknowing" or "unknowable." You could tell them that the position of an agnostic is "I just don't know whether there is a God," as distinguished from that of an atheist (*a*, "not"; *theos*, "god"), which is "I say that there is no God." In addition, you might use the concept of "unknowing" as the central theme of all you had to say. Sometimes a speaker will find in the etymology of a word an archaic meaning which he feels has figurative if not actual relevance, and will use this as the springboard for his modern definition. Whatever use you make of etymology, do not take it too literally. Just because "education" derives from the Latin *e*, "out," and *ducere*, "to lead," does not in any way indicate that our educational system does or should "lead the student out." Word meanings are in a constant state of change.

Three other special methods of definition are by *synonym*, by *classification*, and by *negation*. Although other forms of authority materials are used in these methods, the primary one for all three is analogy.

When one wishes to define a term by *synonym*, he looks for other terms that are very similar in meaning to the one he wishes to make clear. From these he selects those instances which he feels his audience is most likely already to know and understand. Using reference to the experiences of his listeners, he attempts to make a link between terms already known to them and the one unknown. It is analogy not to one other example, as is common, but rather to a number of brief instances. The terms need not be exactly similar to be effective in giving the listener a foothold of understanding. Our use of the word "foothold," should suggest that this method of definition is not likely to be the only one used. More than two or three synonyms usually need to be suggested. As you have already learned, instances gain their effect through accumulation. If a given synonym is to any marked degree dissimilar from the term you are attempting to define, you will want to make sure that you point out the differences.

Definition by *classification*, as the name suggests, attempts clarification through classifying the term by genus and species. If the listener's experience includes any sort of acquaintance with the genus, he can use this knowledge as a means of gaining understanding of the new species. Of the three methods which use analogy, this one uses it in its purest form. Putting the new term into its genus creates the necessary link with the listener's present knowledge; making extended comparison and contrast of it with other species of the genus extends his knowledge and particularizes it. This method is used in the Sample Student Outline, where radio astronomy is placed in the genus "science" and then differentiated from other sciences—given a species—by a number of differentiations of purpose and means.

By far the most interesting of the special methods is definition by *negation*. An anecdote from the life of Samuel Johnson, a great eighteenth-century literary figure, illustrates this procedure rather well. James Boswell, his friend and biographer, had asked the great man for a definition of poetry. "What is poetry? Why, sir," roared Dr. Johnson, "we all *know* what light is, but it is not easy to *tell* what it is. . . . It is much easier to say what it is not." If you were to answer Boswell's question by the method Samuel Johnson suggested (not in this assignment, however; "free verse" would be a better choice), you would cite not those characteristics which poetry has, but those which it does not have. You might say that poetry is not explicit about the point that it is making; it is not given to generalizing; it is not verbose; or it is not undisciplined. Such statements would actually give a clearer idea of what poetry is than any attempt at citing "typical" characteristics. Two poems can have two entirely different sets of characteristics and yet be poetry. What they have in common are the characteristics of prose writing which neither of them possesses. Definition by negation, then, is sort of analogy in reverse. You relate your new idea to a *dissimilar* one which your listeners already understand, not to any similar one. No comparisons are made in definition by negation, only contrasts. For the term which embraces many mutually contradictory elements, there is often no other effective means of definition to use.

Use of Reasoning Materials

You will very probably be using more reasoning materials in the speech of this unit than you have in either of the previous two. While these materials do not really come into their own yet—that they will do in the speeches of persuasion coming up—they are necessary whenever difficult information is being transmitted. The Unit III speech should be liberally sprinkled with such phrases as "that means," "so you see," "it follows therefore," "to repeat," and "to summarize." In public speaking you have to do much more by way of pointing out the relationships and implications of ideas than you do in writing. Even if they had the inclination, your listeners just do not have the time to make the connections themselves. You must do it for them.

We should like to call your attention to repetition and restatement as special reasoning materials that you will certainly want to employ in this speech. If it is kept within the bounds of good taste, your audience will not be the least bit insulted by repetition; they will welcome it. If they are to remember your information, their learning must be reinforced. Repetition and restatement are a simple but excellent agency of reinforcement. Studies indicate that up to five repetitions are effective in aiding listener retention, with three being the most proportionately effective number.[3] Generally speaking, the more repetitions up to the number of five, the better. It is usually wise to vary the phrasings of the idea, but even repetition which uses the same exact wording is better than none at all. If you do not believe this, listen to a few radio and television commercials and note how many times the name of the product and its identifying slogan are repeated.

APPLICATION TO AUDIENCE
AND OCCASION

Once again we suggest that you judge most carefully the exact measure of your audience's present lack of knowledge about your subject. Probably more faults of application of subject to audience in informational speaking occur because this is not done than for any other single reason. Especially when you are dealing with abstractions, you need to know precisely where your listeners' understanding stops in order to start at that exact point and not before or after it. If you start before and lose them for even a minute by seemingly insulting their intelligence or boring them, they may miss some necessary matter of definition of terms or background and be confused all the way. If you start after the point where their knowledge ceases, you will certainly never help them understand; you have forfeited any chance of doing that before you start.

Of equal importance is the necessity of discovering what your audience presently *does* know about your term, concept, idea, or principle; about terms similar or opposite to it; about any subordinate terms, concepts, ideas, or principles you will need to discuss in relation to it; and about the subject area in general. Here again we are only making more explicit a point that has previously been made. As you have noticed, every one of the various ways that we discussed above of making something clear to an audience is based upon reference to their previous experience. You never make anything clear to people by telling them what *you* know, but only by referring to things that *they* know. Your job in informing is not to parade your knowledge, but rather

[3] A. T. Jersild, "Modes of Emphasis in Public Speaking," *Journal of Applied Psychology,* 12: 611–620 (1928), and Ray Ehrensberger, "An Experimental Study of the Relative Effectiveness of Certain Forms of Emphasis in Public Speaking," *Speech Monographs,* 12: 94–111 (1945). The studies agree on the value of repetition in gaining emphasis and the fact that its value diminishes after the third or fourth repetition, but disagree on a number of other points. Although more than three repetitions were shown by these studies to diminish in effectiveness, we feel that the fact that retention value was still being substantially aided up to the number of five repetitions argues strongly for going beyond three if and when possible.

to discover links with your audience's knowledge, and means of showing to the audience those links. Once they make the connection, the job is done.

Dealing in abstractions poses some special problems of audience analysis. There are two items of information that you need to know in connection with preparing this speech that you may not need to concern yourself with in preparing any of your other speeches. This information does have relevance to other kinds of speeches, but not always and not to the degree that it does for this speech.

One of these items of information is how interested in and capable of abstract thought your listeners are. There are some people who thrive on it; more, perhaps, would just as soon leave it as take it. You might suppose that any group of college students would be drawn to it, but such is not the case. They are very much like the general run of humanity in this regard—unequally divided, with the "rather nots" more often than not the majority party in the particular group.

Indications of such interest and capacity are to be found in the prospective occupations of your audience, their ages, and their interests, recreations, and hobbies. Very generally speaking, students enrolled in the "bread-and-butter" curriculums are less at home high on the abstraction ladder than those pursuing less vocationally oriented courses of study. You can say with more certainty that the older the person, the more he will be given to thinking in abstractions and finding the practice to his liking. Interests, recreations, and hobbies are very often excellent indexes. While some of our greatest abstract thinkers may love football, mystery novels, or comic strips, these do not cover the full range nor indicate the general tenor of their avocational interests. They ordinarily also take great interest in such other leisure-time activities as serious reading; chess; discussion groups; and lectures, plays, and concerts.

Should your analysis show you a group not too enthusiastic about climbing an abstraction ladder, our advice is not what you might expect. We do not feel that you need always move down the ladder. Sometimes that may be necessary, but often all that you will need do is to avoid going into the matter as deeply as you would with a more willing group, and develop more fully the fewer points that you do present. The problem is to stay away from any complexities which they would not and could not understand. The advice given in Unit I about ample development of your points becomes even more of a necessity than it would with a group of inveterate abstract thinkers.

The other item of information necessary for this speech concerns the kind of abstract thinking which it is customary for your audience to do. There are two worlds of abstract thinking: a world of verbal abstractions and another world of symbol abstractions. The humanist has his home in the world of words; he uses words mainly as his tools of reasoning. The scientist resides in the world of symbols; his main tools of thought are figures, formulas, designs. What is conceived as a cleansing agent by one is thought of as $Na_2CO_3 \cdot 10H_2O$ by the other. Some abstract terms belong more to one of these worlds, some to the other. Explanation of the term "versification" would relate more to the world of words; explanation of the term "valence" would almost demand use of scientific symbols.

As a speaker you will want to know the correct "abstract world address" of both your subject and your audience. If the addresses match, your problems are smaller than if they do not. But there is no reason for despair if you must talk about a verbal abstraction to a group accustomed to thinking in terms of symbol abstractions, or vice versa. Formulas could even be devised and presented visually to help clarify the term "versification" or other terms related to the verbal world; conversely, entirely verbal explanation can be made of the term "valence" or other concepts that are usually represented by symbols. It may take a bit of doing, but it can be done. In oral communication, of course, you rely mainly on the verbal world. Scientists as well as humanists are forced to live in it much of the time; as a matter of fact, scientists are probably more at home in it than humanists would be in the world of scientific symbols.

As for knowledge of the occasion, the time limit of the speech and the time of day are perhaps the most important conditioning factors. To a large extent your time limit will determine the scope of your efforts; to a lesser extent, time of day will have a limiting effect on them. The effect of time limit should need no explanation. The effect of time of day, while it may be relatively more negligible, can be significant. Mental acuity fluctuates with the clock. The ordinary pattern is for people to be at their mental best in mid-morning, early in the afternoon, and again early in the evening. If you are going to be speaking during one of the "sag" periods, you may be wise to try to do less than if your class meets at a time when most of you are sharper mentally. It will probably involve no more than dropping a subpoint or two, but sometimes even that can make a great difference in terms of the audience's ability to grasp the message.

Ten persons might define the same term and all come up with different but equally valid definitions. The fact that you find your term defined in a certain way in an article or book that you read does not mean that that is the way you must define it for your audience. For them the printed definition might be entirely wrong, or just not the best way of doing it. Use your knowledge of the audience's present ignorance, present knowledge, liking for and ability in abstract thinking, and "abstract world address" to determine where on the abstraction ladder you will finally settle, where you will start and how much you will cover, and what means of definition you will use.

CONSTRUCTION OF THE SPEECH

Moving Up by Going Down

One of the fascinating paradoxes of public speaking is that the best way to help your audience climb an abstraction ladder is by going down it. The first true abstraction on the ladder is usually relatively easy to explain in terms of the concrete data on the rungs below; the progression of syntheses that follow can then be ascended without the wobbling or toppling effect that occurs when the ladder has not been firmly anchored in the ground. Although the downward movement is not the only one—you can move up after you move down, at other times you move up and then back down, and at still other times you cross over to adjacent ladders and then come back again—by and large it is the most common and necessary one.

Let us return to our example of a subject drawn from the area of dramatic acting, "The Method," to illustrate this principle. We will put together a ladder from the related terms that we considered in the hypothetical process of choosing a subject area:

The arts
The fine arts
The performing arts
The theater
The modern theater
The art of acting in the modern theater
The Stanislavski method of actor training
Memory of emotions

We said that some movements would be up from our selected subject area and then back down to it. In this instance it might very well be necessary to acquaint your listeners with some facts about the kind of acting called for in the modern theater, or about what forces in the modern theater make that kind of acting necessary, or even with some background knowledge of the theater that they do not possess in order to clarify the Stanislavski method of actor training for them. It is unlikely that you would have to go higher up the ladder than "the theater," but even that would be possible.

Other movements, we said, were to adjacent ladders. You will have noticed that a number of the terms mentioned in connection with choosing a subject area are not to be found on this particular abstraction ladder. The higher you are on the ladder, the more branchings off into separate and distinct ladders can occur. Going no higher than "the theater," as we saw previously, there are any number of different eras and kinds of theater, each of which would have led off into a different abstraction ladder. Sometimes you will have to go over to other ladders to facilitate your audience's learning. If you were talking to a group of Shakespeare scholars, for instance, you might make considerable reference to the Method's adaptability to the acting of Shakespeare's plays. There are even times when you jump over to ladders seemingly unconnected with your subject, as in comparing the goal of method training in acting to goals in training musicians or even athletes.

The predominant direction of movement, however, should be down, then up. For that to take place on our abstraction ladder, we would have to add more items at the bottom. "Memory of emotions," the present bottom term, is of a rather high order of abstraction. To make it clear, you might want to cite examples of actors using the device to help them in feeling emotions on the stage, or describe the procedure by which an actor calls up an emotion he has felt in the past from the storehouse of his memory, or refer to occasions in the experiences of your listeners when forgotten emotions were suddenly re-kindled by stimuli originally associated with them. All of these means are still somewhat abstract, but you do not have time to demonstrate the technique or have the audience try it themselves. The important thing is that they relate directly to the world of observable fact. Since it is there that most audiences feel most at home, you will want to return to it often in informing an audience.

The Necessity for Being Interesting

Possibly the greatest danger that you face in selecting materials for an informational speech defining a term is that of picking those which, while suitable in every other way, are just plain dull. It was partly to help you avoid this pitfall that we warned you against over-dependence on dictionary and encyclopedia materials. In such sources generalization is likely to have been carried so far that any semblance of the excitement, the wonder, the fascination of real life has disappeared from the treatment of the subject.

Nothing is as fatal to the speaker's purpose as is dullness. He can do almost anything else and get away with it, but he cannot be dull. Our point is that you must take pains to select materials which possess human interest. Having made the point, we must immediately qualify it by saying that, in informational speaking, being interesting should not ever be thought of as an end in itself, but always as a means to an end. You can gain and hold the audience's attention, aid their learning, and make the process of learning more enjoyable to them, but only if you keep your effort within bounds. Almost every college campus has at least one very popular lecturer who keeps his classes laughing every hour of every day he meets with them. It is all wonderful fun, and with superior entertainment being as rare as it is, we would urge you to sign up for the course. But if you do, you must not also expect to learn very much. Such instructors have lost their sense of proportion. We will hope that you do not.

The Factors of Attention

You have already learned a number of ways to gain and hold the attention of your audience. In Unit II two of these were stressed: the use of visual aids and the enlistment of the audience's desires to gain some reward, avoid some penalty, or satisfy their curiosity about some matter. Reference to the previous experiences of your listeners has been, is being, and will continue to be urged. One additional way remains to be discussed. It is choosing and designing materials that inherently possess certain qualities of attractiveness to which the human being is instinctively drawn. The standard term for these qualities is "the factors of attention."

Factors of attention create what the psychologists call "involuntary" attention. It is not a particularly apt name, because it can easily suggest just the opposite of what it means. What it means is that the person cannot help but pay attention, that no effort of will has to be expended.

To be interesting is to create involuntary attention, and vice versa. From whatever vantage point you wish to view it, the moral is the same—you must know the factors of attention and use them in your speaking.

We have just looked at one of the factors of attention from another point of view. In our discussion of the customary downward movement on the abstraction ladder, we said that the audience knows best, understands best, and is most interested in the world of concrete reality. One of the factors of attention is *the concrete*. Whenever possible, refer to actual people, places, and events, and use concrete words rather than abstract ones in explaining them. Talking about people probably creates the most interest. The use of the anecdote about people as supporting material is an excellent means of creating sympathy and a vicarious reliving of experiences on the part of the listeners.

Another potent factor of attention is *the vital*. Anything which significantly affects the audience's welfare or that of those they care about is going to be interesting to them. If what you are talking about touches upon matters connected with the health, wealth, comfort, or other vital concerns of your listeners—including those other persons or groups to whom they feel some strong bond—they will be very much inclined to pay you some heed. Promise of reward and threat of penalty, of course, relate closely to this factor of attention.

The arousal of curiosity relates to a different factor of attention, that of *suspense*. Alfred Hitchcock has grown wealthy on the insatiable human desire to be held breathless wondering how it will all come out. Ordinarily the way the speaker creates suspense is to pose some problem needing solution and then leave the audience dangling as to how it can be resolved. He can also tell stories that have an element of suspense, or promise to divulge some important information later in the speech. A point to remember is that, if your listeners' curiosity is to be sustained, they must be made to care. Also, do not neglect to "complete the uncompleted circle" that has engaged their interest by the time you have finished speaking. Few things are so irritating as being left with an unresolved question; you need to end the suspense.

Conflict sometimes enters into the problems that create suspense, but it need not. On the other hand, suspense almost always is involved in conflict. Human beings are interested in any kind of a fight, and if it is one in which the outcome is in doubt until the very end, so much the better. Better still if that outcome is of vital significance to them. We are not suggesting that you don boxing trunks and assume a pugnacious attitude, but we do suggest that discussing ideas and issues in terms of conflict can make them exciting to your hearers.

Novelty and *familiarity* are equally good at creating involuntary attention, and when they are combined, they have more effect than when used separately. The combination of the two is a dominant note in modern advertising practice: "Good old reliable Brand X has now been made even better by the addition of a new ingredient (you name it). Try the *new* Brand X and you will see that we have made the best product of its kind even better." Your listeners are interested in what is new and different and they are also interested in what is as common to them as an old shoe. A good principle to follow is to look at old ideas from new viewpoints and discuss new ideas in terms of old ones. The attention factor of familiarity is, of course, part of the appeal of any reference to the previous experience of your listeners.

Yet another factor of attention that can be of great importance to the speaker is *humor*. Almost all human beings respond not only with attention but with delight if it is used well, and it can create, as perhaps nothing else does, a sense of well-being that brings speaker and audience together in a happy, receptive frame of mind. Telling a joke just for the sake of being funny, however, is usually pointless. The trite formula of starting out with an outworn, unrelated joke, then suddenly getting serious, is much too transparent. Then too, you must be sure that humor is in good taste so as not to offend the sensibilities of the listeners. Humor that is fresh, that ties in with the ideas of the speech, and that is in good taste is always appropriate. You may be one of those who does not have the knack of telling a humorous story. If so, look elsewhere for a factor of attention, do not strain to get laughs. But if you have any knack at all, use humor whenever possible. Its use can reveal you to the audience as a speaker of wisdom and understanding as well as focus favorable attention on what you have to say.

Activity or *movement* also has the innate capacity to interest the human being. Try paying attention to a sleeping person when another person within view is doing calisthenics. There will have to be other strong factors of attention connected with the somnolent one to make you keep your attention focused on him. The application of this attention factor to your speech delivery is self-evident, but perhaps not so evident is its application to speech content and organization. The things you talk about and your materials should suggest activity, and the speech should be organized so as to give a sense of movement toward a goal.

Finally, there is *variety*. This attention factor should condition your use of the other factors as well as everything else connected with your speech and its presentation. Any kind of a "rut" that you get into, be it of bodily action, voice inflection, word choice, kind of supporting material used, or whatever, will dull audience interest and endanger the accomplishment of your purpose in speaking.

It has already been demonstrated that these factors of attention are not independent of one another. Their interconnections are many and various. A given item of supporting material might very well contain all of them. Your constant job as a public speaker is to find or create materials that have at least a fair share of them.

Organizing the Speech

You were told that, beginning with the speech of this unit and continuing through all the rest of the speeches of the course, the construction of a detailed outline would be advisable. Each of these outlines should represent the result of careful thought devoted to the task of building a speech which will have purpose, pertinence, and point. The outline is both the instigator of your thought about speech composition and its written record.

The purpose of a speech outline, then, is to insure the proper preparation of a speech. It supplies the framework on which the speech is built. It insures logical arrangement and indicates the relationships among ideas. When the speech has been prepared, the outline has done its work. It should not be used as a crutch on which you lean in delivering your speech. Nor is it a strait jacket from which you cannot deviate while delivering your speech. In short, an outline is a means of limiting the subject, classifying ideas, and directing thought so that you can be more successful in achieving your purpose.

The exact form that you will be expected to use for your outlines will be told you by your instructor. The following directions suggest a standard form that we recommend to insure completeness in your outlining procedures:

1. Fill out completely the Outline Page for this unit. You will notice that the questions you are asked to answer in the Preliminary Analysis section are the ones you should think about in preparing the speech.
2. Complete your outline, using separate sheets of paper. Label and develop separately each of the three major divisions, introduction, body, and conclusion. The only section which need be put in outline form, however, is the body. You may write out completely a brief introduction or conclusion. After the outline proper, be sure to list references—sources you consulted in the preparation of the speech.
3. Use conventional outline symbols: Roman numerals, capital letters, Arabic numerals, and small letters. Use of symbols must be consistent. Symbols of the same kind should be kept directly under each other with equal indentations. All statements with the same kind of symbol are coordinate in their relationship if they occur in the same section of the outline.
4. Use complete sentences down to the level of illustrations or specific detail; after that, phrases that will be meaningful to a reader as well as to the speaker may be used.
5. Use only one sentence for each symbol of the outline.
6. Each item in the outline should assert one single idea, not two or more.
7. As a general rule, points should not be subdivided unless they can be broken down into at least two logical subdivisions. This rule cannot be made inflexible in speech outlining, however, because at the level of illustration or specific detail, often only one item is used or is necessary.
8. Refer to the Sample Student Outlines that you will find at the end of this and succeeding units to note how these directions have been carried out in proper form.

In Unit II the general structure of a speech outline and the terminology connected with it were explained. Here we shall attempt to give instruction about the proper procedures to follow in preparing the outline. There will be some reiteration of the previous material, both in order to put it in a new light and to give a sharper focus and greater meaning to the new material that will be presented. Since our purpose will be to help you avoid the common faults of speech composition, we shall group our suggestions around such faults. In an attempt to make the common faults of speech composition more meaningful to you, we shall make some comparisons to similar faults of college students in pursuing their educational goals.

Determining the Specific Purpose.   Probably the most disastrous fault the college student can have is lack of purpose. If he has no idea of why he is going to college, he is not likely to remain there long. Even if he should remain and graduate, much of his four years' time will have been wasted in pointless, undirected activity. The fault is common enough among college students; it is perhaps even more common among public speakers. You have probably heard the speech whose only apparent purpose is to fill up a specified amount of time that the speaker in a moment of folly committed himself to, and which is directed in no way toward gaining a response from the audience. To avoid this fault you should, as your very first step in preparing your outline, determine your *specific purpose.* The word "specific" is important. The more clearly you pinpoint the precise response you want from your listeners, the better you will know how to proceed through the remaining steps. It is not enough to say that you want your audience informed, or even that you want them informed about radiology, but it is perhaps enough to say that you want your listeners to understand the meaning of the term "radiology" by your explaining the development of this study and the present medical uses to which it is being put.

Stating the Central Idea.   Even when the college student has a definite goal in mind, he can go wrong by not choosing the proper major field of study to lead him to that goal. The student whose goal is to train himself to be corporation lawyer would do better to enroll in the Department of Business Administration than in the Department of Political Science. Another pre-law student whose ultimate aim is political office, however, would find his right niche in the political science department. In speaking, the *central idea* is analogous to a student's major field of study—it is the "department" he enrolls his audience in in order to prepare them for the tasks he hopes them to perform. The central idea should be checked to see that if it is developed the right audience response will be achieved. It should be stated in tentative form early in the outlining process. It may be—indeed, most often should be— revised as the speaker goes along, but unless he chooses some special road to travel, he is not going to travel very well at all. All of us have heard the kind of speech the Sunday driver gives.

Even though you were asked in Unit II to determine a specific purpose and central idea for your speech, you may not be entirely sure what each of them is and how they differ from one another. For some reason, they are unusually puzzling concepts to a large number of beginning public speaking students. Since you will be expected to try again to use them rightly, we shall try again to help you. Remember that the specific purpose is a statement of the ultimate accomplishment you hope for, hence is phrased in terms of the anticipated audience response—what you would like them to learn, believe, or do as a result of your effort. The central idea, on the other hand, is a single sentence summarizing the subject matter of the speech. Other names for it with which you might be more familiar are "main theme," "thesis statement," "main point," and "main proposition." It tells in brief what you are going to tell the audience in order to accomplish your specific purpose. It is your speech content in a nutshell. Above we suggested as a sample specific purpose, "To help my listeners understand the meaning of the term 'radiology' by explaining the development of the study and the present medical uses to which it is being put." A central idea by which that specific purpose might be accomplished would read something like, "Radiology, the science of radiant energy and its uses, has known fantastic growth and development since its beginnings in 1896, and now provides our medical doctors with many weapons against disease."

A second glance at the above central idea may give you an insight into the kind of phrasing that will probably be most effective for the speech of this unit. Notice that it is, of and by itself, an embryo definition of the term that the speech will define. It is not enough to give anyone a complete idea of what the term means, but it provides a skeleton definition whose expansion in the speech itself might very well lead to rather complete understanding.

Choosing, Arranging, and Developing the Main Points. In order to get a degree in his major, the student must follow a prescribed course of study. The public speaker also has his course of study, the main points of his speech. No one decides the required courses for him, however. The choosing of main points he has to do for himself. In spite of the best efforts of college registrars, catalogues, and advisers, students can go wrong in choosing their courses. This is especially true of their choices of elective courses. Again, the same faults which plague college students plague public speakers.

Any number of students wind up their college careers having taken all the wrong courses. Courses should be chosen so that, if completed successfully themselves, they will provide the student with exactly the right training for his major, which in turn will allow him to be successful in his chosen job or profession. So it is with main points. They should be chosen so that, if completely developed themselves, they will in turn completely develop the central idea and so accomplish the specific purpose. That is the test that should be applied to the main points you choose.

Let us compare two sets of main points, one very bad and the other a good deal better. We shall take the subject of the Stanislavski Method of actor training mentioned earlier. Our specific purpose is "To enable the audience to understand the purpose and scope of the Stanislavski Method of actor training," and our central idea is "The Stanislavski Method of actor training attempts to give the actor complete control with his mind of everything he says, does, or feels on the stage, so that he may give believable, artistic, and moving performances." The first set of main points is the bad one:

I. The Stanislavski Method of actor training is, basically, systematized training of the actor's imaginative powers.
II. It trains him in the powers of attention, concentration, creation of mental images, observation, memory of emotion, and justification.
III. The Stanislavski Method is taught in practically every acting school in the United States.

Now let us see a better set:

I. The Stanislavski Method of actor training was devised as a means of developing actors capable of giving believable, artistic, and moving performances on the stage.
II. The principal training of the Stanislavski Method is of the actor's imaginative powers.
III. These imaginative powers are developed as a means of giving him conscious control of every action he performs, every inflection of his voice, and every emotion he displays.

It should be rather obvious that the first set of main points could not possibly develop the central idea. They say nothing about the ultimate purpose of the training or to what use the training of the imaginative powers is put. The second set of main points, on the other hand, if completely developed themselves, would in turn say everything that has been planned for in the statement of the central idea.

These same examples can be used to illustrate a couple of other faults of public speakers in choosing main points. You will notice, for instance, that in the "bad" set the second main point is in reality nothing more than a subpoint of the first one; and that the third one is not even very important, being merely background information that one would present in the introduction. Main points must be of coordinate importance. Each should have equal weight. It can be said of the "good" set of main points that they *are* all of approximately the same importance. To return to the analogy of the college student, do not put Underwater Basket-Weaving in the same category as English Literature, History, Zoology, and French.

Another common fault that can be seen in comparing these two examples is in their arrangement. Again, in the bad set we find that, while the second point follows from the first, being really only a subpoint of it, the third one has no necessary relationship with the other two. This is not true of the second set. Main points should have a logical internal organization. Their arrangement should be such that the mind moves by a natural process of reasoning from one to the other. The problem in the listener's mind if this is not done is a bit like that in the college student's mind if he takes first the course in "Shakespeare's Middle Period," then the one in "The Young Shakespeare," and finally "Shakespeare: the Later Plays." Things just do not fit together.

Patterns of Arrangement. Typical patterns of arranging main points that speakers use to make things fit together include the following:

1. Time sequences, such as "24 hours in the day of," "past, present, future," or the one mentioned above, "early, middle, and late." The "step" sequence of "first, second, third" also applies here.
2. Space sequences, such as "moving in a counterclockwise direction around the quad," "on a line from north to south," and "local, state, national, and international."
3. Cause-and-effect relationships moving in either direction.
4. Need, desirability, practicality, alternatives.
5. Problem to solution.
6. A development popularized by Alan H. Monroe, which commonly goes by the name of the "Monroe Motivated Sequence." [4] In it a speaker first draws *attention* to a problem, then shows a *need* for it to be solved, follows that with a suggested solution that will provide *satisfaction* for the need, moves into a *visualization* of the good effects that will result if the solution is adopted and/or the bad effects if it is not, and ends with a statement of the *action* the audience is to take.
7. Advantages and disadvantages.
8. The reporter's questions: Who? what? why? when? how? where?
9. Theory and practice.
10. Purpose and means.
11. Structure and function.
12. Resemblances and differences.
13. Symptoms, prevention, and cure.
14. Extended analogy.
15. ABC's or other letter combinations, such as those taken from spelling a key word.

This is not an exhaustive list, but a suggestive one. Many subjects create their own patterns. If yours does not, select one from this list or from others that you have heard speakers use.

A few of the above patterns were suggested in Unit II as possible choices

[4] Alan H. Monroe, *Principles and Types of Speech* (Chicago: Scott, Foresman and Company, 1962), Chap. 16.

for that speech. These were, to refresh your memory, space sequence, time sequence, and cause-and-effect relationship. They can each apply as well to definition of an abstract term as to concrete objects and mechanical processes.

If you were to define Grimm's Law, for instance, one approach would certainly be through a spatial arrangement which would show the interconnections of the various languages involved and their common origin in the Indo-European "parent" language. Time sequence would apply to many different terms, some of which could only be explained by tracing a time pattern of development. Cause-and-effect relationship is sometimes listed as a special means of definition. There are matters about which we know very little, such as electricity, which ultimately are explainable only by description of their causes and effects.

Purpose and means, structure and function, and extended analogy are other patterns that are sometimes designated as special methods of definition. Certainly they are all excellent for such a purpose. Our suggested set of main points for clarifying the Stanislavsky Method is an example of a purpose-and-means development. A term amenable to definition by structure and function would be "scientific method," which could be broken down into its steps and explained according to the function of each of the steps. Extended analogy is especially useful in explaining a new scientific concept or principle, because it relates the unknown to the known.

Still other patterns that we shall suggest as possibilities for the speech of this unit are the reporter's questions; theory and practice; resemblances and differences; and symptoms, prevention, and cure. The reporter's questions are drilled into every journalism student because they are supposed to get at all the information necessary for a news story. Some terms, such as "McCarthyism," derive from news stories and can be explained by the same methodology. The Back-to-Nature Movement of the middle nineteenth century needs the irony of the sharp contrast between theory and practice to give it full definition. Resemblances and differences are, of course, other ways of using analogy, the efficacy of which we have already discussed. Finally, many mental and physical illnesses are sometimes best explained by detailing their symptoms, prevention, and cure.

The other patterns in the above list which we have left untouched we will have occasion to refer to in succeeding units. They are, by and large, more suitable to persuasive than to informational speaking.

Subpoints, too, should be arranged according to some logical and meaningful pattern. Patterns for these include parts of a whole, lists of qualities or functions, series of causes and results, items of logical proof, and illustrative examples. Again, comparing the procedure with the career of the college student, we can say that he can do little or nothing about the unit arrangements—or subpoints—of the individual courses he takes. The public speaker can.

Number of Points. You may have noticed that in all of the suggested patterns of development of main points, with the exception of the "reporter's questions" which are usually not all used, there are no more than five items, and that in the majority of them there are only two or three. There is good reason for this. Speakers have discovered that the maximum number of main points an audience can manage without the aid of nonverbal means is five, and that even that number can often create difficulties. Two or three main points are usually quite enough for the short speech. Do not commit the fault of the college student who loads himself up with more courses than he can handle. One student in our experience submitted an outline for a five-minute speech that contained 16 Roman numeral headings in the body of the outline! On the other hand, do not take a reduced load just for the sake of making it easy on your listeners or yourself. If a main point is necessary to the development of your central idea, then it must stay. When you find yourself going over three or four, however, see if there might not be some place where you can omit or combine.

Planning the Introduction. Most present-day college students would attest to the fact that none of their four years in college is any bed of roses, but they would also probably agree that the freshman and senior years are the hardest. College students are likely to do most poorly in their academic rankings in these years. This problem also occurs in public speaking.

The speaker's introduction is designed to accomplish purposes similar to those of the freshman year in college—to wake up the student to something new and different, to get him adjusted to it, and to develop a background of information that will help him in his later studies. The speaker in his introduction wants to gain the favorable attention of his audience, promote friendliness and respect, and lead into the subject of his speech. The student needs a period to get used to going to college, to get warmed up to the idea, and to acquire basic knowledge. Likewise an audience needs a period of adjustment, of getting interested, and of acquiring basic knowledge. The introduction, in which this should take place, is as hard for the speaker as the freshman year is for the college student. Very often the speaker falls down in it because he does not work hard enough at it, just as the college freshman fails for lack of effort.

Introductions are of three basic kinds: (1) declarative, (2) explanatory, and (3) motivated.

The first kind, the declarative, which takes the form of a brief statement of the central idea or the main points of the speech, is useful only when the audience already knows you very well, likes and respects you, and is so interested in hearing what you have to say that they do not want to be bothered with any additional introductory material. This state of affairs, you can well imagine, does not occur very frequently.

The second type of introduction, the explanatory, is done by presenting definitions of important terms or the history and background of the subject. This is more generally useful that the first type, but it has some of the same limitations, and if not well handled it can be very dull.

The third type, the motivated, is the kind you will be using the most. It is the type best designed to accomplish all three general purposes of the introduction. Motivated introductions may include: reference to yourself, the previous speaker or the chairman, the occasion, or some recent event; an honest compliment to the audience; an appropriate joke or other humor; unison audience reaction; startling statement; quotation; illustrative anecdote; rhetorical question; visual aids; or development of common ground.

The principal purpose of references to various elements of the speech situation is always to put yourself in a closer relationship to the audience. As they were listed, these included references to yourself ("This is not the first time I have attended a commencement, but it is the first time anyone has ever seen fit to give me a degree at one"); to the previous speaker ("Mr. Green has challenged me to show you a 'single shred of evidence' for my point of view. . . . Ladies and gentlemen, I intend to present you with a whole bolt of cloth"); to the chairman ("Mr. Chairman's introduction was so unduly flattering that, believe me, when he was through I glanced around to see where that other speaker might be"); to the occasion ("I always dread a little speaking on the Fourth of July because I have that irresistible impulse to explode"); or to some recent event ("The murder of Patrolman Brown is still being talked about in my house as in yours"). Sometimes such reference is almost mandatory, as when the previous speaker has spoken on the same subject that you intend to discuss. Most often the reference is brief and coupled with another or several other introductory devices.

An honest compliment to the audience is a technique ordinarily reserved for persuasive speaking, but might be a means of "warming up" the group to you as an instructor. A joke or humorous remark would also have that effect, if it is appropriate. Quotations, illustrative anecdotes, and visual aids you are already familiar with, and their use for introductions has either been previously discussed or is apparent. The startling statement and the rhetorical question, however, may be terms unfamiliar to you. A startling statement, as its name suggests, makes some pronouncement of fact or opinion that literally jolts your listeners bolt upright in their seats. "One out of every ten persons in this room is likely to spend some part of his life in a mental institution," and "I am convinced that this university is on the downgrade" are examples of startling statements. The rhetorical question is one for which the speaker expects no answer, the interrogative form being used only because it is an attention-getter. Ordinarily both rhetorical questions and startling statements are used in multiples, though care must be taken that they do not wear out their welcome.

Any of these devices is suitable for informational as well as persuasive speaking. Reserved for later discussion, because for all practical purposes they are unusable in informational speaking, are the methods of unison audience reaction and development of common ground.

Introductions can vary considerably in length, depending on speaker, speech, audience, and occasion. We have seen that some may consist of only one sentence. Others may be as long as one-third of the total speech, as happened in some of the speeches of Booker T. Washington, the great Negro educator of the early part of our century, in which he was speaking to all-white Southern audiences. In those instances, of course, the speaker faced a difficult task of gaining the audience's liking and respect, and he needed at least that much time to accomplish it. Ordinarily, however, the introduction should be one of the shorter sections of the speech. The head should not seem bigger than the body.

Planning the Conclusion. Poor senior years occur because of the same basic cause that poor freshman years do; that is, lack of effort. The reason for the lack of effort is different, however. By this time the college student knows enough to work hard, but he is just too tired to do it. It is a bad mistake, because the senior year should be the one in which he ties all the loose ends of his training together into a hard core of knowledge and understanding and skill that will stand him in good stead for that first job, and, indeed, the rest of his life. The speaker's senior year, his conclusion, has a similar basic purpose; the cause of failure is the same; and the reason for the cause is also identical. A weak conclusion is a fault fully as bad in speech-making as it is in going to college. The speaker has to spur himself and his audience even harder, battling the fatigue, so that he may tie the loose ends of his speech together and refocus audience attention once again upon the central idea. It is his last chance to drive his point home. He can gain attention from his audience of a kind second only to that which he has in the introduction. He is extremely foolish to waste such a marvelous opportunity to insure the accomplishment of his purpose in speaking.

Conclusions also are of three basic types: (1) the *summary,* (2) the *epitome,* and (3) the *plea for acceptance or action.* Summary conclusions usually take the form of either enumeration of the main points covered in the speech or restatement of the central idea. A quotation, a climactic anecdote, or an epigram (a short, pithy, sometimes humorous statement, such as Oscar Wilde's famous "Divorces are made in heaven") which refocuses attention upon the central idea could all be classified as epitome conclusions. Those conclusions that could be categorized as pleas for acceptance or action are ones like the rhetorical question ("Are you going to meekly stand by and let these demagogues rob you of your birthright?"); prophecy ("I say that if my plan is adopted, within a year we will have gone a long way toward cleaning up both adult crime and juvenile delinquency in our city"); and personal reference ("I know not what course others may take; but as for me, give me liberty, or give me death!"). Whatever type of conclusion you choose, it should ordinarily be the shortest section of your speech. While the conclusion should be brief, however, it should also be a high point, if not *the* high point, in your speech.

The summary conclusion, as you would suppose, is the most commonly used. It is suitable to almost any speech. It is particularly useful for informational speaking, since it directly reinforces the essential idea or ideas you want your audience to remember. Epitome conclusions are sometimes applicable to the speech of information, and might be something that you would want to look into, but for the most part they are heard in persuasive speaking. The same is true of pleas for acceptance or action. There is the off-chance, however, that you will want your listeners to learn more about your subject, in which case you could make a plea for their reading a certain book, attending an upcoming lecture, or in some other way increasing their knowledge.

Testing the Transitions.   A final fault of speech organization is that of lack of effective transitions. Just as college students have difficulty seeing the connections between the different courses they are taking, so audiences have trouble understanding the various relationships of the speaker's ideas unless he takes pains to point them out. Transitions may be single words, phrases, sentences, or even whole paragraphs. They are a type of reasoning material which points out to the audience how one idea ties in with another or what the speaker is going to talk about next and why. Such words as "but," "now," "next," and "because" are often used for transition. More often phrases and sentences are used. Statements like "Let us turn to another similar case," or "Having seen how it all happened and why it occurred, we need now only to" or "To conclude, let me say," or "Why should you know about this?" or "The third and last point is," are transitional ones. They create a bridge by which the audience can quickly and easily move from one idea or section to another. They help insure that no one will be left behind. As a last step in composing your speech, check to see that you have the right transitions in the right places and plenty of them.

Avoid these common pitfalls of speech organization. Make your specific purpose truly specific; phrase your central idea carefully; choose main points of equal importance that, taken together, completely develop your central idea; devise both a good introduction and a good conclusion. Remember that it is the highest type of wisdom in speech-making to lead your audience easily, pleasurably, and unerringly along the path of your thinking so that what you wanted to say about your subject becomes what they understand about it. Good organization helps give you poise and confidence in delivering the speech, and it allows the audience to follow and understand the speech. It is not a task to be taken lightly.

Wording the Speech

Despite what you may have seen in many of your college textbooks and heard in many of your classroom lectures, information need not always be conveyed in drab, dry, completely denotative language. Many time imaginative, lively phrasings pleasing to the ear, rich in associations, and exciting to the imagination are not only possible but preferred. Such wording creates a concentration of attention and an emotional involvement with the subject that leads to successful learning. Connotative meanings, because they are largely emotional in character, may lack the qualities of objectivity and precision; nonetheless, they *are* meanings that can aid understanding. It is not enough that the language of informational speaking be correct, clear, and concise; it needs also to be colorful.

Metaphor is not the only source of connotative meanings, but it certainly is one of the larger suppliers. Metaphor is sometimes mistakenly thought of as an embellishment given to the thought after it has been formed, a sort of varnish that you apply only to give sheen to the finish. On the contrary, it is the ordinary and preferred shape of human thought, and as such the primary means by which our language grows and changes. The metaphor *is* the thought. It is a means of transferring meaning. When it is used, the literal meaning that a word has for one kind of idea or object is figuratively transferred to an entirely different kind of idea or object.

We describe one girl as a "dream" and another as a "nightmare." We speak of "flashes" of temper, "storms" of rage, and "torrents" of feeling. We not only have murderers who slash victims, but flashlights that "slash" the "inky" blackness of the night, "angry" tongues that "slash" out at people, and town gossips who "slash" people's reputations to bits. What is not realized by many persons is that these everyday expressions are metaphors. Our common thought and speech and writing is (to use a rather worn-out metaphor, but a metaphor nonetheless) bursting at the seams with metaphorical phrasings.

Use of metaphor involves downward movement on the abstraction ladder into the realm of the concrete, the particular, the sensory detail. For that reason alone, most people welcome it in the speeches that they hear and the reading that they do. Since it also involves some expression of emotion and attitude, it also tends to enliven matters considerably. Moreover, it does communicate meaning. Through reference to past experience, it transfers the understanding associated with the known object or idea to the unknown one.

To illustrate all of these attributes of metaphor, there is no better example than the Robert Burns poem, "A Red, Red Rose." We quote only the opening stanza:

> O my luve's like a red, red rose,
> That's newly sprung in June:
> O my luve's like the melodie
> That's sweetly played in tune.

It is the abstract special quality of his sweetheart's person and personality that the poet is trying to communicate to the reader. He avoids fruitless attempts to do it with abstract words extolling her "utter loveliness," her "petite figure," her "charm," her "vivacity," or her "sympathetic understanding." Instead he compares her to concrete, sharply detailed sensory experiences that the reader has known and to which he has attached both intellectual and emotional meanings. A transfer of the reader's knowledge of the special quality possessed by the reddest of red roses and by sweet melodies, strengthened by the emotional feeling that is generated by these associations, is made to the girl.

Metaphorical phrasing, then, is one more way that you can give brightness to your speech and help communicate your thought at the same time. Much of what you read about your term may be couched in abstract language, or, worse still, in technical jargon that, like the hardy noxious weed it is, runs rampant in every field of learning. One of your jobs as a speaker will be to "translate" the colorless or possibly even garbled language of your sources into the language of good human speech—direct, clear, and metaphoric.

Here is a paragraph from a student speech in which this was not done:

> The term "pragmatism," as employed in philosophy at the present time, denotes the general tendency to subordinate logical thinking to the ends of practical life and practical circumstances. It is in a real sense an expression

of American culture. The outstanding feature of this philosophy is that it depends on observation rather than science. It accepts ordinary human experience as the ultimate source and test of all knowledge. All concepts, for the pragmatist, are judged valid or invalid by their practical results. In its application to education, pragmatism has fostered the "progressive" movement of "learning by doing, not by listening."

Whatever you might wish to say about the quality of the writing, it does manage to communicate thought. If need be, the reader can go back over it several times and eventually ferret out the message. Orally presented in the student speech, however, the message got nowhere. Some "translating" of this nature needed to be done:

What is pragmatism? It is an adult human philosophy, of course, and it can get very profound, but the basic idea of it is something you see possibly most clearly when observing the behavior of children and animals. Have you ever tried to convince your dog that he should eat "Puppios" because, distasteful as they may be to him, they contain all the vitamins and other nutritional factors that he needs? He barks and whines until you give him the remains of your steak. How successful were you when you told your little brother that eating all those green apples would make him sick? Didn't he have to eat them first and get a stomach ache before he learned about green apples?

The pragmatic philosophy is that of whining for the steak and snarling at the "Puppios" against all logic and reason. The pragmatist is like your dog; he goes by the observations of his own senses: if it looks good, smells good, tastes good, feels good, sounds good, or works well, it has value; otherwise it does not.

Pragmatism, as you may know, is the philosophy underlying John Dewey's "progressive" movement in education. You could call it the "green apple" concept of education. The idea is that students do not learn from being told things, they learn from eating the green apples and getting the stomach ache. Your little brother didn't know he was an educational pragmatist, but that is exactly what he was.

Some writers say that pragmatism is the characteristic American way of looking at things and doing things—so much so, in fact, that our whole American culture could be termed a pragmatic one. I am inclined to agree. Certainly most of the time I myself am disposed to judge things by their practical results rather than abstract theories, and most of what I've learned I've learned by doing. Isn't that the case with you, too?

You will notice that while metaphor is used, it is not so dominant that it calls attention to or becomes an end in itself. Denotative language cannot be dispensed with in informational speaking. It is the vehicle that carries the precise thought you are attempting to communicate. Metaphor is an *additional* means of illuminating ideas, not the only one that must be used. You will notice also however, that the denotative language that is used in the improved version has been changed considerably in the direction of greater familiarity, a more "down to earth" and truly oral character.

PREPARATION FOR DELIVERY

A little while back we gave a bit of counsel concerning the selection of materials which contained the gist of what we should like to say about rehearsing this speech aloud. What we said then was that the speaker must avoid dullness at all costs.

Your delivery of this speech could be dull if you are not careful. The preparation of a detailed outline very often creates as many problems as it solves. The worst as well as the most common of these is the temptation to become dependent on the outline. It would certainly be a grave error to take the outline to the speaking platform with you, reading it almost word for word without varying your voice or attempting to use gesture and movement. Then all the excellent progress you have made up to this point would be lost; deadly dullness would result.

By all means use your outline in your initial rehearsals, but then put it aside for the rest of your oral practice. Steel yourself to this practice; it will be an unsettling experience, but it is an absolutely necessary one. You cannot lead your audience on a road to understanding hobbling along on an outline crutch. Notes, if your instructor permits you to use them, should be minimal. We would suggest notes, exclusive of those needed for citation of exact statistics or quotations, that are limited to a few key phrases that can easily fit on a single note card. When you go to the platform, your speech should exist in your own thoughts and feelings, not on paper.

This means that you will have to put some reliance on your memory for the delivery of your speech. Your memory is one of your most marvelous human abilities, capable of prodigious feats. Probably not many of you have ever exercised it to its fullest capacity. As is true of most human attributes, different persons possess the ability to memorize to differing degrees; but even the person with the poorest memory is able to do much more with it than he might suppose.

Psychologists provide us with a number of helpful hints about how to make best use of our memory. Perhaps the most aid comes from their observation that we remember only what we subconsciously wish to remember or what we consciously will ourselves to remember. Repetition, while it is the principal tool by which we fix things in our memory, is of no avail unless it is done specifically for the purpose of remembering. We must truly want to remember in order to do so. Psychologists also tell us that spaced repetitions over an extended period are best. That means that it is better to rehearse your speech for several short sessions over a number of days, rather than in one or two long sessions. Another thing which the investigations of psychologists have discovered about memory is that the more of our muscles and senses that we involve in the act of memorization, the more likely it is that we will remember. We have previously said that most of your rehearsing of your speeches should be done on your feet, moving and gesturing and speaking your ideas aloud. In large part this procedure was advocated because of the great help it can give you in remembering.

Do not misunderstand our advice about memorization. The very last thing that we would want you to do would be to try to commit the exact wordings of your speech to memory. It is the substance of your ideas and their progression that you should endeavor to remember. Your desire to communicate these meanings to your listeners will provide you with wordings close enough to those of your outline that no damage to audience understanding will be done. Such spontaneous wordings oftentimes are even better than the original ones. We reiterate that you are not to deliver your speech from manuscript or memory of exact phraseology, but extemporaneously. Employing the extemporaneous mode of delivery is the best way for the beginning public speaker to achieve that animated, vital, direct communication which will please his audience best and which will most surely enhance his chances of informing them well.

REVIEW OF PREPARATION

1. Choose as your subject area a significant term, concept, idea, or principle which you are interested in and understand rather well, but which you feel sure your audience does not understand as much as it needs to and wants to.
2. Investigate the subject area by gathering materials suitable for the task of definition.
3. Consider your audience's present "ignorance," present knowledge, ability to do abstract thinking, and "abstract world address," as well as the time limit of your speech and time of day you will speak in determining how much information you will attempt to present and how you will go about doing it.
4. In selection of speech materials, keep in mind the general principle of downward movement on the abstraction ladder and the factors of attention which good materials should possess.

5. Prepare a detailed outline of your speech, following the principles of good speech organization, being especially sure to make your statement of central idea a definition in miniature of your term, and to use an appropriate pattern of main points.
6. Word your speech to have metaphorical phrasing and a generally good oral style.
7. Dispense with your outline as early in your rehearsals as possible, and certainly do not use it in delivering the speech. Commit the more important ideas of your speech to memory. The avoidance of dullness should be a prime consideration in your rehearsal practice as it should be in every other step of your preparation.

Sample Student Outline [5]

Subject: Radio astronomy.
Specific Purpose: The help my listeners understand the science of radio astronomy, how it came to be discovered and developed, and some of its present and potential uses.
Central Idea: Although radio astronomy, the new science of listening to the universe, is barely thirty years old, it has already contributed important scientific knowledge to astronomers and promises to supply answers to many questions concerning the heavens.

Introduction

In the Fifth Century B.C., certain Greek thinkers were convinced that strange and harmonious music was made by the movements of celestial bodies. They believed this "music of the spheres" could be heard by their gods and those humans who were pious.

Today, scientists actually are listening to the universe. The noises they hear would scarcely be called melodious, and those who hear them are not necessarily pious, but it is now possible to tune in on curious sounds from the heavens. These sounds have been termed "cosmic static."

The recently discovered existence of cosmic static has created a whole new science of listening to the universe called radio astronomy. My investigations into this subject lead me to believe that radio astronomy may offer the most significant means yet found for solving puzzling problems concerning the universe. The solutions it finds could profoundly affect your future life and mine. Would we like to

[5] This outline was prepared by Phyllis Woodard for a speech delivered in a beginning public speaking class at Colorado State University. The authors have made some minor alterations in wording. Its use here as illustrative material is with the kind permission of Mrs. Woodard.

know what the people on Mars (if any) really think of us? Would we like to know what George Washington said to his troops at Valley Forge? Radio astronomers listening to cosmic static might just be able to tell us.

Body

I. The principle of cosmic static was an accidental discovery of very recent origin.
   A. Mr. Karl Jansky was the real pioneer in this field.
      1. In 1931 he was experimenting with shortened wavelengths in an attempt to eliminate static from radio receivers.
      2. He discovered a hissing noise emanating from the Milky Way.
      3. He named this noise from the heavens, since it so much resembled the static we sometimes get on our ordinary receivers, "cosmic static."
      4. Jansky's work had little immediate effect because, as the recent *Time* magazine article on the subject put it, "it was done during the great depression, when little cash was available to encourage scientific enterprise."
   B. During World War II cosmic static was rediscovered by radar operators.
      1. In Great Britain the noise was so strong from the southerly direction that radar equipment could not detect enemy bombers approaching from that direction.
      2. Scientists explored the phenomenon and concluded that this cosmic static was issuing from the sun.
   C. Since the end of the war, cosmic static has become the concern of thousands of scientists, and the equipment for detecting it has become more and more elaborate.
      1. Radio astronomy is now a burgeoning science in every civilized nation of the globe, with the United States and England being the chief centers.
      2. The radio telescope—the instrument presently being used for the detection and amplification of cosmic static—has grown from a backyard operation to mammoth proportions.
         a. Although there are several types of radio telescopes, the predominant one in the United States is the parabolic dish type that this drawing illustrates.
         b. The first such radio telescope was one 31 feet in diameter, built in his own backyard by a radio ham, Grote Reber of Wheaton, Illinois, following Jansky's lead.
         c. Just recently completed and now in operation at the National Radio Astronomy Observatory, Green Bank, West Virginia, is the world's largest telescope of this or any other type, standing 23 stories high and with a diameter of 300 feet.
II. Some of the discoveries of radio astronomy already made and the experiments now under way are extremely valuable ones.
   A. Measurements—made by methods like those of radar—of the cosmic static received from the sun and the Milky Way are helping astronomers to reevaluate distances in space.

    B. The discovery of radio stars—those whose light is so weak that they cannot be detected by visual telescopes—is helping astronomers to revise their maps of the heavens.

    C. The recent experiments of U.S. scientists in bouncing radar signals off Venus have demonstrated that radio astronomy can help determine the size of the solar system with an accuracy never before dreamed possible.

Transition: (Radio astronomy is so new that it is impossible to anticipate its full potentialities. According to Sir Edward Appleton, eminent British astronomer and pioneer in this field, however, even the expected advancements are fantastic to contemplate.)

III. Some of the proposed uses of radio astronomy are staggering to the imagination.

    A. Project Ozma is now underway.

      1. This is a project based on the strong conviction held by many scientists that there is intelligent life on other planets in distant galaxies.

      2. Radio telescopes are being tuned in on the universe in a constant vigil to detect any message a more advanced civilization might be trying to transmit.

    B. Scientists who believe in the indestructibility of matter have an even more startling anticipation of future uses of radio astronomy.

      1. The basic contention of these scientists is that no sound is ever lost; that the air around us it literally packed to overflowing with all the sounds that have ever been made since history began—a sort of ladies' bridge party on a cosmic scale.

      2. Through advancements in the field of radio astronomy, they say, we will some day be able to hear the sounds that were made and even the conversations that took place on our own earth thousands of years ago.

      3. If these men are right, perhaps we had better be a little more careful of the things we say now; a future generation may listen in on our static.

Conclusion

We can say, then, that radio astronomy is a new science in which radio telescopes are used to tune in on the radio waves—or, as these waves have been termed, the cosmic static—emanating from the stars in the heavens above us for the purpose of using the sounds received to gain a wider knowledge of our universe. Presently it is helping astronomers remap the heavens. Its possible uses are straight out of the realm of fantasy.

If you would like to dismiss the future uses of radio astronomy which I have mentioned as the mere alcoholic dreams of a science fiction writer, however, consider this truth: the cosmic static from distant heavenly bodies which radio astronomers are hearing today originated before any of us here were born—in fact, before any human beings had ever been born. They pre-date the dawn of man's existence on this planet. I believe we will be hearing of many amazing new discoveries made by radio astronomers, and all of us would be wise to be "tuned in" on their activities.

References

1. Discussion with Dr. Robert W. Davis, Head of Department of Anatomy, Colorado State University, January 30, 1963.
2. Drake, Frank D., "How Can We Detect Radio Transmission from Distant Planetary Systems?" *Sky and Telescope,* January, 1960.
3. Drake, Frank D., "Radio Astronomy Receivers," *Sky and Telescope,* December, 1959.
4. Interview with Professor Leslie Madison, Head of Department of Mathematics and Statistics, Instructor in Astronomy, Colorado State University, January 31, 1963.
5. "Radio Waves from Outer Space," *Encyclopaedia Britannica,* 14th Edition.
6. "View from the Second Window," *Time,* December 14, 1962.

References for Unit III

1. Cherry, Colin, *On Human Communication: A Review, A Survey, and a Criticism* (New York: Science Editions, Inc., 1961).

   A definitive work on communication theory written for the layman. Chapters 1 and 3 would be most valuable to the student of beginning public speaking.
2. Brooks, Cleanth, and Robert Penn Warren, *Modern Rhetoric,* Second Edition (New York: Harcourt, Brace and Company, 1958).

   Chapter 10 on "Diction" has material on abstract and concrete words. Chapter 11 on "Metaphor" we especially recommend for its extended and excellent coverage of a matter we treat only briefly.
3. Hayakawa, S. I., *Language in Thought and Action* (New York: Harcourt, Brace & World, Inc., 1964).

   Valuable as a highly readable and easily understandable introduction to the study of general semantics and its concept of the "abstraction ladder."

Unit IV

Persuasion and Intellectual Appeals

BACKGROUND

Since all oral communication is a kind of behavior and influences other behavior, it may be said that all speaking has elements of persuasion. In speeches whose purpose is not to persuade, the elements of persuasive effect are more often accidental than deliberate; and even when they are planned for by the speaker, they are used as a means to another end rather than as an end in themselves. For instance, in a speech to inform your audience about all the various investment opportunities available to them, you might very well, quite without your intending to, cause some of your listeners to decide that they will invest in municipal bonds rather than in common stock; or, in that same speech, you might try to persuade them to listen by stressing the relevance of your information to their making a wise decision about investing their money. Neither element of persuasion would make of your speech anything but what you intended it to be—a speech to inform. But if the influencing of behavior is the deliberate and principal aim of your speech, if your entire speaking effort is a consciously planned attempt to dispose your listeners favorably toward a goal that you have in mind, you are giving a speech whose purpose is to persuade. It is this type of speech which now becomes the object of our study.

144

A Rationale for Persuasion

Persuasion is a necessary force in a free society. The citizens of such a society, both individually and in groups, believe and act largely as a result of their own decisions. Moreover, dictation and coercion are specifically prohibited as means of influencing those decisions. That means that if you wish to advocate the acceptance of a particular belief or philosophy or policy by other members of your society, you must do it through persuasion or not at all. It is the only morally and legally justifiable means at your disposal.

But, you might ask, should I make such an attempt to sway others to my way of thinking? Is it not their obligation to do their own thinking, as I have done mine? Why should I bother them with persuasive appeals? Do they not have enough to do without my attempting to influence them or to do their thinking for them? Such thinking has much to recommend it, of course; but as a view of the workings of a democratic society, it is rather naive and impractical.

Reticence in trying to impose your views on others, commendable as it might sometimes be on issues of a purely private nature, can be the most shameful neglect of your duties and obligations as a citizen of a free society. Many if not most of our beliefs and actions have public as well as private consequences. Whether we wish to be or not, we are all members of our society, and what we believe and do affects others as their behavior affects us. Those others, left wholly to their own devices, might very well think wrongly about an issue, or perhaps not think at all.

We owe it to our society, therefore, to help in every way we can to guide it toward those principles and practices which we feel will serve it and us best. The consequences of our not doing so on any truly significant issue could be most serious. Let others do their own thinking in order to arrive at their own decisions, by all means, but do not let them do it without the benefit of your best efforts to guide them toward the truth.

On the issues which call for persuasion, there are no infallible guides to truth. These issues are, for the most part, man-made and to be disposed of by man. Even problems thrown at us from the universe or from nature around us are filtered first through human consciousness, then are met by human reactions. Men being as diversified in their backgrounds, circumstances, and predilections as they are, their viewpoints toward any one problem will vary widely, with many different courses of action being urged. From among those suggested—oftentimes widely different in both intent and merit—that solution which will be most expeditious, effectual, and generally beneficial should be found. Seldom is there opportunity to test out the various nostrums in practice, and very often there is a stringent time limit upon decision. Under such circumstances, wise choices are not easily, and certainly not automatically, made.

Ideally, in a free society, each of the advocates on a particular issue will have equal and ample opportunity to present the best possible case for his proposal, after which those who must make the decision will thoughtfully deliberate and choose what would seem to be the most promising course of action. In theory and in the general practice it is a good system, but by its very nature it is liable to error. It can go wrong either if the advocates of all points of view have not been heard, or if they have not been heard to the best advantage, or if those listening are not good at their task of evaluation. A citizen's obligation, then, does not end with advocacy of his point of view whenever occasion for it arises. He should be not just an advocate, but an effective one; and when he is one of those doing the deciding, he needs to be a skilled listener as well.

Aristotle said that the highest calling of the public speaker is to give effective voice to the truth. But too often good causes fail because of lack of effective advocates. Too often truth does not prevail because the advocates of error are better persuaders. Perhaps somewhat naively, Aristotle went on to say that if truth is presented with the same or superior skill as error, audiences will automatically choose truth. We will not make such a guarantee. We will only say that truth must be given an effective voice if it is to have any chance at all for success. Wise, discriminating, open-minded listeners are also necessary for truth to be recognized and accepted. That is one good reason why this is a course in listening as well as in speaking.

One might argue that, once a decision has been made and acted upon, no one can say that another decision might not have worked out just as well. But such speculations do not settle the practical affairs of the world. We live with the fact that decisions must be made and acted upon. We delude ourselves if we do not realize that there *are* such distinctions as good and bad, better or worse, true or false. If we do not believe, at least at the moment of decision, that the one answer we decide upon is the best, we may wind up not adopting any solution at all. This could have tragic consequences. Disaster is never so sure as when nothing at all is done to improve a bad situation.

Purposes of the Assignment

All of this being true, we hope that neither now nor in the future will you ever fail to state your convictions about the way the world should be run. We further hope that when you do speak, you will be the best possible advocate you can be for your point of view. In this unit and the one that follows, we shall try to teach you some of what you need to know about those skills.

Your listening skills should have grown by this time to the point where, with a little more stretching, they will be adequate to the job of critical evaluation of persuasive speaking. In these units, your purpose in listening will be quite different from what it has been up to this point. You will be sitting not as a learner at the feet of a teacher, but rather as a judge of an advocate's appeal. That means that your listening attitude must change. You must listen to challenge arguments, to evaluate their soundness, to weigh them against other aguments, and finally to accept or reject the proposal. Another purpose of these units in persuasive speaking is to give you an opportunity to exercise such listening skills.

The Nature of Persuasion

Quite a few students of the course in beginning speech have some difficulty in understanding the nature of persuasive speaking. This is not surprising, since they are not exposed to this type of speaking nearly as much as they are to informational speaking. To help you gain that understanding, we shall venture the following two statements.

Portrait of a Persuasive Speaker.   As the first of those two statements, let us formulate a capsule portrait of a speaker likely to be successful at persuasion. He is an individual who has a keen, inquisitive mind; who knows how to use it in order to think through and solve problems; who is not afraid of speaking his mind and trying to make his view prevail; who is concerned about the society in which he lives and dedicated to serving its best interests; who is sophisticated enough to realize that conscious thought must be given to the right and wrong approaches to a particular audience; and who is imaginative enough to be able to look at things from a point of view other than his own. Such a person looks upon persuasive speaking as an obligation of his citizenship in a free society, a challenge to his finest intellectual effort, and a force of such power for good or evil that he must treat it as a sacred trust.

Effective and Ethical Persuasive Speaking.   At the beginning of this unit, we defined persuasive speaking as a deliberate and concerted effort to sway your listeners favorably toward a goal that you have in mind. As a concise statement of the essential nature and purpose of persuasive speaking, it served our purpose of the moment quite well. No longer will it suffice, however, for soon we must speak of how the persuasive effect is accomplished, and about that it says nothing. So it is that we present our second statement.

This statement will be not so much a definition of persuasive speaking as a description of it. Its purpose is to give you an overview of persuasive speaking that will better enable you to understand all that we will have to say about the assignment and preparation for the speech of this and the following unit. Here is that description:

> In effective persuasive speaking a speaker attempts to deal with a controversial problem of significance to himself and to his audience through a deliberate, concerted effort to make his audience either immediately or ultimately take his proposed action for solving it. The proposition he advocates has evolved from his very finest reflective thinking, devoted to the discovery of the single best solution to the problem. His effort in speaking is principally aimed at enlisting favorable attitudes toward himself and his arguments through both intellectual and psychological appeals. He designs his arguments to strengthen, alter, or create beliefs that the problem exists and must be solved, that his suggested causes for it are the real ones, and that his solution is superior to the other ones available. He presents his speech in his most vital and winning manner, realizing that his delivery can be as much an argument for adopting his proposal as anything he says. To make his speaking ethical as well as effective, the speaker, while not obliged to be objective, must openly avow his advocacy, be truthful in all of his statements, avoid appeals to base or unworthy motives, be fair in his treatment of opposing arguments, and be devoted to serving his listeners' best interests as well as his own.

In outlining the basic assignment of this unit and its several options, and as we proceed through our advice on preparing for the speech of this unit, we shall be expanding upon this statement in just about everything we say or imply. We will delay detailed consideration of the ethics of persuasion until the next unit, not because the problem does not exist in speeches of the type you will be giving in this unit, but because it is possibly more significant in those of Unit V. If you proceed through the steps of preparation for this speech as we suggest, you will probably be ethical in your advocacy.

THE ASSIGNMENT

In this first unit in persuasive speaking you will be concentrating on manipulating the attitudes of your listeners principally through intellectual appeals. Quite frankly, distinctions between the two types of appeals, the intellectual and the psychological, are extremely arbitrary. There is no so-called intellectual appeal which does not also carry psychological weight, nor is even the most seemingly irrational psychological appeal completely devoid of some kind of logic. Distinction between the two can be made only in terms of greater emphasis. We are asking that in this unit the emphasis be on the intellectual rather than the psychological element. Your proposition, then, should be suited to establishment through logical argumentation, and your contentions should all be well supported with sound evidence and reasoning. You should not rule out the use of psychological appeals entirely, but they should be subsidiary to your basically logical approach.

The next unit of the course will concentrate on psychological appeals. One could argue just as well for switching the order of these assignments. Certainly the persuasive speaker needs to know the techniques of motivating audiences as much as he does the means of convincing them of the logical soundness of his proposal. Since the emphasis of this course is on speaking of high intellectual and ethical quality, however, it might be well to lay the groundwork in logic and then move into motivation. No persuasive argument should ever be made by a speaker merely assuming that it has a logical base; he must be able to demonstrate the soundness of his argument if called upon to do so. Ideally, at least, those persuasive speeches which emphasize psychological appeals do so only because the subject is one not entirely demonstrable by logic or, if it is, because the particular audience neither wishes to nor needs to hear all the substantiating data.

One or more of the following options may be given you for selection of a speech subject in this unit:

Option A: Free Choice. You may choose to speak on any current controversial issue you please so long as it fits the general requirements of the assignment outlined above.

Option B: The Speech Derived from Your Major Field of Study. Almost every branch of study has its own controversial problems that are also relevant to the general public and connect with other more universal problems existing outside its own boundaries. If one of these is to be your subject, be sure to remember at all times that you are speaking to a lay audience, not to fellow specialists.

Option C: The Speech on a Campus Problem. Every college or university campus has more than its fair share of problems. Some of these are purely local, while others are common to almost all institutions of higher learning. Choose a subject of the latter kind, so that you can call upon the experiences of other schools to provide guidelines for your inquiry and advocacy.

Option D: The Speech Suggested by a Newspaper or Magazine Editorial. Browse through the editorial pages in recent issues of some of our more reputable newspapers and magazines until you find an editorial dealing with a problem you feel you simply must investigate further. Try to use the editorial that served as incentive for study of the problem in some way in the actual delivery of your speech.

Option E: The Speech on a Pending Item of Legislation.   Investigate the published proceedings of various legislative bodies, such as the *Congressional Digest* of our national legislature, for a pending item of legislation of concern to you. You may urge the bill's passage, amendment, or defeat, or possibly even draft an alternative bill. At your instructor's discretion, you may either speak to your listeners in their own persons or ask them to imagine themselves the group that is actually considering the legislation.

Option F: Instructor's Assignment.   In order that your assignment may better suit the speech needs of your particular class, your instructor may choose to modify one of the above assignment options, combine features of two or more of them into one assignment, or possibly give you an assignment entirely of his own devising.

SUBJECT AND MATERIALS

Choose a Subject Area

Our description of persuasive speaking stated that the speaker "attempts to deal with a problem of significance to himself and to his audience." The use of the word "problem" should suggest that this kind of speaking exists in the practical world of getting things done, that it is not an idle pursuit. Somewhere someone is hurting because something is not being done or because it is being done badly or wrongly. Moreover, the problem being dealt with is "controversial," meaning that there is more than one way of solving it, that at least two and probably more different courses of action are being proposed as the best way to take care of the difficulty. Nor is the problem a mere pinprick in the tough old hide of the world. It is "significant." That means that the persuasive speaker feels that this is a problem meriting his attention and that of his hearers, most often because he and they are the ones or among the ones who are being hurt the most, and because he and they either now or in the future will be able to do something about it. If there is no problem, or if there is only one possible answer to it, or if you and your audience have no stake in it whatsoever, or if you and they cannot now and never will be able to do anything about it, then there is no reason to present a persuasive speech.

As areas of investigation for persuasive speaking, then, look to the many trouble spots that exist in the world about you. What are some of the evils or difficulties that need to be dealt with? What needs to be changed?

In deciding on a subject area, choose one that is not merely interesting to you, but is one of your really vital concerns. Inquisitive interest in a subject area may be sufficient stimulus for an effective informative speech, but it is hardly adequate for persuasive speaking. If highway traffic deaths mean nothing more to you than momentarily shocking statistics, if you can sleep soundly after reading the grisly news of the most recent holiday weekend slaughter, then this not a likely area of investigation for you. If, on the other hand, you have suffered the loss of loved ones in an automobile accident, or have worked on a job as a policeman, ambulance driver, newspaper reporter, or insurance investigator where the agony, suffering, horror, and tragic waste of ignoring the rules of traffic safety have been brought home to you with the unforgettable impacts of first-hand experience and repetition, then this is something for you to consider as an area for further investigation. No one outside the classroom gives a persuasive speech unless he is trying to solve a problem that he cares about deeply. There is no reason why speeches in the classroom should have any less relevance to the real interests and concerns of the speaker.

Once you have found a subject area that you care about, you have made a tremendous initial stride in the direction of a successful speech of persuasion. Not only should your subject area reflect your vital interests, however; it should also be of significance to your listeners, something worthy of their efforts. If the things which you care about are not too specialized, there is not much likelihood of going wrong here.

Specialized areas of interest that at first you might consider to have no relevance to either persuasive speaking or the general public can with closer scrutiny be seen to be pertinent to both. The student studying irrigation engineering, for instance, might propose that the national government underwrite irrigation programs in the arid areas of our nation as a means of bolstering the economies of these areas and eventually reducing both our food costs and our taxes. Or the student of aesthetics could argue that the proposed building program for the campus should be planned with beauty as well as utility in mind. And why could not the student of business administration present a persuasive appeal for revised corporation tax laws beneficial to the entire nation? However, the wise speaker will want to check to see that there are definite connections between his subject area and his audience before he decides definitely upon it.

Trivial subjects should be ruled out. In the world we know, much skillful persuasion is accomplished in advertising the virtues of particular brands of soap and cigarettes; but for the sake of your own training in speaking and that of your audience in listening, we would hope that you will aim higher in challenging both their and your resources.

There should be no dearth of problems from which to select your subject, for they exist everywhere and every one of us is affected by many of them. All of us have personal troubles; every organization or institution has its dilemmas; each local, state, and national government or agency has more than its fair share of difficulties to resolve; and there are international, and now even cosmic, problems in addition. Such problems make our lives less happy than they could and perhaps should be, and for the sake of our individual and collective pursuits of happiness, we must try to solve as many of them as we can. But they are also an indication of a vital and dynamic person, organization, or society. The one sure way to avoid them is to avoid any kind of purposeful living and doing. Without problems to solve a person, organization, or society stagnates. But there is small danger that you will ever solve all of them, or that even if you did you would be contributing to stagnation. If you, your organization, or your society keep on being vitally and dynamically active, there will always be new problems to solve.

Investigate the Subject Area

Probably the greatest mistake speakers make in investigating their subject area in preparing a speech of persuasion is that of limiting themselves to sources which tend to support their own preconceived position. We have said previously that you always begin by discovering and noting down what you already know, think, and feel about the subject. That advice still holds. It is the logical starting place. But you do not stop there, nor should you be limited in your further study by the narrow vision which you have before you begin investigating the subject.

Try to approach the investigation of your problem with as open a mind as possible. Do not blind yourself to a truth you may discover by a stubborn belief that you already know the truth. Listen to and read what the supporters of opposing points of view have to say as well as the pronouncements of those on the same side of the fence as you now are.

It is the gravest kind of error to think that such practice could do you any harm. If your opponents of the moment are wrong, studying their arguments will only reinforce your conviction of the wisdom of your present position and give you weapons of refutation by which you can the better do battle with them. If, on the other hand, they have the greater truth on their side, then it is to your and everyone's advantage that you discover that fact and ally yourself with them. There is no virtue in holding steadfastly to error and falsehood.

In persuasive speaking, investigating the subject area is in most respects identical with the investigation for informational speaking. As always, you find out all that you possibly can about a general topic, so that later you can pick the most suitable subject for the speech situation in which you will be appearing. As before, you read, listen, and observe in order to discover information, record it, and evaluate it for pertinence, worth, and interestingness. You think about and beyond it to be able to understand it, its interrelationships, and the full implications of all those relationships. But there the difference between informational and persuasive speaking ends. In informational speaking these tasks are to a great extent ends in themselves, your further obligation being only to impart your understanding to others. In persuasive speaking, these tasks are a means to a greater end, which is to discover the best solution to your problem.

The Process of Reflective Thinking

Our description of persuasive speaking, you will remember, makes this statement: "The proposition he (the effective and ethical persuasive speaker) advocates has derived from his very finest reflective thinking devoted to the discovery of the single best solution to the problem." The statement is one of the most important ones we make, and deserves amplification.

A number of years ago, the philosopher John Dewey described the steps of what he called reflective thought—the kind of thinking that results in the soundest decisions and courses of action.[1] The steps he described are these:

1. *A felt difficulty.* A person becomes aware of a problem that must be dealt with.
2. *Its location and definition.* A person examines the problem and becomes as thoroughly acquainted with it as he can.
3. *Suggested solutions.* The individual looks for various possible answers.
4. *Development by reasoning of the bearings of the solutions.* The person tests the answers in an effort to find the best one.
5. *Continuing testing and experimentation.* Once the decision is made, or action taken, it is continually re-evaluated and scarcely ever accepted as final, even though it is put into practice.

An ideal way to investigate your subject area for persuasive speaking would be to follow through with these steps. Only if you have done so can you surely consider yourself to be well qualified to speak rationally.

[1] John Dewey, *How We Think* (Boston: D. C. Heath & Company, 1910), p. 72.

Possibly you already completed the first of the five Dewey steps when you decided on your general problem area. It might be, however, that this area is so large that you need first to do a bit of narrowing. You are exploring the problem of traffic safety, you say. Good enough, but is it campus traffic safety that you are most concerned with, or does the national problem worry you more? Is it unsafe drivers or unsafe automobiles or unsafe highways that infuriate you? Or perhaps you are incensed because you think our laws governing traffic safety are unsound? Before you proceed into the second of the Dewey steps, you had better know. You would be surprised at how many persons deliver ostensibly persuasive speeches without having the foggiest notion of exactly what problem they are speaking about.

Once you have decided upon a "felt difficulty" you will want to learn all that you possibly can about its nature. This is the second step, *location and definition.* It is a step too often hurried through by people who want to make up their minds in a hurry, who are more interested in a quick answer than a good one. It is, possibly, the most crucial step of all, for here you lay the groundwork for a solution that will truly and effectively deal with the problem. Here it is that you discover just how widespread and serious the problem is—who is being hurt and in what ways and how much, and what the history and background of the problem is—when and how and under what circumstances it came about, and what all of the possible causes for the problem may be, and what criteria must be met by an acceptable solution. At the end of this step, you should know precisely what problem you are trying to solve and what kind of a solution you are looking for.

The third step in rational investigation of a problem, *suggested solutions,* is sometimes a lengthy one, sometimes not. Generally speaking, the more controversial the issue, the more time you will have to spend on this step. Of all the steps, this may be the one demanding your greatest effort at objectivity. You may constantly have to remind yourself that you are not as yet an advocate of a particular point of view, that you are still in the act of finding that point of view. Do not look only for the programs presently being advanced for solution of the problem; try to go beyond that and devise others, either wholly original to you or fashioned through alteration or combination of the suggested solutions of others. Like the previous step, this one must not be passed over lightly: it is a prerequisite to discovery of a good solution.

Your mind should be especially keen and your energies at their peak when you approach John Dewey's suggested fourth step, *development by reasoning of the bearings of the solutions.* To accomplish this step well, you will need every resource of imagination and intelligence you have. Your imagination will be devoted to projecting each of the solutions into fully implemented operation in the problem area and speculating upon all its probable

not too broad of a subject

effects. Both your intelligence and imagination will be directed toward giving each solution the benefit of every virtue it possesses and every agency of support it is likely to enlist; and then, conversely, checking out every one of its faults and probable potential enemies. Your intelligence should then take over almost entirely to weigh the merits and demerits of each individual solution, then compare and contrast all the solutions to arrive in your own thinking at the single best remedy. This remedy should be one which will meet all or most of the criteria for an acceptable solution which you set up for yourself in the second step.

The fifth step in the Dewey description of reflective thought, *continuing testing and experimentation,* is the one which will insure that you go before your audience with the very best solution and the most effective supporting arguments that you can obtain. You must not allow yourself to be too easily satisfied. Too frequently in our newspapers nowadays we are reading articles about wonder drugs put on the market without having been thoroughly tested. Such negligence has sometimes resulted in suffering, or deformity, or even death. The reputable scientist does not announce a discovery unless and until he has run every possible test. The reputable public speaker exercises the same caution. Having decided upon a possible solution, then, subject it to even more rigid tests than you did before. Try to find and repair its every flaw. If there are too many flaws that cannot be mended, then obviously you must discard the solution and search for a better one.

Evaluating Your Materials

As you proceed through these steps of reflective thought, you will note that, for the most part, your own attitude and those evident in your sources will be directed toward establishing the validity of disputed truths. You will be looking for the truth, and proponents on all sides of the question will be claiming that what they are offering is the truth. You will be literally bombarded with contentions of truth and evidence and reasoning advanced to establish the validity of those contentions. Your job of evaluating the contentions, the evidence, and the reasoning is a vital, challenging, and—at least for most persons—fascinating task. It has a most serious purpose, of course, but that neither does nor should prevent you from enjoying it.

First let it be understood that in the areas of controversy with which persuasion deals there is seldom, if ever, such a commodity as absolute truth. The best that anyone can do in these areas is to establish a high degree of probability that what he says is so, what he advocates is right. What you are looking for, then, is the likelihood of truth, not its guaranteed presence.

Examine the Contentions.   You will want first of all to examine the contentions of the various advocates whose views you will be examining. There are times when you need to do no more than this in order to reject an advocate. Wild claims and sweeping assertions you should hold immediately suspect. When the snake oil merchant tells you that his concoction will cure every one of the physical ills that has ever beset mankind, you can be fairly sure that the remedy is completely worthless. Or if a spellbinder states that all the professors at X University are Communists out to destroy our democratic system of government, you can usually rest assured that the twisted mind of this advocate poses a danger far greater than any that might exist at X University. People and their ideas and actions are seldom black or white. Be wary of anyone who claims they are. And, of course, if the contentions of the advocate, judged on the basis of what you already know about the world or the subject, seem completely impossible, you may not want to go further in your assessment of what he has to say.

Examine the Evidence and Reasoning.   If the contentions seem reasonable and possible, you will next need to test the evidence and reasoning advanced in support of them. You may find that little or no substantiation of the arguments is being presented. This should serve as a large, flashing, red danger signal to you, for while there may be some few persons too lazy or too neglectful to present their establishing material, most advocates, if they have it and if they have good reason to be proud of it, are only too eager to put it on public display.

Fallacies of Ignoring the Question.   *bringing in irrelevancies*   An early check in your analysis of the advocate's evidence and reasoning should be of its relevance to the issue at hand. A rather large number of fallacies, or errors in logic, derive from irrelevant argumentation. Collectively these are termed the fallacies of *ignoring the question*. They have various different guises, but the common characteristic of all of them is <u>evasion of the real point at issue by diverting</u> <u>attention to other matters which have no bearing on it.</u> If you have heard a statement like "A fine one Professor Slack is to tell us to get our work in on time! It's a month now since we took the midterm and he still hasn't returned the papers!", you have heard one kind of *ignoring the question.* You cannot infer from the character, profession, or conduct of an individual anything about the truth or falsity of his advice. Professor Slack's advice is good advice, whether he himself follows it or not. To argue that we should not do something because it has never been done before; or to claim that the argument is true because the other side either has not or cannot prove that it is not true; or to create a false dilemma, arguing that a proposition should be adopted because it is the only feasible one of only two possible solutions when in actuality there are other alternatives—all of these are additional ways of ignoring the question.

bringing in something that is and argument in itself.

Fallacies of Begging the Question. Other flaws in the workmanship of the general argument you are examining, which could indicate an inferior product, make up a second group of logical fallacies given the special name of *begging the question.* These fallacies, like those of *ignoring the question,* are not associated with any one particular kind of evidence or reasoning, but are applicable to all. Their special identifying tag is the tacit assumption of the truth of a point which is actually in dispute. The oppressors of history have frequently pointed to the more unsavory characteristics of those they are oppressing and said, "Look at them! Wouldn't the better living conditions and opportunities for education that you want to give them be wasted on such a worthless lot as that?" The argument assumes, of course, that these people are inherently unable to improve their status, which is just what those who are proposing reforms are saying they are not. Critics of American teacher-training methods, for another example, will often be heard making pronouncements like this: "Wouldn't it be better for our teachers to be thoroughly grounded in their subject matter rather than wasting their time on a lot of useless methods courses?" Here again something is taken for granted which is really a very hotly contested issue. The advocate had better prove to your satisfaction that "methods" courses are as poor and as unnecessary as he says they are before you even so much as consider his proposal. Test for yourself the "question-begging" in the statement of the college dean who defined panty raids as "a necessary and harmless outlet for the normal spring-time exuberance of the healthy young American male." Such fallacies of begging the question are not easy to spot, especially if you are inclined to agree with the proponent. Keep a sharp lookout for them.

Testing the Documentation. You will want to make one further check on the general quality of the argumentation of the advocate you are evaluating before you proceed to point-by-point analysis of each item of evidence and reasoning. A man, it is said with some justice, can be judged by the company he keeps. How good is the documentation for the evidence being used? How reliable are the men, the organizations, the reference works, the books, the journals, the magazines, the pamphlets, and the newspapers from which the evidence was taken? Are they noted for thoroughness, accuracy, and objectivity or for their opposite qualities? Some knowledge of the reputations of the more generally consulted purveyors of information and opinion—*Time Magazine, U.S. News and World Report, Newsweek, The Reporter, The Annals of the American Academy of Political and Social Sciences, The New York Times, The World Almanac, The Encyclopaedia Brittanica,* the *Mer-*

riam-Webster Unabridged Dictionary and their like—is essential for sound judgment of the worth of an advocate's supporting data.

Another test you should apply to this data is that of *recency*. We will not argue that on some matters the old evidence is still the best, but the odds are not in its favor, especially concerning the more current controversial issues that you will likely be investigating. Circumstances alter cases daily, sometimes even hourly, in matters of this kind.

Methods of Reasoning and Their Tests [2]

We will suppose that you are now satisfied that the advocate's contentions are reasonable, that he has produced enough material for them, that he has not been guilty of ignoring or begging the question, and that his documentation appears impressive for both its reliability and its recency. The next task is to look more closely at his evidence and reasoning, which thus far, at least, appear to be sound. To do this, you will need to know something about the various forms of reasoning and the tests which are ordinarily applied to them.

All of the types of physical and authority materials which you have studied and used in your informative speeches are applicable to speeches of persuasion. In persuasive speaking, however, they are usually used in conjunction with reasoning materials designed to show their relationship to the main contentions of the argument and the relationship of those contentions to the general conclusion which is drawn. Let us look at the various ways in which supporting materials are used as evidence, the reasoning that is applied to them, and the tests which may be made of the quality of the evidence and the soundness of the reasoning.

Reasoning from Example. The basic presumption underlying reasoning from example is that if a substantial number of individual persons, things, places, or events all belonging to the same category have some common characteristic, this characteristic is likely to occur generally in that category. Although all kinds of examples can be and are used, they are usually *real* rather than *imaginary* and *brief* rather than *extended. Fictitious examples, illustrations,* and *stories and anecdotes* are used more in persuasion that stresses psychological appeals, which you will have an opportunity to practice in the next unit of this course.

Let us suppose that an advocate is proposing a bond issue for construction of schools in Yourtown. He is presenting evidence to show the need.

---

[2] For a number of the definitions and tests of reasoning set forth in this section we are especially indebted to William Trufant Foster's classic work, *Argumentation and Debating.* Complete bibliographical information for the book will be found in the References for this unit.

Premise: The schools in Yourtown are unsafe and inadequate.

Example: East School has been condemned by the Safety Board.

Examples: South School has capacity for 200 students and an enrollment of 310; North School is overcrowded by more than 150 pupils; and West School has over 200 more students than it can handle.

Conclusion: There is a need for new schools.

How good is the evidence? You will want to test it before you accept the advocate's contention or use it in your own speech. The established criteria of judgment here, like those for every other kind of reasoning we shall be examining, are the obvious questions raised as a result of a healthy skepticism:

1. *Are the examples accurate?* That is, do these conditions really exist? It is not at all unusual for ill-informed or unscrupulous persons to distort, exaggerate, or even invent examples. Be especially wary of examples for which no specific documentation is given. Demand verifying sources and specific names, places, dates, and other circumstances. When, for instance, was East School condemned? It may be that the conditions that brought about the condemnation have since been completely rectified. If not, how serious are the faults? Might they be remedied at less cost than it would take to build new schools? These suggest the sort of questions you will want to ask to determine the accuracy of the examples.

2. *Are there enough examples to warrant the conclusion?* A few isolated observations are not enough. It is a very human tendency to jump to conclusions, a fallacy in logical reasoning termed the *hasty generalization.* Of course, almost all generalizations are to some extent hasty, since it is virtually impossible to sample every apple in the basket, but the advocate should have bitten into enough of them so that he can legitimately claim that the basket is rotten. How many schools are there in Yourtown? If there are only the four mentioned, or perhaps just a few more than that, then the conclusion may be warranted. But if there are forty schools, or four hundred, then the advocate is making a mountain out of a molehill.

3. *Are the examples representative?* To some extent, this question overlaps with the previous one. There are times, however, when although a sufficient number of examples are cited, the advocate has gone out of his way to find only those which support his contention. You will want to ask if the condition is general or one limited to the atypical examples chosen. Perhaps the three schools mentioned as being overcrowded are the only ones out of nine in which this condition exists. Could some of these students be transferred to less crowded schools at the cost of only an extra bus or two?

4. *Are exceptions at a minimum?* This can be answered "yes" if you get "yes" answers for 2 and 3.

Negative answers to any of these questions mean that the evidence is not sufficient. The reasoning process involved can be seen from the organization given the material. To accept it as sound, you will want to satisfy yourself that the premise, the evidence, and the conclusion are all related to one another, and that the conclusion is warranted by the evidence.

Reasoning from Analogy.   When we first introduced you to the analogy as a supporting material, we said that it was the *literal analogy,* the direct comparison of things in the same general class or category, which could be used most directly to establish the validity of a contention. The *figurative analogy,* or imaginative comparison of unlike things, is used mainly to illustrate or to reinforce a point. Since persuasive speeches need to illustrate points as well as validate them, both kinds of analogies are employed. Of the two, however, the *literal analogy* can be considered more applicable to persuasive speaking, and especially to that which stresses intellectual appeals.

Reasoning from analogy, too, is liable to error and needs to be carefully evaluated. Let us look at analogy being used to establish a different point in the same argument for a bond issue to build new schools in Yourtown:

Premise: Our community can afford better schools.
Analogy: Russia spends more on public education than does the United States.
Analogy: Our community spends more on liquor and tobacco than it does on public education.
Analogy: The construction program in Othertown of three modern schools was financed by a bond issue.
Conclusion: Resources are available to finance the new schools.

How good is this evidence? A convenient set of criteria for evaluation is the following:

1. *Are statements made in the analogies accurate ones?*   It should be noted that each of these statements is in itself a conclusion. Has each of them been established with sufficient evidence and sound reasoning? If not, you should ask for substantiation before accepting them. For the first and second analogies you would want statistical evidence, and for the third you would want to be assured that the construction program in Othertown has been accurately reported.
2. *Are there relevant similarities in what is being compared?*   Although the two items being compared may be similar in many respects, the analogy may still be unsound: the similarities must be relevant to the point at issue. Conversely, there may be many dissimilarities in the items being compared, but if the relevant similarities exist the analogy can be sound. Here you would ask if Russia and the United States can actually be com-

pared in matters of education expenditures. Do they have relatively the same numbers of students to educate, the same amount and type of education, and the same means of financing their educational system? If the answers to these questions are affirmative, the premise is valid, it can be connected to the analogy, and a conclusion of possible significance can be drawn. You would also wish to raise similar challenges against the analogies of money spent on liquor and tobacco with that spent on education, and of Othertown and its building program with the building problem in Yourtown and the proposed solution.

3. *Are there significant differences between points of comparison?* Even if there are a large number of relevant similarities between the items being compared, one truly significant difference can invalidate the analogy. Does Russia have many more students to educate than we have? Is its educational system expensive because it is inefficient and are we actually getting more for a smaller expenditure than they are? Or does Russia have resources for educational expenditure—such as national government funds —not available in the United States? A "yes" answer to one or more of these questions should be an indication to reject the analogy. And how about the money spent on liquor and tobacco: does it come from funds that might be channeled into education, or is it necessary "pocket money" that would merely go for other "frivolous" pursuits if not spent as it is now? As for Othertown, it may be a wealthier community than Yourtown, hence better able to finance a bond issue. It is in this test of significant differences that the fallacy of the *false analogy* is exposed. Quite simply, the *false analogy* is one where the points of likeness used to establish the comparison are outweighed by the points of difference which have been ignored.

Reasoning from analogy, as you can see by now, is the inference that if two items belonging to the same general category resemble one another in all or most known particulars, they will also probably resemble one another in some other particular known to belong to the one, but not known to belong to the other. In our everyday world, it is the commonly heard argument that "If Johnny can do it, Jimmy can do it, too." All of us have been Jimmy at one time or another and know that "it ain't necessarily so."

Reasoning from Testimony. Both reasoning from example and reasoning from analogy make frequent use of what is termed *evidence of fact*. A fact, as we stated in Unit II, may be defined in terms of what can be verified. If it were necessary or desirable, you or anyone else could make the observations or investigations from which a factual statement was derived and arrive at precisely the same conclusion. Although it is the preferred type for establishing the probable truth on a disputed issue, evidence of fact is not the only kind that is used. Advocates also rely on *evidence of opinion*—disputable statements whose claim to credibility lies solely in the character of the person or persons making it—to supplement facts or to support issues where it is impossible to establish facts or when facts are not available.

Quotation, of course, is the authority material which comes into play here. Any and all forms of it are usable, but for logical argument it is *testimony,* both expert and inexpert, which is most appropriate.

Our advocate now is attempting to demonstrate by *reasoning from testimony* that his is the best solution to the problem:

> *Premise:*   Those who should know best support the proposed bond issue.
> *Expert Testimony:*   Superintendent of Public Schools Jones stated, "We need the bond issue and we need it now."
> *Inexpert Testimony:*   Resolutions passed by the five local PTA organizations all urge its passage.
> *Conclusion:*   If those who have studied the problem carefully say that the bond issue is the best solution, it must be.

The tests that we need to apply to reasoning from testimony are three in number:

1. *Is the testimony competent?*   You might assume that Superintendent Jones, because of his competence in his profession, knows what he is talking about in this matter. But resolutions passed by organizations, polls, or surveys are only indexes of group opinion. For these, competence is more difficult to determine. The competence of the individuals represented must be considered to satisfy yourself that the group's opinion is of any worth. Of course, if the group is composed of *expert* rather than *inexpert* persons, its cumulative endorsement carries considerably more weight than that of the single competent individual.

2. *Is the testimony consistent?*   The statement of the individual or group should be consistent with the facts and with the statements of other persons or groups of equal stature and reputation. Reliance on a single item of testimony, no matter how competent its source, is not enough.

3. *Is the testimony unbiased?*   We might assume that, because of his direct connection with the problem of schools, the superintendent would have some bias in favor of the proposal. The PTA groups might also be biased, since they are composed of parents of school children. This does not rule out the use of this testimony material, but the bias must be taken into account. What does impartial testimony have to say on the matter?

A few of the more common mistakes made in reasoning from testimony against which you should be on guard are:

1. *Uncritical assumption of competence for superficial reasons.* A hurried week's trip through France does not qualify a person to speak authoritatively about anything connected with that country.
2. *Accepting the testimony of an expert speaking outside his own field of competence.* The nuclear physicist can speak authoritatively about the nature of nuclear weapons, but he is not necessarily qualified to speak on whether or not they should be used.
3. *The too casual sample of inexpert testimony.* As we have said, cumulatively inexpert testimony can have value as proof, but if it is the "Roving Reporter" kind of hasty and unselective sample, it must be regarded with great suspicion.

Reasoning from Statistics. More often than not, when the ordinary person thinks of logical evidence, he thinks of statistics. Not only that, but he is inclined to accept as incontrovertible almost any statement that is presented within some statistical frame of reference. Advertisers are very much aware of the general public's practically blind faith in statistics. How often we hear radio and television announcers resonantly declare that "The figures on this chart demonstrate the proven fact that Smart Set Cigarettes have 19 percent less tars and other harmful residues than the average of the other brands tested," or "Nine out of ten doctors surveyed said that Nature's Broom is the laxative they themselves use," or "A recent survey made by an independent research organization has once again shown that housewives prefer Scrubbysuds for their deep-down cleaning by a ratio of more than three to one." The evidence and reasoning may be sound or it may not, but the advertiser knows that very few persons will check up on it or even momentarily doubt it. If you wish to become an intelligent speaker and listener, you will need to develop more discrimination.

Statistical argument is inherently neither better nor worse than any other kind. Indeed, it is not so much a separate method of reasoning as a means of reporting and interpreting multiple data for the other methods. That is to say, when in reasoning from example the figures run into the thousands, millions, or billions; or when in reasoning from analogy you are comparing the astronomical expenditures for space research of the United States and Russia; or when in reasoning from testimony you have a veritable army of supporters for your contention; you use statistical percentages, proportions, or correlations to make comprehensible what otherwise might be an overwhelming, confusing, and ultimately meaningless jumble of figures. Naturally, the tests for the particular kind of reasoning in which the statistics are being employed still apply. There are, in addition, tests that apply to the statistical evidence itself.

Here is a demonstration of a need for more schools in Yourtown, with statistics being used as the establishing material:

Premise: The degree of overcrowding in the schools of Yourtown is shameful and will get worse.

Statistic: The classrooms in Yourtown are handling 39 percent more students than they did only five years ago.

Statistics: Two out of three school children are attending overcrowded classes. Sixty-six percent of the classrooms are overcrowded.

Statistic: The average number of pupils in each classroom is 36.

Statistic: The State Department of Education estimates that the school population in this state will increase by 25 percent in the next ten years; this means that our present problem of overcrowding will become even more crucial unless something is done about it and soon.

Conclusion: We must build more schools to take care of the problem of overcrowding.

The special tests of statistical evidence to apply are these:

1. *Are the units of measurement comparable?* Possibly more statistical evidence goes wrong for this reason than for any other. If exact definitions of the units being compared are not given, it may be wise to discount the evidence. Are the bases for the comparison relatively equal? For instance, there may have been 116 classrooms in Yourtown five years ago and 174 now, yet the two figures are equated in the phrase "the classrooms of Yourtown." If such is the case, there are now 50 percent more classrooms to take care of 39 percent more students. Then too, today's classrooms may be larger, or more efficiently arranged, or in some other way different from those of five years ago.

2. *What do the proportions or percentages represent?* In testing the statistics about the number of overcrowded classes and classrooms, the first thing you would want to know is what the advocate considers overcrowding. It might be that no one else would condemn the present conditions. Moreover, you should ask if every one of the classes attended by the "two out of three" is overcrowded, or if perhaps only one or two out of the several they attend each day would fall in that category. Also, are the 66 percent of the classrooms overcrowded for every period of every day or only occasionally?

3. *Is the average the most accurate measure?* Four out of five classrooms might have 23 students each and the fifth be bursting at the seams with 88. The average is the 36 claimed by the advocate, but it gives a false

picture of the situation. Perhaps the mean, the median, or the mode should be used as the standard of measurement.

4. *Are the conclusions drawn from the statistics justified?* It could very well be that the State Department of Education's prediction of school population increase in the state is a good one, but does it necessarily apply to Yourtown? If Yourtown's percentage of increase is likely to be smaller than the state average, then the conclusion which was drawn is not completely justified.

You might now find it interesting to go back to the examples of typical advertiser's use of statistical evidence cited earlier and evaluate them on these criteria.

Reasoning from Syllogism. All of the methods of reasoning which we have discussed thus far have the generic title of *inductive reasoning*. The direction for the movement of thought in each is from the specific to the general. In reasoning from example, after noting a consistently recurring characteristic in a number of specific examples, we formulate a general principle applicable to the entire species. In reasoning from analogy, we compare two examples item by item in all known particulars, then infer that the general similarity that has been discovered can be applied to some unknown particular as well. In reasoning from testimony, we present a large number of items of testimony in an attempt to demonstrate some substantial measure of general agreement on a disputed point. Any of these forms of reasoning can employ statistical evidence, the only difference being that infinitely more specifics are considered before the general truth is assumed.

Derivative from inductive reasoning is another genus which goes by the name of *deductive reasoning*. Once a person has arrived at a general conclusion by means of some form of inductive reasoning, his next logical step is to apply that conclusion to specific items to which he feels it is applicable. In deductive reasoning, then, the direction for the movement of thought is from the general to the specific. The two patterns of reasoning will quite often co-exist in the same argument, sometimes even in the same sentence. They implement, complement, and supplement each other at every turn. Nonetheless, there is enough difference between them to warrant making the distinction.

There is really only one species of deductive reasoning used commonly enough to merit our consideration here, but it is illustrative of all the other species as well. This is *reasoning from syllogism*. "Syllogism" is the name given the specified step-by-step procedure for drawing a conclusion about a particular case from a general law. A proper syllogism is made up of three statements, each of a specified and unvarying kind, and presented in this sequence: (1) A *major premise* stating what is assumed to be an indisputable general law applicable to all cases of a given kind, (2) a *minor premise* stating that the particular case is of that kind, and (3) a *conclusion* stating that what is true of the general category must therefore also be true of the particular case.

Here syllogistic argument is presented to establish that Yourtown would be able to finance the proposed bond issue:

> *Major Premise:*   Any town with a population of 50,000 or more persons is capable of financing a bond issue for the construction of new schools.
> *Minor Premise:*   Yourtown was reported in the last national census to have a population of more than 78,000 persons.
> *Conclusion:*   Yourtown should be capable of financing this bond issue.

Reasoning from syllogism will meet the tests of validity if it satisfies three conditions:

1. *Is the major premise true?*   There are many more general laws asserted than actually exist. In the above syllogism, the major premise should, at least, have been derived from statistically based reasoning from example. You would be wise to ask for demonstration of the evidence and reasoning from which the general law was induced.
2. *Is the minor premise true and logically linked to the major premise?* Unless there has been a mass exodus of citizens from Yourtown since the last census was taken, and if the census figures have been reported accurately, the minor premise of the example would seem to satisfy both conditions. It unmistakably brings Yourtown within the class about which the generalization asserts a truth.
3. *Does the conclusion inevitably follow from the two premises?*   More often than not, if the first two conditions are satisfied, this third one is also. Sometimes, however, a careless reasoner will establish a general principle, then later on, lost in his own wordiness, proceed to deduce a conclusion not from that principle but from another which resembles it. If the advocate using the syllogism we have been testing had concluded with some statement like, "Yourtown should float a bond issue as all the other towns of its size are doing," he would have been guilty of this fault.

Reasoning from Causal Relation.   The third general category of reasoning is reasoning from causal relation. It is given a separate designation for the simple reason that it does not fit conveniently into either of the other two pigeonholes. Sometimes it moves inductively, at other times deductively, and on still other occasions uses both routes to arrive at its destination. It can be said, however, to be primarily deductive in nature. Reasoning from causal relation proceeds from the assumption that nothing ever happens without a reason, and that we cannot do anything without its having a consequence. In trying to solve problems, then, we deal constantly in possible causes for the present intolerable conditions, probable results of leaving the problem unsolved, likely consequences of implementing the suggested solutions, and implications from known events that something happened in the past, is occurring now, or will take place in the future. In this type of reasoning arguments are made from *effect to cause,* from *cause to effect,* and from *sign.*

Let us consider *effect to cause* and *cause to effect* as basically employing the same kind of thought process, hence for the most part subject to the same tests of validity. If we report a fact, incident, or observation as a known effect, we complete the statement by identifying the alleged cause. Likewise, if we describe a known cause, we link it with its anticipated effect. In each instance a direct relationship between the two is assumed by the advocate, but needs to be tested by the one evaluating the argument. With the proposed bond issue again the proposition being argued, the following statements illustrate these two types of reasoning from causal relation:

> *Effect to cause:* The inferior quality of the education being given the children of Yourtown is the result of our inadequate school facilities.
>
> *Cause to effect:* The announced construction of a new plant for United Industries in Yourtown will result in our classrooms being even more overcrowded than they are now.

In examining these cause-effect relationships, you should ask these questions:

1. *Are we mistaking the cause or the effect?* Again the reports of conditions must be accurate; further, they must be directly related. In the instance where the reasoning is from effect to cause, you would want it first established both that the quality of education is inferior and that the school facilities are inadequate; and secondly that inadequate school facilities can and necessarily have to result in education of a lower quality. In the reverse instance, how probable is it that this plant is actually going to be built, and would such construction of necessity overcrowd classrooms?
2. *Are there other causes or effects, some of which are more probable?*

Variables must be accounted for. A consistency of results is as important here as it would be in a laboratory experiment. In the first statement, for instance, you could ask whether other influences besides the lack of facilities are equally or even more influential. What about the salary schedule for teachers? What about the quality of the administration? In the second argument, might not the new wealth which United Industries would bring to Yourtown mean that new schools could be constructed without the bond issue?

3. *Is there a direct relationship, or is the connection mere coincidence?* This test applies only to reasoning from effect to cause, and reveals one of the most common fallacies of causal reasoning, *post hoc ergo propter hoc*. Translated from the Latin, this reads "after this, therefore because of this." Just because two or more events seem to occur simultaneously does not mean that they are necessarily related. The rather indefinite terms "inadequate" and "inferior quality" in the first statement may not always be related. Possibly last year the facilities were just as inadequate but the education was of a much higher quality. And it may be that the year before that the facilities were more adequate and the education of a quality even worse than it is this year. Is it mere accident that the two events have occurred simultaneously this year?

Reasoning from effect to cause is designed to discover why something happened; reasoning from cause to effect is used to predict why something is about to happen. Reasoning from sign, on the other hand, is usually more concerned with the "what" of events. From observing some single circumstance or series of circumstances, we infer a condition which, we feel, always and inevitably follows. Mrs. Smith visits the doctor, resigns her job at the office, and buys a book on knitting; and all the ladies of the neighborhood start organizing a baby shower. Of course, a sign may sometimes tell us the "why" as well as the "what," as in the instance of the *post mortem* examination which discloses cancerous lung tissue. Reasoning from sign is a daily occurrence in the law courts, whenever "circumstantial evidence" is being presented.

One final time let us look at an argument for the Yourtown bond issue, this one using reasoning from sign, and apply the necessary tests:

Signs: Superintendent Jones is the fourth man in that office in the last seven years, and he is leaving us next year; in the past five years the annual turnover for our teachers has increased from 17 percent to 44 percent; and recently many of our wealthier citizens have been withdrawing their children from our schools and sending them to private schools in the East.

Conclusion: Certainly all these happenings should be indications to us that there is something drastically wrong with the schools of Yourtown.

1. *Is there a necessary relationship between the sign and the condition?* There are so-called *infallible* and *fallible* signs. When a man has a fever, it is a sure indication that there is something wrong with him. All of the above signs *may* have some relationship to the alleged condition, but not necessarily. You would have to judge these *fallible* signs.
2. *Have different times or altered circumstances invalidated the signs?* These signs may have been valid when administrative and teaching jobs were scarce and private schools were momentarily unfashionable, but with changing times both these circumstances may now also have changed.
3. *Are there enough signs to establish the existence of the condition?*   Occasionally a single sign is sufficient to establish the existence of the condition, but usually the corroboration of a number of signs is desired. A doctor, for instance, would not base his diagnosis of a serious illness on a single symptom. The three signs presented above, if they met the previous two tests, would probably be considered enough for the ordinary argument.

A Final Word on Evaluating Your Materials

After all that we have said about checking up on the contentions of the sources you will be investigating, the extent and documentation of the evidence, and the soundness of that evidence and the reasoning that is done from it; after all the tests that we have given you to use and the possible fallacies that we have warned you about; after, in short, the fundamentally rather negative character of all that we have said in this section, it probably will seem ironic to you that our last word on this subject is a reminder that what you are seeking is *truth,* not error. With further thought about the nature of your task, however, you may see the wisdom of the negative approach to a positive end. Think of your job as somewhat like that of the physician who, in doing a thorough physical examination of his patient, checks every possibility of disease in the hope of sending the patient out with a clean bill of health. The testing we have advised you to do is always for the purpose of finding good propositions, good contentions, and good evidence and reasoning to aid you in your persuasive task. Discard only the weak arguments; put the strong ones to work for you. The task of evaluating your materials, if conscientiously performed, should give you greatly increased confidence not only in your arguments, but also in your cause and in yourself.

APPLICATION TO AUDIENCE
AND OCCASION

Returning after rather long absence to direct reference to our governing statement about the nature, purposes, and procedures of persuasive speaking, we should like to remind you that it says that the persuader's goal is "to make his audience either immediately or ultimately take his proposed action for solving" their common problem. This part of the statement should warn you that nowhere else do you need to know your audience and your occasion as well as in persuasive speaking.

Action and Belief

The persuasive speaker's job, then, is always to get his listeners to *act*, either immediately or ultimately. There are those who would object at this point, saying, "But can't the persuasive speaker end his speech with an appeal for *belief* as well as for *action?* Aren't there two types of persuasive speech, not one?" Our answer must be that possibly unsettling but honest one, "Yes and no." A persuasive speaker can and often does ask only that his listeners believe along with him in the truth of his proposition, and does not go on to the next logical step and plead that they take an action which will solve the problem. But, we submit, this type of speech is given of necessity rather than desire, and always with hope that someday, somewhere, somehow they will take the necessary action. The speech whose immediate end is belief is given only under one or more of the following conditions:

1. When the speaker has not yet himself found a course of action to suggest.
2. When the speaker feels that it would be wiser not to make a direct appeal and that the listeners will be more inclined to take the necessary action if the plea is made implicitly rather than explicitly.
3. When the speech is part of a long-term campaign of persuasion, and the speaker or another speaker will later present the ultimate plea for action.
4. When the listeners are presently not in a position to act, but may be at some future time.

If the persuader did not wish ultimately for some action to be taken to solve the problem, there would be no reason for him to speak at all. Even when the immediate end of the speech is belief, then, the *seed* for future action can be sown.

It is seldom easy to get people to do something about a situation, even when they are fully convinced in their own minds that the action is one that they should take. It is even more difficult when they are not so convinced. You will need every strategy to shake people from lethargy, dissuade them from error, convince them of truth, and motivate them to action. One of the most necessary of these strategies is thorough knowledge of the speech situation.

In informative speaking all that it is absolutely necessary to know about your audience is their present knowledge of your subject, their ability to comprehend new material about it, and their past experiences and present interests in connection with it. Such knowledge is necessary in persuasive speaking, too, of course, but it is not enough. We have said that the persuader's "effort in speaking is principally devoted to enlisting favorable attitudes toward himself and his arguments through both intellectual and psychological appeals," and that "he designs his arguments to strengthen, alter, or create beliefs." To do these things well, you must endeavor to find out all that you can about your audience's present and potential attitudes and beliefs.

Attitudes and Beliefs

An *attitude* may be defined as "a predisposition to respond to a given stimulus in one way rather than another," and a *belief* as "a conviction of reality." Each of us is filled to the brim with attitudes. We have formed them toward every significant person, place, thing, or event of our lives; and have inferred or borrowed them about matters foreign to our direct personal experience. Depending on the past experiences a person had had with, say, New York City, he might have an attitude predisposing him to avoid any further association with that city at all costs. Or he might turn down a lucrative job offer because he could not bear to leave the place. Depending on his attitude toward New York, he could either dread or eagerly anticipate moving to another large city. His attitude about Camden, Maine might be borrowed from *Holiday* magazine or a neighbor's report of his vacation there. Beliefs, in turn, are the sum total of many attitudes. A series of unfortunate experiences with used car salesmen, for instance, creating unfavorable attitude after unfavorable attitude, might in time convince someone that all used car salesmen are liars and cheats. Another series of experiences, of course, could tend to create an entirely different belief that all used car salesmen are dedicated, ethical persons.

The persuasive speaker wants to know as much as possible about what his listeners' attitudes are toward himself; the cause, organization, or profession he represents; and all the possible intellectual and psychological appeals he can muster for his proposition. He wants especially to know what their favorable attitudes are, because these are the ones he will use to strengthen or build the necessary beliefs the listeners must have to adopt his solution in preference to any of the others that are offered. The unfavorable attitudes, of course, he must either avoid or allay.

The present nature and strength of his listeners' beliefs concerning the problem, its causes, and its solutions are also vital information for the persuasive speaker. He must endeavor to classify his audience as either predominantly *supporting, opposing, skeptical of,* or *indifferent to* his proposition, for almost every choice he makes in his persuasive effort hinges upon that classification. If his audience already supports him, he must use the appropriate means to strengthen their belief; if they are opponents, he needs different methods to alter it; and if they are skeptical or indifferent, still other techniques are required to create a belief.

How does one secure such information? It is really not as difficult as it might seem. Examine, first of all, the ways in which you and your audience are alike. Like experiences create like attitudes and beliefs. Most Americans, for instance, have a favorable attitude toward such things as the democratic form of government, the Constitution, Abraham Lincoln, and the American Revolution. Next, examine what you know about your audience's occupations, economic status, and organizational affiliations. These are perhaps the principal determinants of attitudes and beliefs relevant to public issues. Again the principle "like creates like" holds. You do not have to be especially imaginative to know what the probable attitudes and beliefs of most members of the American medical profession are toward socialized medicine; or how the poor react to social security; or how some of the more conservative members of the Republican Party would respond to accolades for Franklin Delano Roosevelt.

Knowledge of the occasion for your speech can be another effective weapon in your arsenal. There is a time and a place for everything, perhaps, but the time and place of your speech may not be the one for the proposition you advance, the arguments you use, the tie you wear, or the manner in which you waggle your finger at the audience. Think, for an example, of the futility of trying to say anything you really wanted the people on the floor to hear at a national convention of either one of our major political parties. Imagine what your speech occasion will be like, and from that what your audience might be willing and able to hear. You cannot, in any one speech, say everything that could be said or even that you would like to say. What you select and emphasize should be most "right" for the speech situation.

Determining the Purpose

In the light of your knowledge of audience and occasion, your first significant step in direct preparation of your persuasive speech is again to decide upon your specific purpose. You have investigated a problem and found a solution, so a large part of this step has already been accomplished. You know what it is you want your audience either immediately or ultimately to do as a result of your persuasion. But, right at this moment, would your audience be capable of and receptive to a plea for action, or must you satisfy yourself temporarily with securing belief? That answer should come fairly easily with application of your knowledge of audience and occasion to your knowledge of subject and materials.

√ CONSTRUCTION OF THE SPEECH

Accomplishing the Specific Purpose

Frequently we have used the word *proposition* in referring to the subject matter of persuasion. A proposition is usually stated in the central idea, and in persuasion may be thought of as that particular point of view or course of action the acceptance of which is most likely to achieve your persuasive purpose. That is, when you want to influence human behavior by getting listeners to believe or do a specific thing as a result of what you say, a statement of that "thing" contains your entire point of advocacy, the proposal or proposition you are advancing for acceptance.

Kinds of Propositions

Some propositions are classified as *propositions of fact*. You could, for example, argue whether there are such things as flying saucers from outer space. An attempt to persuade an audience what is or is not has its limitations. Lawyers argue propositions of fact in issues of guilt or innocence, justice or injustice. They attempt to influence behavior by appealing for a favorable vote of a jury or judgment of the court. Their arguments about a proposition of fact thus have great relevance to a decision that has to be made. If, however, you choose to discuss a proposition of fact before an audience not compelled to make a decision as a result of it, you will not only have a hard time interesting them, but will have accomplished very little. More than likely your audience for the speeches of this course is such an audience. For that reason you should probably rule out the proposition of fact as a possible subject.

Other propositions are classified as *propositions of value*. These usually center about judgments of good or evil, or right or wrong, or efforts to gain the audience's appreciation of a person or ideal. Arguments about the evils of racial discrimination or cheating on examinations expose the existence of a problem of moral values and motivate action. More frequently advocating propositions of value results in the creation or strengthening of a belief. The use of subjects that involve this sort of proposition is somewhat limited in this speech, since sound evidence and reasoning are many times difficult or impossible to find and since the solution is likely to lack specificity. However, you may wish to speak on such a proposition in the speech of the next unit.

Propositions that may be classified as *propositions of policy* are the most useful for achieving the goals of the speech in this unit. Propositions of policy can be identified by the key word *should:* what should be believed, what should be done. Developing your advocacy of such a proposition gives you an opportunity to use intellectual as well as psychological appeals for acceptance of your proposal, and to ask your audience to choose a specific solution on a rational basis. We urge you then to select a subject that can be worded in the central idea as a proposition of policy: a particular answer to a specified problem. Thus you should not end with establishing a need for "something" to be done; rather you should present a definite, detailed proposal which will accomplish the solution of that problem.

This proposition of policy should, of course, be one that has developed from your thorough exploration of the problem area, incorporating the best thinking that you have found in the speaking and writing of others and that you have done yourself. It should specify a belief or action that you can subscribe to wholeheartedly. But it may not incorporate *all* that you think needs to be believed or done in order to get the problem solved. What is it that this *particular audience* can do to *help* in solving the problem? They will not be able to do it all themselves. Other audiences, capable of different actions, will also have to be persuaded. It would be ridiculous, for instance, to suggest to a classroom audience that they "pass a law." About all they can do is speak or write to their Congressmen, urging them to pass a law. You will also need to consider just how much you can ask for from this audience at this time. If, at the moment, they are unalterably opposed to your proposition, you will have to be careful about the measure of belief or action you ask of them. "Will the occasion influence the phrasing of my proposition?" and "What kind of proposition, coming from a person of my age, background, and position, would not seem presumptuous to my audience?" are other questions that you will want to answer. What we are saying, in short, is that your central idea, or proposition, must fit the speech situation.

Although intellectual appeals are welcomed by almost all audiences, whatever their present beliefs, generally speaking they are most helpful in persuading audiences opposed to or skeptical of a point of view. It would be well, therefore, if your proposition were one that your audience did not presently unquestionably endorse.

The Speaker's Character

It is with attitudes that the persuasive speaker deals most, his job being to call up from his audience those favorable to himself and to his arguments. An attitude lies dormant until it is activated by some new experience. The persuader provides that new experience for his listeners. The means he has for accomplishing this are the very same ones by which attitudes are originally created.

One of these means, and therefore one of your three avenues of persuasion (many would say the most important one), is through the image of yourself which you give your audience. This Aristotle called *ethos,* or the character of the speaker. The earliest attitudes that an individual develops, and many which he develops later, are formed by emulation of the attitudes of those he admires. The persuasive speaker, then, must present himself as a person worthy of admiration. When politicians are casting about for likely candidates for office, one of the phrases that is often heard is "the father image." Many voters, they realize, are more concerned with the man than with the issues. In the last analysis, probably, most audiences are, too.

Are you sufficiently knowledgeable in your subject and convinced of the truth of your proposition to go before this audience on this occasion? Do you presently possess sufficient ethos so that your audience will tend to believe what you say simply because you say it? If not, are you capable of creating that ethos? The freshman Senator, for instance, will never be listened to with the same respect as the veteran with 30 years' service, no matter how hard he tries. And if elements of ethos must and can be created, where do the needs lie? What are the ways by which such elements can be developed?

Of course, ultimately, every bit of material which a speaker uses in his speech, as well as every action he performs in delivering it, adds to or detracts from whatever measure of ethos he might have at the start. He will, however, select certain materials specifically for the purpose of demonstrating to the audience that he has those qualities of character that they admire. As our statement says, the speaker *consciously* attempts to enlist favorable attitudes toward *himself* as well as toward his arguments. Naturally, the qualities that would be demonstrated would differ with differing audiences to some extent. For instance, you might show some aspects of your character at a stag dinner that would not be appropriate at a meeting of the Ladies' Aid Society; and, so long as there was no falsification of the essentials of your personality in either instance, there would be nothing wrong in your doing so. There are some constants, however, applicable to most audiences, which you should know about.

One constant that would apply to almost every audience is that they want, at one and the same time, a speaker who is like themselves and yet to some degree superior to themselves. It is one of the more persistent human tendencies to look with suspicion upon those who are in any large measure different from ourselves, and if you are a wise speaker you realize and act upon this knowledge. You also realize, however, that by the very act of speaking you are setting yourself up in a position superior to your audience and that they know and accept the difference. What you give them should warrant the presumption. You should be able to show that, at least in your knowledge of the question, you are superior to them.

Most audiences want a speaker who demonstrates himself to be a person of competence, integrity, and good motives. If they are to be partially persuaded by the impact of your personality upon them, they want to be assured that you know what you are talking about, that you are honest and straightforward, and that you have their best interests at heart. It would be the very worst form, of course, for you to say outright that you had these qualities. Nor can anyone *pretend* to have these qualities and get by with it for long. The only way to assure your audience that you have the qualities is to *have* them. Selection of materials that imply these characteristics, however, is not only considered good form and ethical behavior, but is many times a necessary part of your preparation.

Finally, as we have previously pointed out in talking about the purposes of the speech introduction, an audience prefers a speaker it *likes* as well as it *respects*. If a choice is necessary on matters calling for rational thought, the discriminating audience will go along with the advocate it respects, the undiscriminating with the one it likes. There is no reason why most speakers cannot gain both the affection and the respect of the audience. If your proposition results from conscientious application of the process of reflective thinking that we have suggested, you will go a long way in this speech toward gaining your listeners' respect. The demonstrations of your own personal warmth that we have previously suggested are as applicable to persuasive as to informational speaking. Logical argumentation can be made human and interesting just as easily as it can be made cold and formidable.

Intellectual and Psychological Appeals

For all the attitudes which we form relatively free of the influence of others, some element of logical thought, minute though it might be, is responsible. Some attitudes are arrived at after far greater cerebration than others, however, and these we might say to be primarily intellectual in character. To activate such attitudes, the persuader must use intellectual appeals of sound evidence and reasoning similar to the methods by which the listener originally formed the attitude. About the nature and kinds of these appeals we have already spoken at length. This avenue of persuasion Aristotle termed *logos,* which applies, fundamentally, to the truth or apparent truth of what is said. It is the primary avenue along which you will be traveling in the speech of this unit. *appeal to listeners by logic*

Other attitudes are formulated with little help from the intellect. Some use of evidence and reasoning is involved when, after a singularly dull and unduly expensive date with a redheaded girl, a boy draws the conclusion that "redheads make terrible dates." Certainly it could not be said to be sound logic, however. Our feelings as well as our rational thought processes go into the making of our attitudes, and sometimes they are the principal ingredient. The stimuli by which the persuasive speaker gets his audience to respond with such attitudes are the psychological appeals that we will be studying in the next unit. This third avenue of persuasion, in Aristotle's terminology, is *pathos.* — *appeal to listeners thru Emotion*

Possibly one of the most misleading phrases ever invented is "cold logic." As long as man is a feeling as well as a thinking creature, the temperature of even the coldest logic will never reach absolute zero. That logic which the persuasive speaker uses must be anything but cold. It must arouse the passions as well as satisfy the intelligence. The distinctions that we are making between the appeals of Unit IV and Unit V are based on relative amounts of intellectual and psychological components, not on absolute contraries. In persuasive speaking do not ever give your listeners a clinical report or the demonstration of a mathematical theorem. The logic you select for use in this speech should come from at least the temperate zones, and, better yet, the semi-tropical areas.

Relationship of Audience and Materials of the Speech

The most important thing to remember about selecting materials for any persuasive speech, however, is that the final test of all evidence and reasoning and of any and every kind of psychological appeal rests not with the speaker, but with the listeners. If your listeners are the discriminating ones that we are hoping to train in this course, they will be asking the same questions of your logic that you did in evaluating it, and unless you manage to satisfy them of its validity as you present it, they will discard it and reject your appeal. The arguments that you select should be the ones most meaningful to both you and your listeners. You must think first of the arguments that had the most telling effect upon you, then pick those that will also probably have the most telling effect upon your listeners. Some that are meaningful only to you may have to be discarded. Then, avoiding every illogical pitfall that you possibly can, you must demonstrate their truth in the speech itself. We have said previously that there would be a point in this course at which reasoning materials would truly come into their own. This is that point.

Physical materials, never ruled out of consideration for any speech, can often be extremely valuable in the persuasive speech stressing intellectual appeals. Certainly if you are doing any reasoning from statistics, you will want to consider the possibility of making your point both clearer and more persuasive by some kind of graphic representation. Taking the original sources to the platform and quoting from them rather than from note cards can also be effective. These and other uses of physical materials can many times lend a helping hand to both your logos and your ethos.

Organizing and Wording the Speech

Organization of the persuasive speech can be a complex and troublesome problem for the conscientious speaker. All those who in their everyday persuasion have failed to win the desired response because they let it be known that they wanted the favor before a sufficient amount of "buttering up" had been done, or because they presented all the right reasons except one, or because they presented a right reason at the wrong time, can testify that it is important to do the right thing at the right moment, to have enough reasons, and to have them in the right order.

These three are the basic problems in the organization of the persuasive speech. The first of them—letting the cat out of the bag too early—happens as a result of faulty audience analysis. There are audiences to which you can state the exact proposition you are arguing at the very outset of your speech, and then step by step establish the soundness of your claim to truth. There are others with which you must proceed as if walking on eggs, gradually building up the validity of your proposition to a point where you have preconditioned acceptance before you actually let them know what that exact proposition is. These differing approaches are called the *direct* and the *indirect,* or sometimes the *deductive* and the *inductive.* The direct approach can be used (although it most certainly does not have to be) with audiences that are not too opposed to or too skeptical of your proposition. The indirect approach almost has to be used if the initial reaction to the statement of the proposition is likely to be negative. Neither of these approaches is inherently better than the other, so long as the audience is not left uncertain at the end of the speech as to what the exact proposition was. Different approaches can be used with different subjects, if you only remember not to antagonize further an already antagonistic audience.

The second problem, the one of not covering enough of the arguments to satisfy your listeners, is a much more complex one. It involves both your investigation of your subject and materials and your analysis of the audience. Both of these preliminary tasks must be done thoroughly, and the connections between the two seen clearly, if you are not to make the mistake of neglecting to cover some point or points absolutely necessary to insure acceptance of your point of view.

Issues. You must understand, first of all, that every proposition has inherent issues, points of contention which will exist between proponents and opponents of the proposition. The issues are the same for both sides of the question; it is the position taken on them that is different. Those beliefs of your audience which our overview statement suggests should be dealt with in persuasive speaking—"beliefs that the problem exists and must be solved, that (your) suggested causes for it are the real ones, and that (your) solution is superior to any and all other ones available"—provide a set of such issues designed to be applicable to almost any kind of persuasive proposition. Issues like these are considered to be *major issues,* ones so general and basic that they do not vary from proposition to proposition.

As a prospective advocate for a proposition of policy, you should be aware of a special set of major issues which has become traditional for propositions of this kind. The "stock issues" of the proposition of policy you have met before as one of the possible organizational patterns for your main points: *need, desirability, practicality,* and *alternatives.* To demonstrate the probability of truth for such a proposition, you must prove that there is a real and pressing need for some solution to the problem, that your remedy will have more desirable effects than undesirable ones, that it can be put into operation without undue effort or expense and will probably make some progress in solving the problem, and that it is the best of all the possible alternatives. To disprove a proposition, the same major issues are considered from a negative point of view. In a very real sense, however, proving is much more difficult than disproving, for while the one supporting the proposition puts himself in the position of having to establish, if need be, the validity of *all* the major issues, the opponent has only to establish *his* truth on *one* of the major issues for the proposition to be invalidated. It is partially for this reason that we so strongly advise investigating the subject area through reflective thinking and careful evaluation of all your sources. You will be a proponent in this speech, not an opponent. The five steps of reflective thinking and the various tests of sources, contentions, evidence, and reasoning are tasks designed to make you ready to do battle on each of the major issues for the proposition of policy.

Even if you are a proponent, not all of the major issues need be covered in a speech of advocacy, and certainly all of them do not have to be covered to the same extent. Which ones you will discuss and how much you will discuss each of them depends upon your analysis of the audience's present beliefs about each of these issues. For one audience, perhaps, the need could be skipped over lightly or not covered at all; for another, it might be the most crucial major issue of them all. Persuasive speakers, of course, can go very wrong in their judgments concerning major issues, but trouble is not so likely with them as it is with what we shall call the *minor issues* and the *psychological issues*.

Minor issues is the term we are giving those subsidiary points in dispute that would either substantiate or disprove the major issues. One advocate's contentions on a set of them would be contained in the statements that "There is a need for a change in our school admissions policy because the state legislature has not given us enough money to handle all the students applying for admission," "The higher-quality student that we would get with a stiffer admissions policy would tend in time to upgrade the quality of the whole institution," and "Considering that trying to make do with what we have would only hurt us in the long run, we have no choice left but to toughen up our policy of admissions." Each major issue can have any number of minor issues, some of them important to one audience, others important to another. Some of these minor issues may be so hotly contested or so important to the welfare of everyone involved that they simply have to be covered in any speech given on the subject. These are the so-called *essential issues* of the question. Often persuasive speakers will defeat their purposes by covering the wrong minor issues for the particular audience, or by neglecting to discuss an essential issue. One student speaker of our experience, for example, actually advocated a policy of aggressive military action by the United States without even so much as mentioning the danger of total nuclear war which such an action might create. It was the one minor issue connected with the major issue of desirability that no advocate could ignore, whatever his audience or his or their point of view. No minor issue could have been more essential. In organizing your speech, do your best to cover the right minor issues for the audience to which you will be speaking, and by all means do not leave out any of the essential issues.

What we are calling *psychological issues* are minor issues given a special name to emphasize a special need. The psychological issues point the direction of the persuasion right into the audience's laps. Contentions on psychological issues attempt to convince the audience that *they* are or are not being hurt by the problem, that *they* will or will not benefit from accepting your solution, that *they* would or would not have to make undue sacrifices should they adopt your proposal. Too often persuasive speakers do not even think about these issues, much less include them in their speeches. This particular kind of error of omission is undoubtedly responsible for the failure of more persuasive speeches than any other one connected with organization of the speech. Unless each persuadable member of your audience is made to feel *personally* involved in the problem in some way, and preferably in all of the major issues, no one will be likely to do what you want them to.

The Problem of Order.   The third basic problem of organizing the persuasive speech, we said, is having the reasons in the right order. A fault here can be the secondary result of any one of the faults of omission, or it can be one of misplacement. When either of these faults occurs in a persuasive speech of the kind which this unit calls for, it can have fatal consequences. The need for a tight logical structure is nowhere so great as it is in the speech of persuasion which stresses intellectual appeals.

Whatever specific pattern of organization is used, the kind of structuring which is given the speech materials in a speech of this kind is always the same, that of a chain of logical reasoning: if this proof is good, then the contention on this minor issue stands; if all of the contentions on these minor issues stand, then the contention on the major issue is valid; and if all of the contentions on the major issues are demonstrated to have validity, then the proposition is established. We have said that all an opponent has to do is to show one significant flaw in this chain of reasoning to invalidate it. The proponent can be his own worst enemy by leaving out a link in the chain or by putting it someplace where it does not fit, thus himself creating that one fatal flaw.

We are not saying that in the structure you give your argument each point must follow from the one before and lead to the next as inevitably and infallibly as they do in a lawyer's brief. For that kind of thoroughness you have neither the time nor the necessity. A modified version of such a construction, however, is not an impossible goal to shoot for. Remember always that your outline is your primary instrument of logical argumentation, and that the discriminating listener, knowing it to be such, will be looking most carefully for any holes or flaws which it might have. You should not be any less thorough.

We have no preferred pattern of organization for your main points to suggest. Any of three standard patterns—*problem to solution;* the "stock issues" of *need, desirability, practicality,* and *alternatives;* or the *Monroe "Motivated Sequence"*—could be made to serve your purpose admirably. We would also like to present for your consideration one additional one.

Although somewhat similar to the Monroe "Motivated Sequence," this pattern is not identical with it. Paralleling as it does John Dewey's five steps of reflective thinking, it would seem to us to be one that might be useful in reasoned discourse. This is the pattern:

1. The audience is made aware of the problem.
2. The problem is analyzed in a way to point up the necessity of making a decision about it.
3. Various answers are suggested, but the best one is strongly advocated as being the most complete and most beneficial.
4. The values of that one solution are made clear.
5. The responsibility for action is then given to the audience.

There might be another pattern that would suit your purpose better than any of these; if so, by all means use it.

It could probably be said without too much qualification that the introduction and conclusion must be made to serve their purposes even better in persuasive speaking than they do in informational speaking. In the next unit, we will discuss the psychological appeals which can be incorporated in them or which they can be made to serve. For the present, we will only specify that these are the two points when the persuader has the most time and the best opportunity to present appeals designed to strengthen his ethos; and that the persuader's conclusion must drive home his point with such force that it will not only be remembered, but will cause the listener either immediately or ultimately to act.

Wording.   Probably the two most persistent faults of wording that beginning speakers make in speeches of the type you will be giving in this unit are those of phrasing their points with too much objectivity or too much separability.

What is forgotten in making the wording too objective is that the persuader is at all times an advocate of a particular point of view, and that therefore every word he utters must be designed to serve that point of view. The persuader does not say, "This summer's drought conditions in X County are estimated to have cost the farmers of that area over 15 million dollars in lost revenue." Such phrasings are for newspaper reporters, whose job it is to be objective. What the persuader says is, "The water diversion project for which I'm asking your endorsement is going to save us from more of the 15 million dollar 'pinches' that all of us here in X County have been feeling this year." Wording the point for persuasive effect is the only way to make the point have that effect. Information presented in the persuasive speech is not presented for its own sake; it is presented to prove a contention. The relationship of your materials to the establishment of your proposition must at all times be stressed. Your proposition is much more likely to be an impelling one if you word it in terms of the desired audience reaction.

The error of separability in phrasing points involves failing to point out the chain of reasoning of logical persuasion. Transitions should abound in this kind of speech. Check for words and phrases like "therefore," "it follows, then," "now the only thing that I have left to prove to you," "we have seen that all signs indicate," and "from this we can see." In the wording of rational discourse, you show not only the relationship of materials to the proposition, but also their relationships to one another by use of carefully worded transitions. No single point that you are making should be an island.

PREPARATION FOR DELIVERY

> "My strength is as the strength of ten,
> Because my heart is pure."
>
> Alfred, Lord Tennyson, *Sir Galahad*

Both the sentiment and the author of this poem are now considered to be a trifle out of style. But the sentiment is not as laughable as you may think it to be. In public speaking, when you are infused with the zeal of championship of a worthy cause, your strength on the public platform can sometimes be almost as great "as the strength of ten." The power that comes with sincere conviction is something that we expect and look for in any persuasive speaker. Failing to find it, we judge the message as well as the speaker to be weak and hence unworthy of belief. A large measure of your ethos, especially if you are young, derives from the apparent sincerity and conviction you demonstrate as you deliver your persuasive message. As the overview statement puts it: "He (the persuasive speaker) presents his speech in the most vital and winning manner of which he is capable, realizing that his delivery can be as much an argument for adopting his proposal as anything he says."

The delivery should be "vital," the statement says, *and* it should be "winning." Sometimes the speaker can be extremely vital, but not at all winning. In preparing yourself for delivery of your speech, watch for and avoid the tendencies, noted in too many advocates, of belligerent bellowing, argumentative shouting, dogmatic asserting, and pompous know-it-all–ism. Showing your zeal in these ways is more irritating and possibly even more damaging than the faults of excessive timidity or apparent indifference. In the eyes of any audience, the brighter the armor, the nobler the knight.

Also, as you prepare for delivery, refine the wording of your points to have both the individual persuasive effects and the over-all effect of unity and coherence that we talked about as necessities in this kind of speaking. A caution in this regard is necessary, however. You can claim too much, and you can structure too tightly. In the first instance, you will be rejected as a blind and foolish zealot; in the second, the audience becomes either bored or fascinated by the workings of the machinery, and in either case pays little attention to the persuasive product you are trying to manufacture. Never forget that you are talking to *people,* and that your purpose is to *persuade* them, not to harangue, bore, or fascinate them.

REVIEW OF PREPARATION

1. Choose a subject area that involves a problem or problems of significance to both you and your audience.
2. Investigate the subject area following John Dewey's five steps of reflective thinking and carefully evaluating your sources for soundness of evidence and reasoning, trying always to find the best answer to the problem.
3. Consider the audience, the occasion, and the purposes of this assignment in determining the limitation of your subject.
4. Determine whether your specific purpose will involve belief or action in terms of the audience's capacity for and susceptibility to a plea for action.
5. Determine a specific proposition of policy as the central idea for your speech, and select the necessary materials of *ethos, logos,* and *pathos* for enlisting favorable attitudes toward yourself and your arguments.
6. Organize the body of the speech to be appropriately either direct or indirect in its approach, to cover all the necessary issues, and to have the form of a logical chain of reasoning. Any one of several patterns of main points are usable.
7. Pay special attention to the introduction and conclusion as places for developing ethos and to the conclusion as needing particularly strong development.
8. Word your points to have persuasive effect both individually and collectively.

9. Familiarize yourself thoroughly with the message you have now composed.
10. Rehearse the speech a number of times to make your delivery both vital and winning and to insure that your wording will be persuasive.

Sample Student Outline

Subject: Farm surpluses.

Specific Purpose: To cause my audience to believe that our farm surpluses should be maintained because of their importance to our national security, our future, and our prestige abroad.

Central Idea: Because our farm surpluses can keep America going against Russia in the event of nuclear war, insure that millions of Americans may not go hungry in the not too distant future, and continue to win friends for us abroad, they must be maintained.

Introduction

Possibly you read the cover story about Secretary of Agriculture Freeman and his efforts to solve the problems of American agriculture in the April 5 issue of *Time*. As an Agriculture Economics major, of course, I couldn't pass it up. *Time* calls the problem of our large and growing farm surpluses a "mess," deplores the cost to the taxpayer of present support, control, and storage programs, and voices despair of anything ever being done to solve the problem. I think most of you probably feel the same way about the situation. I'd like you, if you can, to consider with me a different view of this whole matter.

Let me pose three questions. Question number one: How would we manage to feed ourselves and keep fighting if a nuclear attack were to destroy our food sources? Question number two: How can we be sure that we will have enough food to feed a population of 230 million people in 1975, an even more fantastic number of 370 million people in the year 2010? And the final question: How can we help feed starving peoples all over the world and win them to the cause of democracy? I say that all of these questions can be answered in a simple phrase: maintain our farm surpluses.

Body

I. Our farm surpluses could feed us in the event that a nuclear attack immobilized our mechanized agricultural industry, thus preventing the Soviets from having the advantage over us they otherwise would.
   A. Nuclear war could cripple or even completely paralyze our agricultural production for a period of years.
      1. Our mechanized agricultural industry depends heavily on rubber tires, tractors, trucks, and many other industrial products.

       2. The industrial plants that produce these products would be among the first targets of any nuclear attacking force.

       3. Restoration of those industrial facilities would require one or two years, and it would take longer than that for agriculture to get back on its feet.

   B. Vincent Sauchelli, in a relatively recent article in *Agricultural Chemicals,* estimated that our present food surpluses could bridge the time gap.

   C. This might affect our survival as a free nation, for if we did not have the surpluses, the Russians, whose agriculture is still that of the horse and plow, would have a great advantage over us.

       1. In the latest issue of *The Reporter,* Allen B. Ballard, Jr., who lived in Russia and attended Moscow's Timiryazevskaya Agricultural Academy, says that Russia is at least 35 years behind the United States in mechanization of agriculture.

       2. Although this may not be an enviable position for Russia to be in now, it would be very advantageous should our nuclear bombs destroy her industrial plants.

Transition: (Now let's consider that second question concerning an increased American population.)

 II. We may need our farm surpluses to feed the millions of people that will be living in our country before too long.

   A. By the year 2010 we will need an agricultural production capacity two and one-half times greater than the present one, according to agriculture expert R. L. Skrabanek.

       1. Skrabanek bases this estimate on the predicted population figures I gave you before—370 million people, or just about twice as many as there are in the United States right now.

   B. Sooner than that—in 1975, as Skrabanek sees it—we may be in trouble, with 230 million people, or a 20 percent increase in population.

   C. Other experts say that, if experimentation now going on designed to increase our agricultural production potential is successful, there is no need for concern.

   D. You may be willing to feel secure in such happy predictions, but I can't help thinking that things don't always go as well as they should, and it might be very helpful to have some food surpluses to fall back on just in case.

   E. I am concerned because famine is never a pleasant prospect, and I expect to be around in 2010 and certainly in 1975; and I imagine you do, too.

Transition: Even if neither of these unhappy events ever took place, however, there would still be an excellent reason to maintain our farm surpluses.

III. Our farm surpluses are presently being used, and should continue to be used, to feed starving people in foreign countries, aid the cause of democracy, and improve our prestige abroad.

   A. Each year the United States exports to foreign countries about 40 billion tons of surplus food.

       1. These exported food materials help feed the starving nations of the world.

       2. Also these exports are one of our most vital weapons in a battle with

Russia to win the friendship and respect of the uncommitted small nations of the world.

B. Surpluses unnecessary for our own survival can and should be used for this purpose in the future.

Transition: (It may be that something will need to be done about our agricultural surpluses if they get completely out of hand, but for the present I think we should be very grateful that we have them.)

Conclusion

We had better not be too hasty about reducing beyond a reasonable level our American food reserves. They may be necessary in the future in case of nuclear attack or inability to feed our mammoth future populations, and they are presently needed to promote better foreign relations. The cost of maintaining our food surpluses is not small, but then, good insurance is never cheap. Don't forget that what you eat in 1975, or possibly next year, or maybe even tomorrow, may depend upon our farm surpluses.

References

1. "A Hard Row to Hoe," *Time,* April 5, 1963.
2. Ballard, Allen B., Jr., "A Barnyard View of Soviet Agriculture," *The Reporter,* May 23, 1963.
3. Heady, Earl O., and John F. Heer, "Why and How Do We Produce So Much?", *Iowa Agriculture Experiment Farm Science,* October, 1960.
4. Sauchelli, Vincent, "The Importance of Food Surpluses in a Nuclear War," *Agricultural Chemicals,* October, 1961.
5. Skrabanek, R. L., "Future Population and Production Needs," *Texas Agricultural Progress,* July–August, 1960.
6. Thompson, Leon E., "Farm Problem, Eat Up or Export the Surplus," *Iowa Agricultural Experiment Farm Science,* February, 1960.

References for Unit IV

1. Foster, William Trufant, *Argumentation and Debating* (Boston: Houghton Mifflin Company, 1945).
   Although the illustrations are now perhaps somewhat dated, this book still holds up very well against the more recent entrants in the field. It has the admirable virtues of clarity, cogency, and soundness. The section of the book most interesting to the student of public speaking would include chapters 5 through 9.
2. McBath, James H., ed., *Argumentation and Debate: Principles and Practices* (New York: Holt, Rinehart & Winston, Inc., 1963).
   The pick of the more recent works in this area. It suffers from the unevenness of multiple authorship, but many of the chapters are excellent. Chapters 1, 4, 6, 9, 10, and 11 are most apropos to this unit.

3. McBurney, James H., James M. O'Neill, and Glen E. Mills, *Argumentation and Debate: Techniques of a Free Society* (New York: The Macmillan Company, 1951).

   Like the Foster book, one of the acknowledged classics. Chapters 4, 7, 8, and 9 would probably provide the most immediately useful information.

Unit V

Persuasion and Psychological Appeals

BACKGROUND

We shall examine in this unit a kind of persuasive speaking that is legitimate and often desirable. Yet often when persuasion is being talked about, and especially when the tenor of the remarks is disapproving, the reference is to the kind of speech which stresses psychological appeals. It is often called, somewhat inaccurately, an "emotional appeal" to an audience. You have heard it many times. Unfortunately, the frequency of its occurrence is not directly proportional to the frequency of its usability. Many persuaders substitute it for the persuasive speech based on logical argument either as a shortcut or as a result of mistaken audience analysis. Those who believe that it is the "smart" way to persuade on any and all occasions are not nearly so wise as they think. There are audiences who will deeply resent a speaker trying to work upon their emotions, just as there are those other audiences who need and want such an approach.

As we have said, the amount of difference between the two types of persuasive speeches is hardly absolute. The persuasive speech devoid of any and all intellectual appeals is hard to find outside the worlds of demagogy, charlatanism, and cheap salesmanship. Nevertheless, the two types of persuasive speeches *do* take fundamentally different approaches. The speech of this unit, as differentiated from that of the previous one, will be, generally speaking, one employing a looser logical structure and supports, considerably more use of *ethos,* and a much more concerted attempt to evoke and use for persuasive purposes the feeling responses of the listeners.

The Ethics of Persuasion

The fact that the persuasive speech stressing psychological appeals is usually (though not invariably) the type preferred by the champions of false and misleading doctrines, and the additional fact that it has often been almost unequivocally condemned by well-meaning persons and groups who were attempting to alert the public to the practices of unethical persuaders, have tended to give this type of persuasion a very bad name. Like some other bad names, it is only partially deserved. Psychological persuasion is not inherently bad; it is only when it gets mixed up with bad companions that it goes wrong. We hope that you will welcome it as a friend rather than an enemy.

From the earliest days of public speaking practice and study until the present, there have been many good citizens who have not been its friends. Plato was one of these. At one time he would have excluded all rhetoricians from the ideal republic ruled by philosopher-kings that was his dream. Another time he relented somewhat and said that the study of rhetoric would be acceptable if it were combined with and made subservient to the study of philosophy. Never, however, was he counted among the strong allies of psychological persuasion.

The tragedy of such persons is that they often do not do an effective job of persuasive speaking because the whole concept of consciously attempting to manipulate the emotions of others seems to them morally reprehensible. They and the society of which they are a part are the losers, for these same persons are usually among the wisest, most thoughtful, most responsible, and most influential of its citizens, the very ones who should be guiding its destinies.

What repulses such persons most is the thought of deliberately fashioning their speaking efforts to impress a particular group of hearers. They are quite willing to argue the truth of their proposition and to go to great pains in doing so, but they want to do it completely on their own terms, without the slightest effort to "win friends and influence people." They dismiss any and all techniques of psychological persuasion as morally degrading. Possibly you yourself hold this opinion. It may be that your experiences with sleazy salesmen of shoddy wares, or your reading of books like Vance Packard's *The Hidden Persuaders,* or your study of the list of propaganda devices put out by the Institute for Propaganda Analysis (and what a magnificent job of "name-calling" they themselves did!)[1] has made you suspicious and unfriendly toward this means of influencing human behavior.

Aristotle, we feel, saw the moral issue clearly, as he did so many other matters in rhetoric. He expressed a longing common to most persuasive speakers when he said that a good cause *should* be accepted with the speaker doing no more than presenting it in a straightforward and objective manner. But, he went on to say, with audiences being what they are—an assemblage of imperfect, only too fallible human beings—the speaker must learn how to handle them as well as his subject. Indeed, his definition for the art of public speaking is the discovery, in the particular place, of all of the available means of persuasion. As Aristotle went on to demonstrate and as we hope also to do, this not only must be done, but can be done without undue sacrifice of either the speaker's or the listener's integrity.

There is no better way of insuring your own ethical conduct in persuasive speaking than for you to be guided by your conscience in every choice you make and every word you say. To make doubly sure that you do not commit a breach of ethics, we shall spell out some of the possible ways in which the speaker can either willfully or inadvertently go wrong. Remember that our definition of the persuader is that of Quintilian previously noted: "The good man skilled in speaking." Even if the ethical speaker could not also be the more successful speaker, which he can, we would hold no brief for charlatanism.

There might be times when, in order to sway a particular audience, it would seem necessary for you to resort to lying, trickery, or deceit. In such cases, we would advise defeat with honor rather than success with dishonor. Audience adaptation does not mean catering to their every wish and desire, selling your soul to them for the sake of making converts. There are sometimes things which an audience *must* be told, whether they particularly want to hear them or not. Winston Churchill, for instance, when the fortunes of the British cause were at one of their lowest points during World War II, told the British people that he could not offer false hopes, but only "blood, toil, tears, and sweat."

In no instance of unethical conduct would we say that the end justified the means. But, we hasten to add, instances where it is necessary are very rare. Usually persuasive speaking can be both ethical and effective.

Our condensed description of persuasive speaking, presented in the pre-

---

[1] In case the student is not familiar with the Institute's list, it includes seven devices: "Name Calling," "Glittering Generality," "Transfer," "Testimonial," "Plain Folks," "Card Stacking," and "Bandwagon." In the same order, they are unethical versions of what we discuss in this book as "negatively loaded words," "positively loaded words," "borrowed ethos," "expert testimony," "common ground," "presenting the best possible case for yourself," and "majority opinion." The Institute's own summary of these techniques is to be found in Alfred McClung Lee and Elizabeth Briant Lee, *The Fine Art of Propaganda* (New York: Harcourt, Brace and Company, 1939), pp. 23–24.

vious unit, had this to say: "To make his speaking ethical as well as effective, the speaker, while not obliged to be objective, must openly avow his advocacy, be truthful in all his statements, avoid appeals to base or unworthy motives, be fair in his treatment of opposing arguments, and be devoted to serving his listeners' best interests as well as his own." Let us take up this statement point by point, each time trying to show as best we can exactly what is being said.

Ethical behavior in the persuasive speech situation does not mean presenting as good a case for the opposition as you do for yourself. If you have identified yourself as an advocate of a point of view, your audience expects you to present the best possible argument for it that you are able to muster. Their further expectation is that your opponents will in turn present to them the best possible argument against that point of view, and that they will then have to make up their own minds about where the greater truth may lie.

However, you must openly avow your advocacy. If you masquerade as an impartial observer when in reality you are grinding away mightily at an ax, you are guilty of unethical behavior. To use the trite terminology of the sea, you are "sailing under false colors." Such practice is considered one of the most serious violations of maritime law. If you use the indirect approach in organizing your speech, you may not really hoist the flag until you have lowered the boarding ladder, but you should have been flying it high enough to be seen and acknowledged by the audience at the very first sighting.

Perhaps qualification of the phrase, "truthful in all of his statements," is necessary. The statements should be true *to your best knowledge*. As we have said before, in persuasive speaking truth must always be considered to be a matter of greatest probability, not of absolute certainty. As in the law courts, you are not convicted of perjury unless your misrepresentation has been willful. But, also as in the law courts, you are expected to speak certainly only about things on which you feel absolutely certain. You will probably speak a lot of error in your time (even the best speakers do), but if it is honest error, you need not ever feel ashamed.

In this unit you will be introduced to motivation as it applies to persuasive speaking. It is the most direct means by which you affect the feeling responses of your listeners. As you know from your own behavior and what you have observed in others, both right and wrong desires can motivate human actions. It is not enough that the persuasive speaker's cause be right: every persuasive means he uses, including the motives to which he appeals, must be right. In T. S. Eliot's play, *Murder in the Cathedral*, St. Thomas à Becket, when contemplating the motivations impelling him to martyrdom, dismisses one of them as the "greatest treason," because if he were to be actuated by it he might be doing the right thing for the wrong reason. It is an excellent illustration of the moral scruple that we are speaking about here.

"Fairness" in the treatment of opposing arguments is a rather slippery concept. How fair is fair? On that your own conscience should be your guide. One course which some speakers take is to ignore the existence of opposing arguments completely. That would be all right if it were not also foolish. Those arguments are going to exist in the minds of some or all of your listeners whether you want them to or not, and you had best do something about refuting them if you want to win your case. The main thing you will have to remember is that opposition to your point of view does not automatically make your opponents or their arguments idiotic. It may well be that you can show some of their arguments to be totally unsound; but if you are ethical, you will probably acknowledge other arguments as having an element of truth, and still others to be ones on which opponents seem to have the best of it. Such fairness will help your cause, for the simple reason that the gain in ethos which will result will far outweigh the loss of a few conceded points. You do not have to be right on every point, after all; you only have to be right on more of them than your opponents are.

This leads us into our final criterion for ethical persuasion, devotion to your listeners' best interests. Here we have two items to consider, the first having a direct relationship to refutation. A good part of persuasion may well be an attack, a tearing down of what is wrong or unfavorable. But the appeal cannot end there. Something positive must be advocated, or the audience is left completely in doubt as to what decision to make. Part of the speaker's ethical responsibility is that of positive advocacy. Persuasion that is completely negative results in destruction, real or implied, that can do the listeners no real good. The decisions made by the audience should be constructive ones. Our second item concerns the more obvious kind of violation of ethical responsibility in this regard: those decisions which the audience makes should be ones which will lead to results favorable to them as well as to yourself. The ethical persuader does not sell the secondhand car that will get the buyer only as far as the street.

Purposes of the Assignment

Since psychological persuasion is a rather frequent and necessary task of any public speaker, you, as one learning this art, should gain some practice in it. You should also be assured that this kind of persuasion can be made to serve good ends without violation of moral principle. Most of the devices of psychological persuasion are neutral ones, suitable for serving either the cause of good or the cause of evil. We want you to learn the use of these devices and the ethical principles involved in their use by giving and hearing speeches that attempt to be both ethical and effective.

As listeners, we will want you to be as honest as you are when speaking.

If the speaker has misjudged your beliefs on the proposition, your attitudes, or anything else about the speech situation, react accordingly. You will be doing him a disservice if you pretend not to notice any errors of application to the audience. On the other hand, if you are sure that he has judged the situation correctly, go all the way with him. Continue to be critical in your listening, of course, but let your emotions be active as well as your intellect. Be on the alert for fallacies in argument and breaches of ethical conduct, but do not go out of your way to find them. It is this kind of listening, we feel, which will serve both the speaking and listening purposes of the assignment best. In the last analysis, those purposes are identical: we want you to learn to both speak and listen with your emotions as well as your intellect.

THE ASSIGNMENT

The nature of the assignment for this unit of the course should be fairly clear to you already. You are again to give a persuasive speech on a controversial proposition designed to solve a problem of significance to both yourself and your audience, with your aim being either immediate or ultimate action. Your basic persuasive approach, however, will here be psychological rather than logical. You should endeavor to use all avenues of persuasion, but pathos will be the predominant one, and ethos will probably also figure in more strongly than it did in the speech of the previous unit. There should be no violations of your own ethical code or the one which we set up for persuasion.

One or more of the following options may be given you for choice of a speech subject in this unit:

Option A: Free Choice. You may choose to speak on any proposition you please so long as it fits the general requirements of the assignment outlined above.

Option B: The Encore. Your subject will be chosen to meet the requirements set up by the one or more of the options of Unit IV specified by your instructor. You will, however, use the more psychological approach to persuasion which this unit calls for.

Option C: The Lip-Service Speech. To what cause or principle does your audience claim devotion, but deny by its actions every day? Does this cause or principle mean enough to you to make their inconsistency hurt you deeply? Form a proposition to which your audience can subscribe and see if you can get them to acting as well as talking.

Option D: New Teeth for an Old Saw.   There are in persuasion timeless as well as timely subjects, problems so basic to human experience that they have always been timely. You do not often read about them on the front pages of the newspapers, but they are of vital concern to every human being. "What is the good life?" could probably serve as the prototype for all such subjects. Most of our slogans, maxims, mottos, axioms, epigrams, and other "wise sayings" are actually propositions dedicated to the solution of these timeless problems. "Honesty is the best policy," "A penny saved is a penny earned," "The largest ball of twine unwinds," "You judge a man by the company he keeps"; these are some of the "old saws" we mean. They are appropriate subjects for a speech, except that they have been literally "talked to death." People talking about them have usually said the same old things in the same old way. Your job will be to give "new teeth" to the "old saw." Try to look at the subject freshly, giving new and different substantiation for the old wisdom. Try, in other words, to make the timeless subject truly timely.

Option E: The Speech of Tribute.   This may be your only assignment in this unit, but it is more likely that your instructor will use it for a second speech if time is available. In this speech your purpose is to share with others your admiration for some outstanding, wonderful person still alive today. There is no limitation to the field of endeavor in which he may have achieved excellence; there is not even the necessity that he be a "great" person in the eyes of the historian. The occasion is a testimonial dinner being held in his honor and you are the principal speaker. Tell your audience of the achievements and character traits that you admire and point out to them the lessons of right conduct that they can learn from his example.

Option F: Instructor's Assignment.   In order that your assignment may better suit the speech needs of your particular class, your instructor may choose to modify one of the above assignment options, combine features of two or more of them into one assignment, or possibly give you an assignment entirely of his own devising.

SUBJECT AND MATERIALS

Choose a Subject Area

You may be wondering when and why the type of speech just assigned is used in speaking situations outside the classroom. "Where may I have heard or given this type of speech? Under what circumstances in the future might I be hearing or giving it? What kinds of propositions are talked about, and under what circumstances?" These questions may be troubling you.

One answer is that this type of speaking takes place on the same kind of proposition that you argued in the preceding unit if and when the audience is made up of *supporters* who do not need much by way of logical evidence and reasoning (just enough, you might say, to reassure them that their previous decisions on the matter were sufficiently logically oriented). Such an audience might be bored to tears if you went over all of it again, but they do need emotional reinforcement of their beliefs. Often this sort of speech is given to such a group when they are at that crucial point when all that is needed is one last little push to make them take the plunge. They are all set to dive, but do not have quite enough heart for it. As Patrick Henry did in his famous address before the Virginia Convention of Delegates, the speaker designs his speech to give them that heart.

There is another occasion for a speech stressing psychological appeals. It is when the speaker is facing an audience that (in the mixed-metaphorical phrasing of one student speaker we once heard) is a "hotbed of apathy." The *indifferent* audience will often need a good deal of emotional prodding before they get at all excited about the problem, much less want to do anything about it. If there are only a few latent elements of skepticism and opposition in such an audience, they can sometimes be converted by one speech to supporters, and even warm ones, provided the speaker can come up with a skillful blend of psychological and intellectual appeals. More often, however, follow-up speeches are necessary.

Propositions different from those specified in the last unit also call for persuasive speaking of a more psychological than intellectual character. These propositions can fall into any of our three categories—fact, value, or policy—but they are likely most often to be those of value. They are propositions which just do not lend themselves well to intellectual argumentation.

Where, for instance, are you going to find well-documented evidence to support the assertion that "Honesty is the best policy"? No one that we know of can produce statistics from which you could reason about the probability of a dishonest person eventually being caught and punished. Police records would tell you only about known crimes. Can anyone actually prove that honest people sleep better at night than dishonest ones do? Has anyone conducted experiments, collected data, and come to a conclusion about the relative duration, depth, tranquillity, and restorative power of the sleep that each group has? Yet this does not prevent those speaking on the affirmative side from asserting that dishonest persons usually are found out in the end and that, even if they are not, they do not sleep well at night. On the other side of the fence (we are not, incidentally, advising that you climb over) you will hear it argued that "only suckers play it straight." How about clear definitions of terms and enough examples of a truly representative nature to substantiate that claim?

Substantiating evidence aside, propositions of value are necessary and worthwhile subject matter for persuasion. They need to be talked about. Each of us must formulate beliefs about them as a guide to the conduct of all our personal affairs. Also, in the collective units of society—the organizations to which we belong, the school we attend or the company for which we work, and the government to which we swear allegiance—these propositions and the decisions we have made on them have their place. When all is said and done, group morality is nothing more nor less than the majority of the individual moralities of the persons composing the group. The person who "goes along with the group" must be counted as one of the group, not as a person apart.

A rather specialized occasion for this type of persuasive speech would be the one assumed for Option E: "The Speech of Tribute." This option, if it is used, will introduce you to a type of speech that some writers feel merits an entirely separate designation. These writers say that there is a type of speech whose immediate end is only to stimulate feelings favorable to a belief already firmly held by the audience. When given a separate designation, this type is usually called *the speech to stimulate*. We would quarrel with the title, just as we objected in the last unit to complete separation of the ends of belief and action, because it is our feeling that all persuasive speeches are generically the same, seeking action as their ultimate if not their immediate goal. But we certainly would not argue against the existence of speeches whose immediate goal is to stimulate emotions, or the desirability of your learning about and possibly even trying your hand at one of them.

For a speech of this type the occasion is often a ceremonial one; the audience is made up of ardent supporters of your proposition; your purpose is to arouse them to the greatest height or depth of whatever the appropriate emotion might be; and so quite naturally you use little else but pathos and ethos in your approach. One example we would suggest is Lincoln's Gettysburg Address. While speeches like the Gettysburg Address may be the furthest extension of the type of approach you will be using in this unit, we feel that they are an extension and not a separate approach.

Most so-called speeches to stimulate are also, as we have suggested, speeches for ceremonial or "special" occasions, such as memorials; commemorations; dedications; and testimonial, award, fund-raising, or "kick-off" banquets. In turn most "speeches for special occasions"—speeches of introduction, welcome, presentation, eulogy, nomination, acceptance, or keynote—are some variation of the speech of tribute. Option E, if it is used, can provide you with experience that should have considerable carry-over value to other speeches of its kind.

Choosing a subject area for this speech is, as you have probably already gathered, quite a different task from that of the previous unit. Generally speaking, you will probably spend less time on it for this speech, and correspondingly greater amounts of time on some of the later tasks of preparation. The principal reason for this is that you should be further along in the job at the start. If you intend to move an audience emotionally to the degree expected of you in this speech, the truth that you are propounding should be one that not only affects you deeply but that you have had strong belief about for some time. You may know at the start what your tentative specific purpose and central idea are. As we see it, the major task will be determining that the subject area you are considering is one which will provide you with a speech appropriate to the particular assignment you have been given.

Investigate the Subject Area

You might think that reflective thinking and source evaluation can be dispensed with on those propositions for which really solid evidence is next to impossible to find. That will be true only if you have already gone through these tasks on some previous occasion. Otherwise, they may have to be pursued even more diligently. Always, on any kind of proposition, evidence of some kind is presented and reasoning is done from it. If the evidence is skimpy, the reasoning done from it is even more liable to error than if it is plentiful. Your investigation of one of these more speculative subject areas could well provide a field trip for the observation of many different fallacies. The more your audience has to depend upon the quality of your thought for the quality of the solution, the more hard thought you should give the matter. You need especially to consider how much the strength of your own feeling may be affecting your thought. Try not to allow your emotional involvement to blind you to error. Your obligation to your audience is always to present them with the soundest thought possible on the issue.

Thought of another kind must also be given to investigation of your subject area in preparing this speech. This thought is directed toward finding those speech materials which will have the effect of arousing the feeling responses of your listeners along with or apart from satisfying their critical thinking about the proposition. What you will be looking for will be materials which either inherently possess or can be made to have qualities of psychological effectiveness. To help you do this well, we will first discuss the major qualities of psychological effectiveness, then the speech materials in which they are most likely to be found.

The Qualities of Psychological Effectiveness [2]

What qualities must materials have to make them effective stimuli for strong feeling responses in your listeners? Three basic ones, one or more of which any item of psychological proof should possess, are: *motivation value, attention value,* and *suggestion value.*

Motivation Value. Psychologists in their studies of human behavior devote a great deal of effort to attempts at analyzing what motives are, classifying them into categories and types, and understanding the ways in which they influence what we do. Rather than being literally "reasons for" what we do or believe, motives are usually described by psychologists as nonrational desires or impulses that impel us toward certain behaviors. Our choices are not always selfish and willful, however, because our likes and dislikes are influenced greatly by the particular society in which we live. Motives have their roots in society as well as the individual psyche.

As a matter of fact, there is no one of our human motives, no matter how primitive and self-serving it might seem, that is not to some extent a product of civilization. Man was born with *drives,* or the strong stimuli of the tensions created by his basic animal needs; he created *motives* as the learned behaviors by which to satisfy his drives. The tensions created by hunger, thirst, sexual impulses, temperature extremes, fatigue, bodily waste materials, danger of bodily injury, and basic emotional responses need always to be released or removed in some way. Around each of these drives and various combinations of them have grown many motives, desires that impel us toward actions which will bring about that release or removal. Primitive man would satisfy the hunger drive by stalking game, killing it, and eating it. One reason civilized man works in the office, factory, or store is to satisfy his money motive, the learned desire which takes care of relieving the hunger drive and wholly or partially a number of the other drives as well.

The persuader must be aware of the primitive drives of man. Appeals made directly to such drives, however, are rare. They usually occur only in times of war, famine, pestilence, or other extreme emergency which strip away the outer coatings of civilized behavior and reduce man to his animal nature. Most often as a persuader you will use the same indirect approach that your listeners use in satisfying their drives: you will make your appeals to their motives.

Some motives can be considered to be more *selfish* in nature than others.

---

[2] For the distinction made here between drives and motives and for the enumeration of drives that is given we are indebted to Winston L. Brembeck and William S. Howell, *Persuasion: A Means of Social Control* (New York: Prentice-Hall, Inc., 1952), pp. 64–76.

These would probably lead any listing in number and variety, if not always in strength of appeal. Among these would be our desires for personal prestige, money, popularity, sexual attractiveness, and winning out over the other fellow in competition. Others would be our liking for adventure, for independence of action, for creative expression, and for various personal satisfactions of comfort, pleasure, and emotional release. Selfishly, also, we want to satisfy our curiosity and flirt with fear but not be overcome by it.

There is nothing wrong with using any of these or other selfish motives in persuading your audience, if the satisfactions you promise will come about in socially approved ways and are "right" rather than "wrong" reasons for the action you are asking them to take. We could not survive if we were not selfish. Selfishness in a man and in your persuasive appeals should be condemned not for its presence, but for an excessive degree of presence.

Other motives are predominantly *altruistic*. In these we are influenced by our desire to help others and to promote the welfare of the groups to which we belong. The welfare of our families and friends can sometimes be of greater concern to us than our own personal welfare. We frequently read in the newspapers of a parent giving up his own life to save his children from a burning building. Such concern can extend to persons we do not know, even to those we have not seen and never will see. Whether or not these motives may have a strong concealed element of selfishness in them is beside the point, which is simply that your persuasive appeal should often be made on the basis of the good your proposal can do for the persons or groups whose welfare your audience cares about or can be made to care about, rather than the good it can do for them personally. From the persuader's point of view, altruistic motives are neither better nor worse, more nor less preferable than selfish motives. They are simply another means of accomplishing your goal, ready at hand when their use seems called for.

Still other motives are *idealistic*. Most societies and most people believe in principles such as honesty, loyalty, justice, and patriotism that condition many of their choices of action. Do not dismiss them as "weak" motives. They can predominate in a person or an audience. Countless men and women have suffered ostracism, calumny, deprivation, torture, and loss of life in serving these ideals. Again, the persuader will use idealistic motives only if and when they are appropriate for the circumstances. They, like altruistic motives, may seem more inherently attractive to you than selfish ones; but they may not seem so to a particular audience on a given occasion with regard to your specific proposal.

You have a better chance of persuading others to accept what you propose if the proposal appears to satisfy their motives. Look about you to see how it is being done. Advertisers use selfish motivation quite obviously in their appeals. Radio and television commercials and printed advertisements constantly remind us, "Buy our product to save money, to be popular, to get ahead in the world." Appeals for charitable drives employ altruistic motives of generosity and sentiment. Political speakers plead with us on both selfish and altruistic grounds when they urge us to elect a candidate who will serve our interests and those of our "fellow Americans." On other occasions we are persuaded to support national or international policies for the sake of our own lives, the security of our loved ones, and the cause of peace. In this instance, of course, the appeal is to all three types of motives. Be advised by what you observe that motivation value is one of the most necessary qualities of psychological proof. In investigating your subject area for this speech, search diligently for materials that have this value or can be made to have it. They are going to be your greatest stock in trade in this speech.

Attention Value. Materials that have motivation value are also likely to have attention value. You will remember that in Unit III we introduced you to the factors of attention which your materials can have, and that one of these factors was the *vital*. Any appeal which will motivate your audience, you have just seen, must strike at one or more of their vital concerns. It follows that this particular factor of attention, in the long run, plays a larger role in persuasive speech than any of the others. But it does not follow that, simply because motivational material involves vital concern, the speaker can afford to ignore attention value.

For one thing, the motivational material can be presented in such a way that it repels rather than attracts attention. Unless the audience is attending— and with even greater concentration of effort than required for any of your other speeches—the motivational material has little chance to work. The necessity for attention value in the materials of psychological persuasion, in fact, is that of providing a condition of heightened emotional receptivity in which motives can be aroused, sustained, and directed toward accepting the proposition. You know from your own experience that when you are truly "wrapped up" in a novel, a play, a movie, or a television dramatic program, your capacity for emotional response is considerably greater than when you are reading or observing with a bored attitude. Condensing it to a slogan, we can say: "Without attention, no motivation."

Materials, then, must be found and fashioned to keep your audience's attention as you have never kept it before. All of the means of gaining and holding your audience's attention which you have learned—reference to experience; visual aids; promises of reward, penalty, or satisfaction of curiosity; and the factors of attention—are as applicable here as they were in the speeches of the units in which they were introduced. You must not forget that your learning in this course is designed to be cumulative, not piecemeal. Basic methodologies of speechmaking are learned to be used repeatedly, not just once.

Suggestion Value

Do not delay another minute! Go to your drugstore now, while our special introductory offer is still on, and get your bottle of Hirsute's Hair Restorer! Remember, you get this amazing new scientific discovery, the only hair restorer containing secret ingredient F-26, at half its usual price and with a guarantee of your money back if you are not completely satisfied!

Does this sound familiar to you? Probably entirely too familiar, for it is one of the most commonly used closings for the "hard sell" commercial. We could use it to illustrate any number of things about the nature of psychological persuasion, including motivation and attention values, and possibly unethical practices (if the product were not as good as it is claimed to be), but we feel that its best application probably is in helping to make clear to you the nature of suggestion value.

You are not told in this commercial that Hirsute's Hair Restorer is going to give you a bushy head of hair overnight; that it is the best product of its kind on the market; that it contains one of the great medical discoveries of all time, the result of years of laboratory research by great bearded scientists; that you have nothing to lose by trying it; or that it is right now the greatest bargain in town. These beliefs, if they are created in you at all, you build yourself from suggestions, direct and indirect, positive and negative, that are given.

In effective psychological persuasion, there is much more than meets the eye. Many appeals are specifically designed *not* to meet the eye, but to be taken in from the fringe areas of attention. The idea is that if this can be done, there is much greater likelihood of its being accepted without critical examination. "Isn't she perfectly lovely in that dress?" for instance, will not meet with nearly the amount of skepticism and resistance as "That's the dress you must buy for her!" Because it does not, it will probably sell the dress. We all like to feel that we have made up our own minds to buy "Hirsute's Hair Restorer," that "perfectly lovely" dress, or whatever. Suggestion allows us to do that. It also provides the speaker with a shortcut to persuasion that accomplishes much in a very short time.

Four categories of suggestion were mentioned as being used in our hypothetical hair restorer commercial: *direct, indirect, positive,* and *negative.* They are all concerned with the *direction* the suggestion takes.

Direct suggestion does nothing to disguise the fact that it is being made. Slogans like "Every litter bit hurts," "Fight cancer with a check-up and a check," and "Drive safely, for the life you save may be your own" are all examples of this kind of suggestion. The aim is apparent, but the means is a clever slogan rather than a well-developed argument. Such devices can work with supporters or those indifferent to your proposal, but will not work as well with opponents or skeptics.

The usual direction of the suggestion in the commercial is direct, but there is one notable example of *indirect* suggestion. Our commercial claims that Hirsute is the "only hair restorer containing secret ingredient F-26." Nothing is said that is directly derogatory of any other product, but the implication is that, without secret ingredient F-26, they must all be inferior. Generally speaking, the more indirect the suggestion, the more likely it is to be accepted without quarrel or question.

The commercial begins with an example of *negative* suggestion: it tells you what not to do. Although its use may be effective, it is seldom as successful as a *positive* suggestion, telling you what to do. We tend to resist a "Thou shalt not" approach. Inexperienced persuaders will sometimes unwittingly create a negative suggestion harmful to their purposes, like the little boy who knocks on the door and says, "You wouldn't want to buy any Christmas cards, would you?" The easiest answer to give him is "No." "Do not" may sometimes be a necessary approach, but "do" is preferable, and should probably be combined with "do not" if the negative approach must be taken. That is what is done, you will notice, in our commercial.

One other direction for suggestion is possible, which is even more potentially dangerous for a persuader than the negative direction. It is *countersuggestion*. With this you attempt to deal with persons who are negatively suggestible, ones who are inclined to do the opposite of what you request. Jonathan Swift, the famous satirist, suggested in "A Modest Proposal" that the best way to relieve the Irish famine was for the hapless inhabitants of that country to sell their babies as food. He hoped by this writing to shock the sensibilities and stir the conscience of his British readers. His effort did not meet with success. You may at some time want to try countersuggestion, and it may work, but if it goes wrong, you have defeated your own aim.

Again, from the persuader's point of view, there is nothing inherently good or bad about any of these different categories. They are tools designed for different tasks, each with its own individual strengths and weaknesses. An ethical persuader can feel free to use them all, being careful only to use the right tool for the job.

On a somewhat more exalted plane than the imaginary television commercial we used to illustrate use of suggestion is this quotation from a speech of the great British Parliamentary orator, Edmund Burke, who was speaking in behalf of the American colonists:

> Now if the doctrines of policy contained in these preambles, and the force of these examples in the Acts of Parliament, avail anything, what can be said

against applying them with regard to America? Are not the people of America
as much Englishmen as the Welsh?

The implication is that the American colonists should be treated as fairly
as other British citizens. Are you able to identify the kind or direction of the
suggestion used here?

If motivation is the chief aim which an item of psychological proof is
attempting to accomplish, and attention is a necessary condition for reception
of the motivational stimuli, then suggestion is the path along which those
motivational stimuli must travel to arrive at their destination. It is the shortest
route home. The shortest route, we would remind you, is not always the best
route; but it is not at all smart to go the long way around when you can get
there faster and maybe even better by going over the back fence. Look for
materials with suggestion value.

A single item of material you find might well have all three values of
motivation, attention, and suggestion built right into it. Another might have
two values, or one, or seemingly none. Sometimes the temptation is strong to
save only the "ready-made" items, throwing the others aside. What is forgotten
is that the speaker always has it within his power to use materials to serve his
persuasive purpose best. With thought and imagination given to the task,
materials can be made to have these values.

The Best Materials for Psychological Effectiveness

From what was just said above, you can see that any kind of speech material
can either have or be made to have the psychological values of motivation,
attention, and suggestion. We will discuss, however, only those which we feel
to be most adaptable.

In the realm of *examples*, probably nothing will do so well for psychological persuasion as illustrations or extended examples. Better still are those
lengthy illustrations that we gave a special designation as *stories* or *anecdotes*.
Indeed, of all the various forms of authority material, the story or anecdote,
other things being equal, is probably your single best bet.

The reason for stressing length in examples is that it gives the speaker
opportunity to build up sensory impressions about a person, a place, a thing,
or an event. Any artist, including the speaker, must deal in strong sensory
impressions if he wishes to create a powerful emotional response. The story
or anecdote, being usually even longer than the illustration, allows for more
and better sensory impressions; hence for that reason alone it is superior.
What raises it to the heights of supreme excellence is that, in addition to the
motivation value of its sensory impressions, it has also the inherent attrac-

tiveness and indirectness of a narrative format to give it both attention value and suggestion value.

Let us attempt to show how sensory impressions and the narrative structure do their work. We will suppose that you are advocating some improvement in medical care for the aged. You could develop the argument in any one of several different ways. You might, for instance, do it as one student speaker did, by reasoning from statistics thusly:

I. The problem of medical care for the aged is a very grave one.
  A. Our old people are beset with many problems of illness and essential hospital care.
    1. Eighty of every 100 people over 65 suffer from some chronic ailment.
    2. Sixteen of every 80 are hospitalized one or more times annually.
  B. Voluntary health insurance is not taking care of the financial problems which this high incidence of illness and hospitalization causes.
    1. Only half of the people over 65, and but 30 percent of those over 70, have such insurance.
    2. Only 10 to 15 percent of the health costs of our aged citizens are reimbursed by insurance.

Such an approach could well be the preferable one for some audiences and occasions. For any one of the situations specified by this assignment, however, it would not suffice by itself. You would also want something of the sort that another student speaker did on the same subject by this anecdote:

> I worked in a rest home taking care of old people last summer. It was a job, and I felt I was doing some good in the world, and after a while I even got to like it. But there were some things about that job and about that place and what that place represents that I didn't like at all. The things I didn't like are the point of what I'm going to say.
>
> I didn't like the smell, for one thing. That smell still haunts me—my whole experience haunts me. The smell was musty and sour-sweet and a little bit ammoniacal. It clung to everybody and everything, and made you want to change all the beds and open all the windows, except that you knew it wouldn't do any good—the smell would still be there.
>
> It wasn't only the smell of the place that bothered me so much. It was the old people themselves. There were so many of them. I hadn't realized how many there are. You know, you don't see them on the streets. I guess that's because they're either sick in bed at home or in a hospital or in a rest home, as all these were.
>
> It makes you feel a little strange to be near a really old person for the first time. I suppose that's because you know that it will happen to you that way, too—age, I mean; and the wrinkled, sagging, blue-white skin; and the squinting dull eyes, and the soft, limp arms and hands. But then you get to know them,

and it's different. They're people like anyone else, and you like them or you don't.

What really haunts me though, is what happened to Mrs. Davidson. She was one of those I didn't like. She was always whining and complaining and threatening to kill herself because she was nothing but a burden and an expense. I thought she was just a bothersome person. But now I don't think she was. She did kill herself, late in August, just before I came back to school. She did it with her wish to die probably more than her fall from a high window. And do you know what her husband said when they called him? The head nurse told me. He said, "Oh no! All those doctor bills and now a funeral, too!" It was the first thing he said. It must have been the biggest thing on his mind, just like it had been the biggest thing on her's.

An audience usually does not respond with any great amount of emotion to a statistic, unless it is aimed right at one of their most vital spots. But if the speaker makes the statistics into real people whom the audience can feel with and feel for—usually with a story or anecdote concentrating on an individual—he will get an emotional response. The above anecdote held the class's attention as it probably never had been held by any speaker before. Moreover, it suggested much of what the other speaker's statistics had stated outright, and its motivational effect was actually observable.

It is almost always preferable if the speaker can deal with real illustrations, stories, and anecdotes, since the audience can identify more easily. Fictitious ones, however, are often necessary in persuasive speaking to illustrate a general truth about a group. If, in your persuasive speaking, you are illustrating with Mr. Average Farmer, or telling a story about him, the main thing to do is to make him as real as you possibly can. Give him human characteristics that make him someone the audience can care about, not a meaningless abstraction.

Quite often an illustration, story, or anecdote serves as one of the examples being compared in the persuasive speaker's use of *analogy*. Even analogies that do not employ such materials can often have telling persuasive effect. Just the fact that two examples are being compared is something of a dramatic event that excites attention and concentration, and the connotations surrounding the comparison can have both suggestion and motivation value. We said previously that figurative analogies were more prevalent in persuasion stressing psychological appeals than in persuasion which is more intellectually oriented. The reason for this is that the kinds of comparisons used in the figurative analogy are likely to appeal to the imagination much more than literal comparisons would, and thereby relate more closely to suggestion value. To call the situation in Cuba a threat to Latin American security is one thing, but to call it a "cancerous disease" has broader implications touching upon motivational and attention values as well as suggestion value. Analogy can be a potent weapon in the persuasive speaker's arsenal.

Quotations are another form of supporting material that can be of value to the persuader. Literary quotations have the attention value of *the familiar,* and often other attention values as well. We are all aware of the motivational force of our impulses to revere and want to be guided by the thoughts of great men, and the immense suggestion value generated by the feeling that "if these great men say it's so, then it must be." Some of the same values, of course, can be found in expert testimony, although the attention value of the familiar might not exist. Multiple inexpert testimony, or majority opinion, gains its psychological effectiveness mainly from our strong motivations to belong, to be one of the crowd, to be influenced by what everybody else is doing. Such material also has attention and suggestion values. Because we want to be "in" rather than "out," we are always greatly interested in reports of what the "in" group is thinking, saying, or doing. And if it can be inferred that the way to be "in" is to do what the speaker is advocating, the audience may need no other form of suggestion.

Materials for Ethos. If an audience is laggard in fulfilling its duties and obligations, it is not going to pay much heed to another laggard telling it to reform. If it "couldn't care less" about the proposal, the speaker must care a good deal more than it does to get it to feel that it is a matter of real concern. For indifferent audiences, your ethos must be especially high.

Most of the essentials of this value of persuasion were presented in the previous unit. All we will attempt to do here is to suggest materials that help establish ethos best in psychological persuasion. They are, essentially, the same ones that were mentioned as being psychologically effective. However, illustrations, stories, or anecdotes, if they are to create ethos as well as pathos, should preferably derive from the speaker's own experience. If you have had no experiences worth telling, of course, you must make second-best do; but if you have had, by all means use them. Not just *any* experience will do, however. The story of the accident that almost happened will probably have a negative rather than a positive effect. The accident must have happened, and it must have had rather serious consequences, if the audience is to be moved. Skillful use of analogy will also tend to reflect favorably upon the audience's estimation of the speaker. But when you are young and relatively inexperienced, when you do not have the gray hairs that are supposed to accompany wisdom, there is probably no better way of building ethos than to borrow it from persons and groups whose testimony you present in your quotations. Make sure that such persons and groups are held in high esteem by your audience.

Other Materials. Physical materials of a dramatic character are quite often used in persuasive speeches stressing psychological appeals. Highway accidents, for example, can become more than dull statistics if the speaker shows us enlarged pictures of a few of them. One student speaker whose topic was litterbugs made an indelible impression on his audience by bringing to class and dumping on the desk the litter that he had collected around that particular building that morning. Such means reinforce your listeners' emotional involvement. The charts and graphs mentioned in connection with the previous unit are another type of physical material that you might wish to consider, especially if speaking on a proposition of policy.

Although reasoning materials may be rare occurrences in many of the persuasive speeches that you hear given, this is not what should happen. Emotion should give strength to thought, not weaken it. This is not to say that the character of the thought for psychological persuasion is not different from that given intellectual persuasion, however. Essentially, the difference is that imagination plays a larger part in it, critical analysis a smaller part. It is a difference that has already been made apparent, and that will become even more apparent in the sections to follow.

APPLICATION TO AUDIENCE
AND OCCASION

With the progression of this course moving, as it does, from the more simple to the more complex, it is not strange that this final speech should be the one for which you will need to know more about your audience and occasion than for any of the previous ones. You might be lucky occasionally in employing psychological appeals without giving thought to the speech situation in which they are to be used, but more often you would fall short of accomplishing your specific purpose. That the emotions of persons are tricky matters to deal with is a truth that by this time in your life you probably understand.

Emotions

You have always touched the emotions of your hearers when you spoke. A human being cannot speak to other human beings without there being some emotional interchange. But in this speech your deliberate and concerted efforts at persuasion are centered around exciting your listeners to deep feeling about your proposal. Can the audience be made to feel deeply? What motives are operating or can be made to operate in them? What will make them give maximum attention to you? What are the shortest pathways to emotional response? In addition to all the information about your audience and occasion that you needed in previous speeches, you will need to have answers to these questions.

Again you will want to know where the answers are to be found. Occupation, economic status, and group membership, we suggest, are quite as useful in giving you clues to your audience's motivations, vital concerns, and degree of suggestibility as they are in supplying you information about their probable beliefs. An audience of accountants, for example, would probably be shocked by figures showing a grossly unbalanced national budget, whereas the same figures might have little emotional impact on a group of English teachers. "Money talk" might be boring to those who were born with ample inherited wealth, but fascinating to a group of self-made men. The "Knights of Dedicated Service" you would imagine to be more suggestible than the "Citizen's Council for Civic Improvement." As with all such estimations, you could be wrong, but you are playing the percentages and should win a fair share of the time.

You can also look for answers to these questions in the age and sex distribution of members of your audience.

The impulses that motivate our actions, the things that we care about, and our responses to suggestion vary a good deal with age. Attractiveness to the other sex might very well be the driving force for a person in his teens, and the smallest of his concerns at 80. The advertisement of a new hair lotion with magnetic powers would probably have that same person's rapt attention as a youth, but would pass unnoticed in his old age. And a "scientific survey" on what young girls considered the "ideal date," which precipitated a frenzy of self-improvement when being an ideal date mattered to him, would, if read, produce a laugh when it did not. Nor is this the only matter on which age might make a very great difference. Older persons tend to be more interested in security, serenity, and comfort; less interested in the urgent problems of the day; and less suggestible. Consider both the age span of your audience and the predominant age group, if any.

Are women more emotional than men, or vice versa? It would be interesting to debate the question, but not very profitable. Certainly both men and women are emotional enough (and sometimes more than enough) for any persuader's purpose. More to the point are the questions of whether women are more demonstrative than men and whether their emotions are excited by different appeals. A woman's traditional role in our society, modified though it is by careers after marriage and electric home appliances, is still a conditioning factor of her emotional responses. Generally speaking, she will show what she feels more than a man will, if for no other reason than that society allows her to. Moreover, altruistic motives, especially those associated with home and children, will usually be more operative. Observers differ as to whether idealism is more deeply ingrained in the woman than the man, with the modern, more skeptical view of woman threatening to overthrow the older concept of her inherently idealistic nature. However, women *can* be said to be on the average more suggestible than men, but not so interested in and concerned about the world's woes. When attempting psychological persuasion on audiences in which women predominate, then, the most important things to remember are that ordinarily you will have more difficulty creating interest in a public problem, altruistic appeals are more likely to prove effective, suggestibility will be higher, and you will have to shift to a higher reading on your gauge of observable response to determine your real effectiveness.

Knowledge of your audience's level of basic intelligence and of knowledge may also give you clues to probable psychological effectiveness. It is not that greater intelligence and knowledge necessarily make a person less emotional, but rather that they make it more difficult to excite his emotions. Usually the less intelligent and educated the person is, the more he will be governed by his motives, the easier it will be to gain and hold his attention, and the more suggestible he will be.

Overriding all these considerations of occupation, economic status, organizational affiliation, age, sex, and intelligence, however, is the fact that men are fundamentally alike in their emotional responses. *Your* emotional involvement is good indication that your audience might become involved. But before making your decisions, put yourself "in the other fellow's shoes," become as much like him as your imagination will help you to be, and try to see whether, looking at the matter from his point of view, you would still care as much.

Social Facilitation

In psychological persuasion there are times when the nature of the occasion for the speech assumes importance equal to and possibly even greater than the nature of the audience. The occasion, as a matter of fact, can be used to change the audience, whatever its initial complexion, into the kind receptive to the persuasion. If this sounds fantastic, read the historical accounts of Adolf Hitler's mass meetings, then the sections in *Mein Kampf* in which he sets forth the techniques of manipulating the speech situation by which he managed to create frenzied hysteria in normally staid, sedate men and women. Or observe any skilled religious revivalist at work. The ultimate purposes may be as different as night and day, but the phenomenon and the way in which it is achieved are similar in both instances.

Accounting for the phenomenon is the psychological principle which Floyd Allport [3] termed "social facilitation." Essentially what is meant by the term is the tendency of the individual human being to be influenced in his behavior by the behavior of those around him. When surrounded by people all saying, doing, or feeling the same thing, the individual will find it well-nigh impossible not to respond in kind. But social facilitation goes beyond that, for each individual joins in more lustily than if he were alone. Attention upon the speaker-stimulus is heightened, and emotionality and suggestibility are considerably increased.

The speaker who wishes to fashion such a "psychological crowd" uses every means possible to make the individuals feel identification with the mass, and to get the mass acting in concert and paying attention to him and him alone. Among other things, he crowds people together as closely as he can, having them stand rather than sit; he plays music to stir them up emotionally; he gets them singing, chanting, clapping their hands, stamping their feet, or performing some other such act in unison; he displays objects or symbols to which they owe a common allegiance; and he avoids competing stimuli of any kind. By these methods, as we have suggested, either storm troopers or soldiers of the cross can be created. In and of themselves they are neutral techniques; it is the ethical behavior or misbehavior of the speaker that makes them either "good" or "bad"

It is not likely that you can make a psychological crowd of your speech class. It is not even likely that in the future you will be doing much speaking before audiences numbering in the thousands. However, the principle of social facilitation, the crowd behavior which it produces, and the means by which it is accomplished all have relevance to every persuasive speech occasion, no matter how small the room or the audience assembled. Social facilitation is something you can accomplish anytime, anywhere. The results achieved with smaller groups are not dramatic, perhaps, but they certainly can aid your persuasive effort.

Determining the Purpose

Because in psychological persuasion the speaker is usually dealing with audiences either favorable or indifferent to his proposal, he can develop a false sense of security, feeling that the determination of his specific purpose is an easy matter. If the audience believes that honesty is the best policy,

[3] Floyd Allport, *Social Psychology* (Boston: Houghton Mifflin Company, 1924), p. 261.

or at the moment has no strong inclination not to believe it, why not state the specific purpose as "To make my audience believe more strongly (or just believe) that honesty is the best policy"?

It would be convenient if it were that simple. But audiences are not just favorable, they are *more or less* favorable, and degrees of favorability vary within a given audience as well as among different audiences. Some will believe that honesty invariably is the best policy; others that it usually is; still others believe that, given the choice and other circumstances being equal, it probably is. The specific purpose must be truly specific, recognizing the degree of belief as well as the existence of belief. It could be that the audience's present degree of belief suits you well enough, in which case you would have few troubles; on the other hand, you might have to treat them almost as opponents in moving them toward a more favorable degree of belief.

The occasion may also dictate qualification of your specific purpose. How much time will you have? How receptive will the audience be and can you make them be on this occasion? As we have said before, you cannot always do it all in one speech. Make the specific purpose one that can be accomplished with the particular audience on the particular occasion with the particular persuasive avenues and means at your disposal. Starting out tentatively with the aforementioned broad and absolutely unqualified purpose of strengthening or creating belief that honesty is the best policy, you could very well wind up with a much narrower and also much more manageable one: "To make my audience believe more strongly (or just believe) that they should own up to their mistakes rather than to try to cover them up."

CONSTRUCTION OF THE SPEECH

Accomplishing the Specific Purpose

The advice we have to give about statement of your central idea so as to achieve your specific purpose is relatively brief. It will introduce a recurrent theme in this section and the next, which is that the person attempting psychological persuasion should try to use every ounce of imaginative and creative skill he has in building his speech and readying it for delivery. Motivation, attention, and suggestion values are important not only in supporting materials, but in everything about the speech and its delivery. Certainly the central idea, as the statement of the belief or action you are trying to secure, should have these values in more than sufficient quantity and quality. Imaginative wording will help.

Not just any phrasing of your central idea will do. One wrong word can decrease motivational power, dull interest, or make a command out of a suggestion; it can make the audience balk because too much is asked of them or bored because not enough is being demanded; it can alienate friends and create enemies. If your purpose is to persuade the audience that they should own up to their mistakes rather than to try to cover them up, your first impulse might be to put your central idea in those words. While there could be worse wordings, that is not the point. The point is that there can be better ones. We suggest "The best place to hide your mistakes is in the open." It is catchy, easy to remember, and carries with it both motivational and suggestive power. The central idea in psychological persuasion should very often be phrased as a catchword or slogan.

Organizing the Speech

At the beginning of this unit we made the statement that persuasive speeches of the type we are describing here are likely to have a looser organizational structure than those emphasizing intellectual appeals. The principal reasons for this are rather obvious. One, of course, is that with most audiences supporting or indifferent to your proposition, logical precision and inevitability are not necessary. But such a negative reason would not be reason enough. The better reason is that tight organization does not create an atmosphere conducive to emotional arousal through suggestion. For that you need uncritical attention. Borrowing Coleridge's famous phrase, the psychological persuader, like the storyteller, tries to create "a willing suspension of disbelief."

Patterns. Many different patterns of organizing main points are available for use in a speech of this type. Conceivably almost any pattern could be used with success. The more usual ones, however, are less rigid variations of the patterns suggested for propositions of policy. For the other propositions, as well as occasionally for those of policy, there are such patterns as time sequence, space sequence, cause-and-effect relationships, advantages and disadvantages, extended analogy, and ABC's or letter combinations taken from spelling a key word.

If you are arguing a proposition of policy, we would suggest that you give serious consideration to the Monroe "Motivated Sequence." It is to the persuasive speech emphasizing psychological appeals, we feel, that this pattern of speech organization is most legitimately applied. True, it is somewhat of a "recipe" approach to organization, but if you want that kind of cake and follow the recipe closely, you might win the blue ribbon. The chief benefit of this pattern for the beginning speaker is that it systematizes the achievement of the key steps of the process of psychological persuasion. These steps are:

1. The speaker gains and holds attention.
2. He arouses desires useful to his purpose.
3. He demonstrates how these desires can be satisfied by acceptance of what he advocates.
4. He tries to produce the specific response to his specific purpose.[4]

The achievement of these aims in this order is your organizational goal whatever pattern you choose and whatever kind of proposition you might be arguing. The Monroe "Motivated Sequence" can be an excellent way of achieving it for a proposition of policy.

Let us look at some of the ordinary uses of the patterns introduced here for the first time in connection with persuasive speaking.

The persuader may use time sequence for demonstrating that matters are either better or worse than they once were, or in tracing the growth and achievements of a person, organization, or government. He will sometimes employ space sequence when the problem involves a number of different divisions or levels of some large organization of people or process, or when there are spatial differences in the nature and extent of the problem. The problem of racial integration, for instance, might be approached from the point of view of its local, state, national, and international implications; or, in another way, by considering the differences in its nature and extent in the North and the South.

Cause-and-effect relationships, of course, can be discussed for any problem; and if an indirect speech development is desirable, the pattern based on them can effectively lead up to or merely imply the persuader's advocated solution to the problem. The same would be true of the pattern of advantages and disadvantages, which likewise allows the persuader's specific purpose to be withheld from complete view until the end of the speech.

The extended analogy has application to propositions of all kinds, and can be made to have strong motivation, attention, and suggestion values. Any problem involving the application of a solution previously used elsewhere, a comparison of differing or changing viewpoints, history repeating itself, or a contest or race of some sort might well be discussed in terms of an extended analogy.

The patterns of ABC's or other letter combinations derived from spelling out a key word are ordinarily reserved for the "speeches for special oc-

4 Brembeck and Howell, *op. cit.*, pp. 26–27.

casions" discussed above in connection with Option E of the assignment. These patterns can be quite dramatic and effective, but they also can fall very flat. If you use one, avoid triteness, overblown claims, and obvious straining to find a word to match the letter.

Although the speech of this unit may not require you to cover as many issues or to cover them as thoroughly as did the previous one, the matter of knowing and discussing the pertinent issues must be taken into consideration. The major issues will still serve as a guide to your choice of organizational pattern and to your investigation of the minor issues. But the issues dealt with, both major and minor, will differ with differing audiences and occasions. You will need to be concerned about the possibility of neglecting a necessary psychological issue and the danger of a major break in your chain of reasoning. To simplify, however, it could probably be said that in most instances your principal worries about issues here need only be that they be suitable to the speech situation, that no "essential" issue be left undiscussed, and that predominating among minor issues be psychological ones that will serve to motivate the audience.

In the last unit we attached great importance to the introduction and conclusion of the persuasive speech and promised further development of their functions. Let us proceed to that amplification.

Introductions. With the gaining and holding of attention being the first step in the process of psychological persuasion, it follows that the attention-getting task of the introduction becomes more crucial in persuasion than it is in informational speaking. For this reason, the type of introduction we called "motivated" is used even more generally for persuasive speeches than it is for speeches of information.

Although such introductions are designed principally to motivate the audience to pay attention, their motivational value can extend to the speaker's proposition as well. Indeed, motivation connected with the purpose of the speech is often the means used to get the audience to listen. Startling statements, quotations, illustrative anecdotes, rhetorical questions, and visual aids serving as introductions to persuasive speeches are usually directed immediately and primarily to the speaker's proposition, with the expectation that the inherent attention value of the devices themselves, coupled with the motivational impact of their vital content, will be sufficient to create and for a time hold the necessary amount of attention. Thus the second step in the process of psychological persuasion, creating desires useful to the persuader's purpose, can also be aided by this kind of introduction.

References by the speaker to himself, the previous speaker or chairman, the occasion, or some recent event, or paying an honest compliment to the audience, are designed mostly to create a warmer, more intimate relationship between the audience and himself. These devices, even though they may have ethos as their main goal, contain also the attention factors of familiarity and the concrete.

Humor can be used more often in persuasive speaking than most beginning speakers realize. There are, after all, many qualities and kinds of humor, ranging all the way from the most warm and sentimental to the most bitter and satiric. Few subjects are so serious that there is not an appropriate kind of humor for them. Moreover, the human being can switch from laughter to tears with amazing facility. Although the introduction is not the only place appropriate for humor, it is the place that is most commonly used. Your humorous introduction may be either a direct or an indirect route to your proposition. The caution to observe with the indirect route is to make absolutely sure that it does lead eventually to your persuasive goal. One of the most compelling factors of attention, as you remember, is that of humor.

As you may also recall, we delayed explanation of two kinds of motivated introductions until this unit because, we said, they are most important for the type of speech you will be giving now. One of these, unison audience reaction, has already been touched upon in connection with the discussion of the psychological persuader's use of social facilitation. Getting the audience to perform some action together is a useful warm-up tactic if you want to mold your audience into the semblance of a psychological crowd. The technique, of course, should give you attention of a very concentrated kind.

The other kind of introduction left unexplained was that designed to create common ground. As generally used, it is essentially an extended attempt to create ethos. In it the speaker demonstrates to his listeners how he and they are alike in one or more ways. Likenesses can be pointed out in age; occupation; economic, political, or social status; geographical, organizational, or institutional identification; or experiences, attitudes, beliefs, or motives. Personal reference of any kind usually holds attention; when it is allied with the audience's interests, its attention value is compounded.

The common-ground approach is not necessarily limited to the introductory remarks of the speaker. It can run throughout the speech and condition his language, his manner, and his dress as well. The problem of ethics arises only if the likenesses are artificial rather than genuine. While this approach can be used on opposing audiences, unless they are so antipathetic that they would be inclined to reject even the genuine as artificial, it is probably most beneficial with audiences that are initially friendly or inclined to be so. Although an audience may see eye to eye with you on the proposition at issue, they may not give you a completely sympathetic ear. There may be some kinds of people that they do not want on their side. The common-ground technique takes you out of that category.

Conclusions. As you now know, it is important to command maximum attention in the conclusion as well as in the introduction of a speech; and as you now further realize, ethos should also again be stressed, especially if the speaker's purpose is a persuasive one. But you should also realize that a good conclusion is not an end but a means, its real purpose being to strengthen the speaker's reinforcement of his central idea and thus help insure the accomplishment of his specific purpose. In psychological persuasion, then, it can be said that the end result of the conclusion should be completion of the fourth and final step in the process of psychological persuasion. After your introduction has gained attention (which the rest of the speech must be designed to hold) and it and the body of the speech have aroused desires useful to your persuasive purpose and demonstrated how these desires can be satisfied by acceptance of what you advocate, your conclusion should try to produce the specific response to your specific purpose.

The most direct means of doing that, of course, is the summary conclusion. In persuasive speaking, however, this type of conclusion is somewhat different from what it was in informational speaking. A bare recital of main points covered or a bald restatement of the central idea might prove adequate, if barely so, for the speech of information, but it would have no chance at all of doing the job for the persuasive speech. Again, motivation, attention, and suggestion values must be incorporated into the summary statements; this must be done with consummate skill so as to strengthen ethos; and the progression of statements must produce in the listener a reaction of, "Of course, there could be no other possible conclusion drawn than the one which the speaker is presenting." Here again we are saying that imagination and creative skill may often prove desirable in psychological persuasion.

Quotations, climactic anecdotes, and epigrams, as we have said, are all excellent means of concluding the persuasive speech. Unlike the summary conclusion, such epitome conclusions usually have built-in motivation, attention, and suggestion values. Even if they do not, they can more easily be made to have them. In using quotations and epigrams you are also more likely to have ready-made ethos, though admittedly of a secondhand variety. The climactic anecdote, if it derives from your own experience, will have to be told in a way that establishes ethos for you; and if it is borrowed, in a way that transfers the ethos of the source to you. The key to any successful conclusion, however, is a forceful reiteration of the main theme of the speech.

The third category of conclusions, the plea for acceptance or action, is suitable for almost all persuasive speeches, but is particularly applicable to those in which the speaker is trying to get immediate action. Since all of these kinds of conclusions—rhetorical question, prophecy, and personal reference—are of the speaker's own devising, he must, as with the summary conclusion, see to it that all the necessary qualities of a good persuasive conclusion are incorporated into it.

One final word about introductions and conclusions may be necessary to clear up any possible misunderstanding that might arise from the rather rigid categories that we have given them. You must not think that you are limited to one type per speech. In the longer speech, and more especially in the longer persuasive speech, you might very well use several of the introductory and concluding devices in combination. In your introduction, for example, you might make reference to a previous speaker, establish common ground, tell an anecdote, and come out with a startling statement, all by way of leading into your subject. In the conclusion you might summarize, use a literary quotation, ask a rhetorical question, and answer it with a declaration of the action you yourself intend to take. Since warming up the audience and driving the point home to them are more necessary tasks in persuasive speaking, more effort—which sometimes includes using several devices, not just one—must be expended upon them.

Wording the Speech

A number of times we have talked about creating motivation, attention, and suggestion values in materials which do not inherently possess them; and on other occasions we have mentioned the necessity of using your imagination and whatever measure of creative skill you might possess in phrasing your statements to create these values. Our inability to reserve comment about wording the speech of psychological persuasion until this section should serve to emphasize the all-pervading importance of this step of your speech preparation. "Give me the right word," wrote the great English novelist, Joseph Conrad, "and the right accent, and I will move the world." There is nothing the least bit hyperbolic about the statement. It is no exaggeration to say that in psychological persuasion, how you phrase what is said is often more important than what you say.

Everything that you have learned in this course and outside of it about language will be useful now. Correctness, clarity, and concreteness are as necessary in persuasive as in informational speaking, for the message must be understood before it can have any emotional effect. Metaphorical phrasing, because of its power to stimulate sensory impressions, tends to be an habitual recourse of the psychological persuader. And certainly the persuasive slanting of your language that you were told about in the previous unit has even more relevance to psychological than it does to intellectual appeals.

Slanting, as a matter of fact, takes on much greater importance in the speech of psychological persuasion. It can reach the point where practically every word is examined for its possible persuasive effect, and used or discarded on this ground alone. We do not expect quite that much diligence from the student speaker, but we do expect more than is usually given to the job. Not every one of your words may be a gem of psychological effectiveness; but you should at least avoid such gross errors as terming your own solution "probably too idealistic ever to work," or speaking of yourself as one who "knows less about this problem" than the audience does, or referring to your opponent as "a much wiser man" than yourself, or calling "moronic" the fraternal organizations to which most of the members of your audience belong—all of which, and more, we have heard from student speakers attempting persuasion. The right words must be applied to the right ideas or those ideas will come out wrong.

Sensory Impressions. In his use of stories, anecdotes, and analogies, the psychological persuader is constantly called upon to seek words which will conjure up sensory impressions. Often, as we have said, he will find what he wants in metaphorical phrasings. But more often it is the single word necessary for accurate and persuasive description or narration that he must have. If at all possible, he should try to find words which stimulate more than one sense. "Smooth," for instance, stimulates only the sense of touch, whereas "silky" produces reactions of both touch and sight; "tearful" creates only a sight image, but "sobbing" preserves the image and gives it a sound track in addition; and "sweet" activates only the taste buds, unlike "sugary," which affects the eyes and the fingers as well. But in any case the words should stimulate at least one sense. There should be no "happy" looks or "good" smells or "pretty" girls in your narration and description. Such words do not affect the senses, and therefore do not stir the emotions.

In Unit III connotative meaning was discussed. Connotation has significance for the persuader as well as the reporter. Not only can it clarify meanings; it can also help create motivation, attention, and suggestion values.

Loaded Words. Writers on persuasion suggest as one of its techniques the use of so-called "loaded words," by which are meant words having strong emotional overtones, words that are literally "loaded" with positive or negative connotations.

Such words are tied up with our most stereotyped notions of what the world is like. Lacking complete knowledge of the world, and yet wishing to have a system of thought by which to operate in it, all of us early in life create images of that world which are really incomplete reflections of the economic, political, and social reality they attempt to represent. These are the "stereotypes" which we never really lose, to which we have strong emotional attachment, and which condition our thinking and feeling on almost every problem.

We may never have seen a Russian, but we know that Russians are evil; we may have not the slightest knowledge of communism, yet we are firmly convinced that it is the worst system of government ever devised; we may think the Kremlin is an organization rather than a building, but no one can tell us that any good ever came out of it. Conversely, we know that all Americans are good, that democracy is the best system of government for everyone, and that the White House has always been a staunch defender of what is right and true and good. Stereotypes like these exist for almost every people, government, occupation, organization, movement, or activity on the face of the earth. You do not need to tell the college freshman what college professors are like; he knows even before orientation week. Nor do some college professors need any first-hand knowledge of athletes to know that none of them is capable of passing his course.

The psychological persuader must realize the power of such stereotypes and the "loaded words" which can create them in the audience's mind. Calling something or someone "communist" may excite maximum attention and cause us to reject it or him without giving the matter the slightest conscious thought, just as calling it or him "democratic" may create acceptance in the same way. The more uncritical the audience, of course, the more effective are such "loaded words." Like almost everything else in psychological persuasion, "loaded words" are dynamite, but you can learn to use them both effectively and ethically.

Pay close attention to your wording. It should be correct, clear, concrete, slanted for persuasive effect, and evocative of both sensory impressions and stereotyped reactions. Check always to see that your words are carrying the motivational stimulus desired along the shortest possible route.

PREPARATION FOR DELIVERY

Rehearsing Aloud

Pathos must emanate from the persuader as well as from the content, organization, and wording of the speech. Motivation, attention, and suggestion values are as vital to the delivery of the message as they are to the message itself. By supreme effort the listener may learn information presented in a lackluster manner, but by no amount of effort can he make himself feel deeply if the speaker's presentation does not communicate deep feeling.

There are actors and public speakers (and, for that matter, ordinary people) who have the ability to feign an emotion so skillfully that they can move others without themselves being moved. They are fewer than is generally supposed, however, and the discriminating listener can very often detect the false note. Modern actor training, as a matter of fact, is devoted more to ways and means of feeling the emotion than to techniques of expressing it. Indeed, the modern public speaker might well learn from the ideal of the modern actor, which is to communicate only feelings that he himself deeply believes in, letting a relaxed and responsive body react naturally to the impulse. Most of the best actors do not try to shape themselves to the role, but rather act themselves in it. The persuader has an even greater obligation to express only his true feelings. Certainly it is the only sure way in which he can carry enough conviction to influence belief and spur others to action.

Empathy

If you really feel the motives that you want your listeners to feel, and have begun to be able to use your body with true freedom and expressiveness, the problem of giving your delivery motivation value should pretty well take care of itself. Operative in every communicative situation is a phenomenon which the psychologists have called "empathy." Briefly, empathy is the tendency we have to imitate physically whatever is engaging our attention. Empathy explains the uncomfortable feeling you have whenever one of your fellow students is ill at ease in delivering his speech. It can and should work the other way, not only making the audience feel generally at ease with the speaker, but causing them to respond to his every physical cue. By imitating your physical responses, your listeners should tend to feel the same way that you feel. They will actually tremble as you tremble, groan as you groan, smile as you smile, laugh as you laugh, and frown as you frown.

Your delivery, of course, can have either positive or negative attention value. The delivery of most highly successful persuasive speakers is animated. Watching such a speaker, one gets the feeling that his whole body is alive and vigorous, that even the smallest gesture is a total rather than an isolated action. You need not always be a constant whirlwind of activity on the platform. The amount and size of your gesture and movement will vary with subject, audience, and occasion; but you should always be active. Your voice, too, should command attention with its vibrancy of feeling and responsiveness to all kinds and shades of feeling.

It should be fairly well understood by now that your delivery has an effect upon your ethos, and that your ethos in turn can strengthen or weaken the effect of any suggestion you might make to the audience. What may not be understood, however, is how suggestion can be conveyed through delivery. The speaker can use a gesture to suggest the action of signing, and the listeners will the more easily sign his petition. Or he can with a laugh or a lifted eyebrow refute the opposition argument he has just finished presenting. His smile can strengthen his own case, his frown help to negate that presented by his opponent. Do not forget that the suggestion value of your speech content can be both implemented and supplemented by your use of gesture, movement, and voice.

Joseph Conrad's statement included the "right accent" as well as the "right word" as necessary for moving the world. All aspects of your delivery should be fashioned in rehearsing aloud to give your persuasion those qualities.

REVIEW OF PREPARATION

1. Choose a subject area involving a problem about which you have had strong convictions for some time. You may even start out with tentative statements of specific purpose and central idea.
2. Investigate the subject area by gathering materials possessing motivation, attention, and suggestion value, looking most especially at illustrations, stories and anecdotes, analogies, and quotations. Also consider ethos in your selection of materials.
3. Consider the emotional receptivity of your audience and your possible ability to heighten it by manipulating elements of the occasion in determing how far you can take your audience on this occasion.
4. Determine a specific purpose for your speech in terms of emotional receptivity and their present *exact* position on the proposal.
5. Phrase your central idea in a compelling way, and organize your speech to accomplish psychological more than logical goals.
6. Plan carefully an introduction that will attract maximum attention to you and your subject.
7. Plan just as carefully a conclusion that will produce the specific response to your specific purpose.
8. Pay more attention to wording the speech than you ever have before, aiming at correctness, clarity, concreteness, persuasive slanting, and the creation of vivid sensory impressions and stereotyped reactions in your listeners.
9. Practice the speech to give the delivery as well as its content the values of motivation, attention, and suggestion.

Sample Student Outline

Subject: Professional Boxing.

Specific Purpose: To get my audience to write letters that will help bring about the creation of a Federal Boxing Commission.

Central Idea: Unless you demand that Federal government step in to exercise control over professional boxing, the bloodiest, most bestial, most inhumane sport of them all will continue to destroy human lives, minds, and bodies.

Introduction

If you read the newspapers at all, you know who the late and too little lamented Benny "Kid" Paret was. It was only last month that he died, but I wouldn't be too surprised if most of you have already conveniently forgotten how and why it happened. I am going to remind you. Benny died defending his welterweight boxing championship against Emile Griffith. Probably you were, like me, one of the 15 million Americans watching their TV sets as Griffith, seeking the fame and fortune of a world's championship, drove Benny to the ropes, and pounded and pounded and pounded away until Benny, his face a mass of blood and more streaming from the eyes, nose, and mouth, slumped to the mat in a coma that never lifted, but only moved into the final, complete immobility of death.

Who was to blame? Some said Referee Goldstein, because he did not stop the fight. Others said the ring physician for not seeing that Benny was a tired, sick man whose previous fights had made him unable to take another beating. Still others blamed Manager Alfonso, who should have known Benny's condition better than anybody. There were those who blamed Griffith. There were those who said it was just that filthy boxing racket. Not many blamed themselves. I do. I blame myself. And I blame you, too.

Transition: (I think all of us—you, me, and the rest of those 15 million at their TV sets, and the many more millions of others who only read about it in the newspapers—are to blame because we didn't long ago demand some kind of Federal control for professional boxing.)

Body

I. There not only is now, but there has been for years a crying need for something to be done about the blood and mayhem of professional boxing.

A. Since 1947, there have been 174 deaths from injuries received in the boxing ring.

B. Just a few years ago, in 1959, Johnny Saxton, another one-time welterweight champion of the world, broke under the strain of boxing, attempted suicide, and was committed to a mental hospital, only one of many boxers to wind up in that condition.

C. Punch-drunk boxers are supposed to be funny, but there is nothing the least bit amusing to their wives and children about these shuffling, befuddled wrecks, mockeries of the strong young physical specimens they had once been.

D. There is no doubt about it, professional boxing as it now exists is a disgrace not only to the world of sports but to our human condition.

   1. An editorial in *America* magazine describes it as "The manly art of mutual mayhem."

   2. Paul Pender, himself a boxer, uses the words "cruel, filthy, dirty" in describing his trade.

   3. Professional football star and sports commentator Kyle Rote compares boxing in bloodthirstiness, cruelty, and just plain inhumanity to the Roman gladiatorial contests.

Transition: (I used to be a boxing fan—maybe I still am, I don't know—but I think I could get along without it, and I think most of you could, too. We are not the only ones involved, however.)

II. To ban boxing would be too drastic a measure, as well as an impossibility.

A. Boxing has millions of fans who would not stand for its complete abolishment.

B. There would also be irresistible pressure against such a move from vested interests like TV, radio, sports arenas, fight promoters and managers, and the boxers themselves.

C. The move would not do any real good, anyway, because it would only force boxing underground and conditions would be worse than they are now.

   1. James Farley, Jr., son of the former Postmaster General of the United States and himself a member of the New York State Athletic Commission, is my authority for saying that boxing would go underground.

   2. Conditions, if boxing were to become another "closed doors" affair like gambling, are frightening to contemplate.

      a. Fights would be staged in garages and empty sheds with no supervision of any kind.

      b. There would be no such thing as a pre-fight physical.

      c. There would be even more hoodlums connected with the sport than there are now.

Transition: (If something needs to be done about controlling this man-killing, man-crippling, man-debasing sport, and we can't abolish it entirely, what can we do? What I said we should have done long ago—demand some kind of Federal control. I think you and I and a lot of other people need to start agitating for a Federal Boxing Commission and strict rules and regulations that would humanize the sport.)

III. A Federal Boxing Commission is the only salvation we have; and it could be just that—a salvation of the sport and of our human dignity.

A. Kyle Rote, Chicago fight promoter Joe Kellman, and many other responsible men of the sports world say that the only solution to the problem is a strong Federal Boxing Commission, since the states cannot cooperate among themselves.

B. Such a commission could do many necessary things that are not now being done.

    1. Thorough pre-fight physical examinations could be made mandatory, with negligence a punishable crime, thus insuring that only fighters who were in top physical shape would go into the ring.

    2. Stricter rules and regulations, such as those requiring padded headgear, heavier gloves, and shorter rounds; prohibiting blows to the head; and providing for another judge to free the referee for closer supervision of the fight, could be made and enforced, thus reducing the present terrible toll of death and injury.

C. The commission would not please the really blood-thirsty fight fans, of course, but such fans helped create this legalized bloodbath and can be well done without.

D. Under Federal government supervision boxing could hold its head up high, and so could you and I and the rest of our supposedly civilized world.

Transition: (Can we make this happen? Yes! How can we make this happen? Let me tell you.)

Conclusion

The way to do it is to ask the Federal Government to set up a regulatory body for boxing. I don't say write to your Congressman. That could be 20 different letters to 20 different men. I ask all of you to send a letter of support, as I have done, to Mr. Kyle Rote, care of *This Week* magazine, 485 Lexington Avenue, New York 17, N.Y. I think that we can trust him to carry on from there. I am sure he is getting and will continue to get thousands of letters like yours and mine.

I don't care to watch any more real-life murders on TV. Do you? I don't want to have to think about other Benny "Kid" Parets dead at 25 years of age because we didn't take the time to care. Do you? I don't want to have to think about any more murdered boxers, or the ones who are luckier and only wind up insane or beaten into brainless hulks; or their wives and children, for that matter, either. Do you? I want a Federal Boxing Commission badly enough to have written to Mr. Rote. Do you?

References

1. Farley, James A., Jr., "My Fight in Defense of Boxing," *Sports Illustrated,* April 23, 1962.
2. "Magnified by TV," *Time,* April 6, 1962.
3. Massaquoi, Hans J., "Should Boxing Be Abolished?", *Ebony,* June, 1962.
4. "Murder by TV," *Christian Century,* April 18, 1962.
5. "Ring Requiem," *America,* April 21, 1962.
6. Rogan, Gilbert, "The Deadly Insult," *Sports Illustrated,* April 2, 1962.
7. Rote, Kyle, "Can We Stop Boxing Brutality?", *This Week,* January 13, 1962.

References for Unit V

1. Brembeck, Winston L., and William S. Howell, *Persuasion: A Means of Social Control* (New York: Prentice-Hall, Inc., 1952).

    The most complete and authoritative treatment of persuasion from the standpoint of the public speaker readily available to the student. Has thoroughness and an eminently practical approach.

2. Minnick, Wayne C., *The Art of Persuasion* (Boston: Houghton Mifflin Company, 1957).

    Shorter and consequently less comprehensive than the Brembeck and Howell book. It is soundly documented and has a considerable number of items of information and advice helpful to the student of persuasion.

3. Monroe, Alan H., *Principles and Types of Speech* (Chicago: Scott, Foresman and Company, 1962).

    For the student wishing to know more about the Monroe "Motivated Sequence," Chapter 16 provides the basic information about the sequence, and Chapters 21 and 22 discuss its application to speeches of the type assigned in this unit.

4. Oliver, Robert T., *The Psychology of Persuasive Speech* (New York: Longmans, Green and Company, 1957).

    Good insights into the persuasive process based on applicable research outside the field of persuasion as well as that done in the field itself.

Optional Unit C

Discussion

BACKGROUND

"Come, now, let us reason together," wrote the Hebrew prophet, Isaiah. Ideally, that is the invitation being offered to the participants whenever a discussion group assembles to share knowledge, conciliate disagreement, or decide policy. Such invitation might be said to describe discussion at its best.

Too often, however, discussion falls far short of that ideal. Someone once facetiously remarked that he would define discussion as "the friendly pooling of ignorance." Another commentator observed rather cynically that "the best way to meet a problem is to ignore it; the best way to ignore it is to discuss it; the best way to discuss it is to assemble a group of uninformed individuals bent on impressing each other, then have them depart amiably, each one being most impressed with his own erudition." Such observations certainly describe discussion at its worst. It is the purpose of this unit to help you avoid "the friendly pooling of ignorance," and achieve rather the mutually beneficial sharing of well-reasoned thought.

Basis for Discussion

What do we mean by discussion? Explanation should not be too difficult, since in a very real sense, the greater proportion of the speaking you do could actually be called a type of discussion. In ordinary conversation and in your everyday communication, you for the most part speak and listen in alternation with one or more other persons who also alternate listening and speaking. This kind of communicating is the basis of discussion. Discussion we define as oral communication by two or more people talking and thinking together in a group. Through this kind of oral communication, people try to understand one another, get along with one another, and solve problems that affect groups of people as well as individuals. Although discussion can be and unfortunately sometimes is used to evade individual responsibility, its proper use should be to share responsibility. Such use is consistent with our continuing emphasis in this course on the shared responsibilities of both speaking and listening.

This kind of activity, in both its everyday conversational form and the more organized form that this section of the book deals with, is especially important in a free society. The very essence of a free society is freedom of speech. Not only does each individual in a free society have full and free rights to think for himself and to express his thoughts and feelings to others, but he also has some responsibilities to give consideration to ideas expressed by others and to work with them in the cooperative solution of problems. Organized discussion tries to provide a means to that end which is similar but superior to ordinary conversation. It is a more or less formal speech activity designed for cooperative problem-solving through the sharing of ideas. It is *organized* so that the kind of oral communication that takes place will have some purpose, point, and pattern and hence more will be accomplished.

Organized discussion has a tradition ranging as far back as the councils of primitive man around the campfire. The tradition also includes Socrates, the ancient Greek philosopher, asking his probing questions in an effort to get men to understand themselves and to search for truth, and the New England town meetings where community matters were decided. But it is also as new as group psychotherapy, group dynamics, and brainstorming by a group of advertising executives. Scholars in the fields of psychology, sociology, and education, and investigators in business and industry have done much work in recent years studying and experimenting with various types and methods of discussion as means of instruction, decision-making, and improving relationships among individuals. Discussion is also taught and practiced as a part of modern speech instruction, since it obviously involves direct oral communication.

This section of the book will give you a brief introduction to organized discussion so that you may become acquainted with its more basic forms and uses. It must be understood, however, that a great deal of study and practice in discussion is required before you can become truly skilled as a participant or leader in various kinds of discussion groups.

Forms of Discussion

Discussion takes many forms, ranging from the most informal social conversations to the formal kind of oral interchange that takes place in a business meeting governed by rules of parliamentary procedure. Definitions of the various types of discussion can be made according to the particular makeup of the group, the purposes or tasks of the group, or the distinctive kinds of subject matter or procedures that are used. We shall introduce you to three general categories of discussion forms, but concentrate mostly on the first of these.

We can say, generally, that one form of discussion takes place mainly for the benefit of those taking part in it. This kind of discussion, whether it is called a round-table discussion, study group, or panel, has as its main purpose a shared learning by the participants. A group of people, made up usually of from four to eight members, working together and motivated by a common interest in dealing with a question or problem, discuss it among themselves. What they learn from each other and through the cooperative problem-solving method of group discussion is entirely for their own benefit, not for the benefit of an audience nor as a prelude to making recommendations to some agency or organization for action to be taken. They have come together only to learn. For sake of convenience, we shall call this a *discussion-learning group*.

Another form of discussion takes place mainly for the benefit of an audience. Information is also shared, but here the discussion group, composed of two or more participants, deals with a particular question or problem so that the audience may learn something from what the group has to say about it. Various kinds or styles of programs can be arranged for this general form of discussion. A discussion of this type between two persons is called a *dialogue*. Another kind of presentation is to have two or more (usually not more than four) individuals present prepared statements on a subject, each one representing a particular aspect of the subject or point of view on it. This kind of program is called a *symposium*. A third method is to have four to six persons discuss an issue. This technique is similar to that of the learning group, except that the discussion is for the benefit of the audience rather than the participants, with the introduction and conclusion of the discussion usually being directed entirely to the audience. This is called a *panel* discussion. These programs may be given to an audience which is actually present or over radio or television.

Discussion that includes members of an audience taking part by asking questions or making statements from the floor in the town-meeting tradition is called a *forum*. The forum is often combined with other kinds of presentation. That is, a program of some kind, not necessarily a discussion, is presented, followed by questions or statements from the floor. Thus we can have a public speech followed by a forum; a demonstration-forum; a film-forum; a debate-forum; or a dialogue-forum, symposium-forum, or panel-forum.

We shall call this general form of discussion that includes an audience either as active or passive participants a *discussion-instructional group.*

The third general form of discussion is one which involves a group having an official task to perform. It is required to make a decision or recommendation for action or to take action itself on a question or problem. Staff or board meetings in a business or other type of organization hold discussions on items of business; frequently several items are included in a single session, and are called items on an agenda. The more common kind of group in this category is the *committee.* Committees are often looked upon as necessary evils in the functioning of an organization; some argue that they are not even that. Nevertheless, their multiplicity can scarcely be denied. A committee is an organized smaller group that is part of and responsible to a larger organization. Meetings of boards or committees may be open to the public, but the proceedings are not for the benefit of any audience that may be present. The distinguishing characteristic is that the decisions made by the group become "official" decisions, often made so by a formal vote taken after discussion of the item or items. Other variations, such as investigating committees, arbitration or mediation groups, and public hearings, could be mentioned. We shall call this third general category a *discussion-decision-making group.*

We are going to consider discussion mainly from the point of view of what is involved in the first form we described, the *learning group.* What you learn about and practice in this kind of discussion should give you a good foundation upon which to build your future experience in the other forms.

Pattern of Discussion

Basic to all these types is a pattern of problem-solving that gives direction to some kind of systematic consideration of a question. This pattern is one that parallels the Dewey five-step description of what takes place in reflective thinking that we described for you in Unit IV. You will recall that these steps include:

1. Realizing a felt difficulty.
2. Locating and defining the difficulty.

3. Suggesting possible solutions.

4. Developing by reasoning the bearings of the suggested solutions.

5. Further observing and experimenting which will lead to accepting or rejecting a solution.

These steps in reflective thinking apply to cooperative thinking that takes place in group discussion, as well as to individual thinking in dealing with particular issues. Whatever the form of discussion or particular group doing it, then, a basic problem-to-solution sequence of thought development is followed. Sometimes it is carried through to completion, other times not.

The pattern of a complete discussion can be described in the following manner:

1. The group is either assigned a question or decides what question it should discuss that represents a significant problem affecting the members of the group or the society in which they live.

2. The group decides on the exact wording of the question (best stated in question form) to indicate the limitation that is being imposed on the issue being discussed. Agreement on definitions of confusing or ambiguous terms is sought. An analysis of the problem is attempted by presenting and exchanging information that describes conditions as they are, why these conditions exist, why they constitute a problem, and what needs to be done to bring about a solution to that problem.

3. The group then considers what various answers to the question may be given in light of the analysis they have made. Various alternatives may be suggested as a preliminary step in selecting the "best" solution.

4. Then the group considers each answer in an effort to evaluate and judge its comparative merits. A consensus may be arrived at as to which is the most complete and satisfactory solution.

5. The group may agree on means of implementing the solution. Participants may well realize that the answer agreed to is not necessarily the complete, final answer for all time. Further examination of the solution may have to be made, and some reexamination done after the solution has been put into practice.

Not all discussion groups complete all these steps. Most learning groups get as far as the first two, and may just begin the third one. Most decision-making groups that have assigned duties of deciding a policy or recommended course of action continue through the fourth and often the fifth steps.

We shall consider subject matter, the role of participants, and the role of leadership to show how organized discussion can work constructively and purposefully.

Subject Matter

What sort of subject matter is appropriate for discussion? The easy answer is to say that anything can be discussed; and in the unorganized, highly informal kind of discussion called conversation, we must admit that just about anything is. Passing up the easy answer, we would suggest two possible limitations: the limitation of one's knowledge, and the avoidance of matters that may offend the sensibilities of those taking part. The second of these qualifications usually limits conversation, but the first hardly ever does. However, both these qualifications apply to organized discussion. Certainly the participants in organized discussion need to know what they are talking about, and this necessity presupposes knowledge derived from their own experience, investigation and research, and specific preparation for taking part in the discussion. A third limitation applies to discussion-instructional groups. For them the matter of adapting the subject to the particular audience has to be considered.

Some criteria for consideration of subject matter can be suggested:

Is the subject suited to the group? Asking yourself what kind of group is involved in the discussion and what its general purpose is can help supply an answer to this question. If the group is a learning group, we assume that the subject matter is to be worthy of their time and efforts and that discussion of the subject will add to their knowledge and appreciation of it. The actual topic being discussed may therefore suggest a question of value rather than one of policy. A topic such as, "What is the real worth of a college education?" implies a search for goals and values rather than a decision about what should be done. A topic such as, "What should be the length of women's skirts?" might be an appropriate one for a conclave of dress designers, but not particularly useful as subject matter for general education.

A panel or symposium appearing before a particular audience must deal with a subject of either general or particular interest to that audience, and one that conforms to the purposes of the meeting where the discussion takes place. For instance, let us suppose that a public meeting of citizens is called, to which anyone and everyone is invited, in order to consider the matter of public recreational facilities in the town. A panel appearing before that group would have no choice but to discuss the problem that has brought them together and probably should have a forum or question period following their presentation.

A committee, staff, or board engaged in decision-making discussion usually has a specific task assigned to it. The discussion topic is an item on the agenda, or a particular task or problem related to the jobs that the individuals making up the group or the group itself must perform. For example, a committee may have been assigned the problem of investigating parking facilities around the Student Union and of reporting its findings and recommendations to the student legislature. The limits of its task are rather clearly defined, and the directions of the discussions that take place are determined mainly by the nature of the assignment. A staff or board meeting usually has an agenda that lists items which will require discussion before a decision can be reached. Discussion on such an item lasts only until general agreement on its disposition is arrived at, then the group moves on to the next item on the agenda.

Does the subject suggest a recognizable problem? This question applies more to learning or instructional groups than it does to decision-making groups. One test to apply is whether the statement of the topic suggests more than one possible answer. Wording the subject correctly will probably be a helpful means of meeting this criterion. Most books on discussion agree that the topic for discussion should be put in the form of a question. This form gives more specific direction to the group's deliberations throughout, and particularly aids at the outset in refining the wording of the question so that it states a problem clearly and impartially. A discussion group that had the topic "Capital Punishment" would probably be at a loss to limit the area of its discussion. But not just any question will do. If the topic were worded as a question, "Should the death penalty be abolished or modified?" a little clearer direction would be given the group, but some confusion would still exist because of the ambiguity of the statement and the difficulty of defining or distinguishing between abolition and modification. Were the question reworded as, "Why should the barbaric practice of capital punishment be abolished in the state of Kansas?" there would certainly be greater specificity, the direction the discussion would take being made rather clear. But partiality and bias are also evident in the wording. A better statement might be simply "Should capital punishment be abolished in our state?" One problem in this wording is that the question could easily be answered "yes" or "no" by the discussion group; they could conceivably take a vote without bothering to discuss it at all. The wording suggests only two possible answers to the problem; it leaves no room for half-way measures. Yet the discussion could take place, and would probably not deal with the so-called "pro's" and "con's" of the question, but more with reasons *why* capital punishment is the better or worse of the answers, and whether a change should be made. Possibly a still better alternative would be "What is the best way of dealing with criminals guilty of first-degree murder?" This wording allows the same discussion as before and, in addition, several alternatives to consider, including imprisonment, rehabilitation, or capital punishment.

Many writers in the field of discussion state rather definitely that discussion should deal with questions of policy rather than of fact or value. Such advice may be justified if the goals of the group or the purposes of the meeting where the discussion takes place conform closely with the steps suggested earlier: definition, analysis, alternate solutions, decision about the best of the solutions. Yet there are possibilities of dealing with problems of fact alone in learning groups and even in instructional discussion groups. Questions of value, as mentioned earlier, may also be as appropriate.

Is the subject a practical one for the group to handle?   An answer to this includes consideration of whether the topic can be dealt with in a reasonable length of time, whether adequate information is available to the participants, and whether any decisions arrived at are within the province of those making the decision. The question of whether nations deficient in their payments of assessments for support of the United Nations should be dealt with in some particular way may be discussed in terms of desirability by members of a learning group or instructional group, but actual decision about what action to take could scarcely be accomplished.

Participants

We can say categorically that the success of any discussion is directly proportional to the quality of the participation. The idea that anyone can discuss any issue at any time or in any place is just as erroneous as the assumption that public speaking requires no preparation or acquired skills. From the point of view of either the participants or listening audiences, the failure of a discussion may often be ascribed to the following faults: (1) the participants are unprepared, (2) the participants have attitudes not conducive to constructive accomplishment, or (3) the discussion procedure is mishandled. To eliminate these possibilities of failure, certain requirements for participation are necessary.

First, the participants cannot rely on guesswork or good intentions; they must prepare. The steps of preparation, however, differ from those made by the public speaker. They are directed almost entirely toward gaining knowledge of and insights into the subject matter, not toward formulating a point of view.

Each participant should do some reading, observing, and listening of his own, just as a public speaker does in getting materials for his speech. The information he gathers is for use in analyzing the nature of the problem. He should be prepared to contribute that information during the analysis phase of the discussion. Further, he needs to do some thinking about the subject. Since discussion involves cooperative thinking and the sharing of ideas and information, successful discussion demands that he should do some preliminary cogitation of his own up through, but not beyond, the stage of determining possible alternate solutions. Should he go beyond this point and decide for himself what the one and only answer to the question is, he will probably miss the whole point and purpose of the discussion, which is to have the group, rather than any one member of the group, arrive at a decision. Further, if he considers himself in possession of *the* answer, he may place himself in the role of an advocate, arguing that his answer is the best one. Also, by so doing, he may find himself in direct opposition to the points of view of other participants and will probably close his mind to whatever they have to say. Such attitudes and procedures, needless to say, do not make for a happy situation. Short of making himself an advocate for a point of view, then, the participant should be knowledgeable of the subject. He has as much obligation to document his information, to provide examples, quotations, analogies, and illustrative anecdotes to help enlighten the group as a public speaker has in developing the central idea of his speech.

The participant also needs to have a constructive attitude. He does not necessarily have to be an avowed or unavowed advocate to be lacking in this regard. The good participant's openmindedness toward other ideas, other participants, and other points of view will aid in building and maintaining a friendly, cooperative atmosphere throughout the discussion. He should give courteous attention to others who are making their contributions, listen carefully to what they say, and give them credit for the worth of their ideas.

This does not mean agreeing with everything that is said just for the sake of keeping harmony within the group, however. Participants must be as willing to share areas of disagreement as they are to share areas of agreement. Conflicts are a necessary part of discussion and can actually help promote its constructive course. After all, if everyone were in full agreement with and had complete understanding of everything that was said, there would be no reason to waste time in discussing the matter. Helpful conflicts are those of ideas, points of view, or proposed solutions. Harmful conflicts are ones of personalities, those created by outbursts of uncontrolled emotional responses, or displays of antagonism toward those who disagree. Although agreement could be said to be the ultimate goal of all discussion groups, it should be considered in terms of arriving at understanding, not in terms of compromising one's considered point of view for the sake of "getting something done."

The participants also contribute to the discussion procedures. Management of a discussion is not the sole responsibility of an assigned or elected leader. Each participant should be thoroughly acquainted with the pattern of systematic problem-solving that applies to discussion. He should have a clear idea of what steps are involved and in what order they come and be aware of what stage the discussion is in at any given time. For example, he needs to realize that analysis precedes solution, that one needs to understand the nature of a problem before he comes up with an answer. Therefore, he needs to suspend judgment to a degree, and certainly to delay proposing a solution, until the analysis is completed and understood by the group.

Participants may also be called upon to make summaries at any stage of the discussion, or to summarize the entire discussion at its conclusion. Further, individual participants may assume various roles designed to aid the course of the discussion, such as expediter, conciliator, creative thinker, or critical tester of ideas that are advanced.

Leadership

Efforts are sometimes made to hold discussions without a leader. The assumption is that the group can lead itself. These "leaderless groups" produce chaos more often than accomplishment; either the members do not know what to do or else everyone tries to do everything at the same time. Until the participants acquire a good deal of skill and sophistication in discussion methods, it is better to have an assigned or elected leader to keep things under control.

The degree of the leader's control can either help or hinder the course of the discussion. If he pursues an authoritarian, "strongman" type of leadership and tries to dominate or manipulate members of the group at each stage of the discussion, he will not only inhibit the work of the participants, but probably defeat the primary goals of discussion. Very weak leadership, on the other hand, puts the group in an even worse position than if it starts out knowing it is leaderless. Time is wasted discovering the fact that the leader refuses to accept responsibilities; participants are hesitant to "take over" for fear of offending him. The proper degree of control lies in between the extremes, and is given the name of "group-centered leadership."

The concept of group-centered leadership really means that the leader should contribute to the work of the group and help give them direction, but not make decisions for them. Such a leader does have certain distinct responsibilities. Some of them are standard ones that can be made a matter of routine; others that serve to facilitate the discussion are a good deal more flexible.

Procedure. We shall discuss the responsibilities of the discussion leader in terms of two categories. The first category might be called matters of organizational procedure:

The leader must do some preplanning. This includes acquiring knowledge of the subject, becoming acquainted with the participants, taking responsibility for the physical arrangements for the discussion, and preparing an agenda or tentative outline for the discussion period.

In acquiring knowledge of the subject, his preparation should be as complete as that the participants make, so that he is as well acquainted with the background and areas for analysis as they are.

He needs at least enough acquaintance with the participants to enable him to introduce and refer to them by name. Beyond that, a recognition of their previous experience, knowledge, and background will be useful for him in eliciting their participation.

He is also responsible for the physical arrangements. If the discussion takes place without an audience, the most practical arrangement is a closed circle. The group either arranges chairs in that manner, or seats itself around a table. This kind of arrangement puts everyone on the same level and directs communication toward the center of the group rather than to any one side. If an audience is present, the more practical arrangement is that of a semicircle, with the leader near the midpoint of the arc. This enables the participants to direct their communication partially to each other and partially to the audience so that they can best be seen and heard by all concerned.

The leader is also responsible for preparing an agenda or outline for his own use in maintaining a degree of organization during the proceedings. For business sessions involving committees, boards, or staffs, an advance notice of the meeting must be sent out notifying members of the time, place, and items to be considered. For learning or instructional groups, preparation of a tentative outline is desirable. The main headings probably will follow the steps of the discussion cycle. The subtopics can take the form of questions that might be put to the group as a means of eliciting participation and to serve as transitions to new aspects of the subject.

The leader starts the discussion.   Usually the first thing that he does is to state the question, then introduce the members to each other or to the audience. He then introduces the subject by giving a brief background of the question, commenting on its significance, stating clearly and accurately the limitations of the question decided upon by the group, and giving definitions of terms that might be misunderstood. The next step is to get the members started. He will ordinarily do this by asking a question related to the analysis of the problem, directed to the group as a whole, or to some individual member of the group if he notices in them a general disinclination to lead things off voluntarily.

The leader closes the discussion.   His most usual method is to summarize briefly what has been accomplished. The leader often presents the summary himself, endeavoring to make sure that it represents what the group has decided, not what his own personal interpretations of the discussion may have been. He may ask a member of the group to make the summary; or if there has been some divergence in points of view at the conclusion, he may ask individual members to make separate summaries of their differing points of view. If an audience is present the leader should thank them and dismiss the meeting. If a forum follows the discussion it then becomes his responsibility to elicit questions from the audience and direct them toward individual members of the discussion group or to the group as a whole, so that one or more of the participants may volunteer answers.

Control.   The second category of leadership responsibilities has to do with the conducting of the discussion while it is in progress. Each of these responsibilities suggests a measure of control exercised by the leader.

The leader should give some order and direction to the course of the discussion. He will be helped in this if he has planned his outline of procedures carefully. The means of keeping the discussion on track most commonly used is that of internal summary, in which a brief summation of a just completed phase or of the entire discussion up to that point is given and the next phase to be considered is introduced. If the discussion gets off the track and irrelevant issues creep in, the leader must bring the group back to the main question itself.

In getting the group to stick to the more important matters, the leader needs to be alert to the progress of the discussion. It is his responsibility to see that the over-all pattern shows progression of thought and that the participants have an idea of what progress is being made. Once the group has decided what limitations they are going to put on the question and what their goals in the discussion are, he should take them into the phase of analyzing the problem. He may introduce this portion of the discussion by asking a leading question of the group and encouraging participants to contribute. During the analysis of the problem, the leader needs to insure that the offering of solutions is delayed. After all, an answer cannot mean much until the group has an understanding of what the question is and a basis for judging how good an answer may be. The leader can conclude the analysis step by giving a brief summary, then asking the group what some of the answers may be in light of their analysis of the question. Thus he will proceed through as many of the steps of reflective thinking as are necessary or possible.

A leader can also encourage members to examine critically their own and others' contributions. Let us say that a group is discussing raising the minimum age for granting of drivers' licenses. A member says that the minimum age should be 18 rather than 16 because most accidents occur among drivers who are 16 or 17 years old. This member could be asked to give the source of his information or if he has some evidence to back it up. Further, he might be questioned about some of the reasons for the frequency or infrequency of accidents occurring at any particular age level. This kind of questioning and the answers that are given help contribute to the substance of the discussion. In addition, they help determine whether a member's contribution has been based on something more than a sudden inspiration or expression of an unsubstantiated opinion.

The leader should handle the participants.   Discussion leadership includes not only management of ideas but, to some extent, management of people. Since the participants speak and listen in alternation, some kind of balance in the amount of participation needs to be maintained. It is, of course, the duty of participants to speak up, not just sit there and enjoy the benefits of the work of others. Yet one or two persons—possibly even the leader—could dominate the whole proceeding, with others willingly or unwillingly keeping quiet. One of the tasks of the leader is to watch and listen carefully to determine if the discussion has some balance, encourage the reluctant to take more part, and tactfully restrict the overtalkative members.

Another important obligation of the leader in handling participants is to make constructive use of conflict of ideas. He can challenge a participant's statements and assumptions or elicit such challenges from other participants by encouraging critical thinking. Intrinsic conflicts—those that arise from misunderstanding of information, definitions, or systems of values—can be resolved during the discussion by exploring the ideas more completely. Extrinsic conflicts—those that arise when participants may just not like each other or may take sudden offense at something someone says—need to be handled tactfully by the leader and eliminated if possible.

THE ASSIGNMENT

Whatever assignment is given by your instructor should allow time for critical evaluation. We suggest a time limit be set for each discussion, perhaps about half a class period, so that the remainder of the time may be used for class discussion of what took place.

Option A: The Learning Group.   Your instructor will divide the class into groups with five or six members in each group and with one member designated as the leader. The groups should meet separately for a preliminary session as described in the section, Preparing for Discussion, then conduct the discussion proper in the presence of the class.

Option B: The Panel.   One or more groups are organized and proceed as in Option A, except that a forum period involving the entire class follows their presentation.

Option C: The Recorded Discussion.   Groups are organized as in Option A. Discussions are recorded and played back to the class for their analysis and evaluation.

Option D: Business Session.   Your instructor will help the class organize a mock business session conducted by parliamentary procedure.

Option E: Instructor's Assignment.   In order that your assignment may better suit the speech needs of your particular class, your instructor may choose to modify one of the above assignment options, combine features of two or more of them into one assignment, or possibly give you an assignment entirely of his own devising.

PREPARING FOR DISCUSSION

Successful organized discussion, we have said repeatedly, calls for adequate preparation on the part of everyone involved in it. If the discussion is to have purpose, point, and pattern, the preparation must include some planning by the group, by individual participants, and by the leader.

As a Group

In the preliminary session your main tasks are to decide about the precise wording of your question for discussion and the definitions of terms, and then arrive at some understanding of how far you will want to or be able to go in discussing it.

Let us say you have the general area of Federal aid to education to talk about. You may decide on a wording such as, "Should the Federal Government give direct aid for public education?" If you agree on this wording, the next task of your group in its preliminary session is to decide the definition and limitation of the question and to define the separate terms contained within it. You should have little difficulty agreeing upon what is meant by the "Federal Government," but would probably want to get an understanding of what you mean by or will include in "direct aid." You may decide to confine your discussion to the kind of aid proposed in bills pending before Congress.

In considering the term "public education," you may decide to limit yourselves to elementary and secondary public schools and eliminate discussion of aid to parochial schools—an issue that could very well warrant separate handling as an entirely different discussion question.

You may then want to talk over rather generally the significance of the question and to consider how far you would be able to go with it. For example, you may decide to deal with only current needs in public education and the extent of present state and federal support, thus limiting the problem to existing needs and their causes and possible solutions for those needs. You may even decide to stop short of deciding on a single answer which could be tested out by further analysis and eventually worded as a concrete recommendation for action.

Once you have arrived at these decisions, the preliminary planning of the group is done; you do not want to go further at that time. Any decision about what members are to say or any preliminary rehearsal of the discussion proper would destroy the spontaneity you will want later on. Moreover, you need additional preparation before you get into the actual subject matter of the discussion.

As a Participant

As an individual participant, your preparation consists of both investigating and thinking. These tasks in many ways parallel your search for materials for a public speech, but in other ways they do not. One important difference is that in discussion these procedures are governed by the limitations that the group has decided upon rather than by your own choice of subject, analysis of audience and occasion, and selection of specific purpose.

Since the questions for discussion are more likely to be ones of current significance, your best sources for materials will be current periodicals. Current issues of the *Reader's Guide to Periodical Literature* provide an index for materials of this kind available in most libraries. Records of interviews with experts on significant current problems in such news magazines as *U.S. News and World Report* are often quite useful. Almanacs and yearbooks can be used as supplementary sources for factual information. Also, do not neglect any chance to listen to or view public service programs on radio or television. Both network and local stations can provide you with a variety of discussion programs that can be valuable not only as sources of information, but also as examples of various discussion techniques. Finally, depending upon the kind of question you are discussing, you may find that interviewing one or more of your professors, or perhaps someone in the community, may provide you with useful information and points of view.

Many discussion participants neglect to keep an accurate record of what they learn from their investigation. The feeling is that since they are "just talking," they have no need for precise information. Do not make this error. Takes notes on what you read and hear, and arrange them by topics so that you can refer to the specific items of information and give the source for them during the discussion session. As in public speaking, you should compile much more information than you could actually use. The amount you use and the selection of particular items is largely decided by you or for you during the course of the discussion.

In analyzing your materials you will find it useful to compose an outline entirely for your own use. This outline will aid you in organizing your own ideas about the question. Although there is no standard form for you to follow, we will suggest some major headings that can be helpful. Note that these headings are in the form of questions rather than the declarative sentences you use in your speech outlines. The reason is that in preparing for discussion you are not giving answers to questions in order to influence the thinking of an audience as you do in a public speech, but instead are searching for possible answers to contribute to an organized process of group reflective thought.

    I. What is the actual problem?
   II. What is the extent or nature of the problem?
      A. Is this problem widespread, or confined only to particular areas or states?
      B. What segments of the population are affected by it?
 III. What are some likely causes?
 IV. What are some likely effects?
  V. From what is known, what appears now to be the direction that various alternative solutions may take?
 VI. What are some possible solutions worthy of consideration?
VII. What tests will need to be applied in evaluating these solutions?

These steps of preparation involve each member of the group including the leader, but the leader has some additional planning to do.

As a Leader

If you are a discussion leader, your preliminary investigation and thinking about the question should be done mainly to learn about its background. This information you do not acquire to use, but as a means of "briefing" yourself. Your steps of preparation are guided throughout mainly by considerations of what can be done to encourage a maximum amount of constructive contribution in the time available. This does not mean that you cannot take part at all. Your role, after all, is that of guide, not presiding officer. Yet your contributions to the content of the discussion should be less than that of the other members, and should be phrased to encourage fuller and more meaningful contributions on their part.

For these reasons, your preliminary outline takes on a different form. It should serve as an aid for you in planning how you will guide the course of the discussion. Again, it is in the form of a series of questions. Some of the questions are ones you may actually use in guiding the course of the discussion, but you must never feel bound by its wording or progression of ideas. After all, the group is the final arbiter on all matters.

Here is a sample general outline that might be helpful for you to use as part of your planning. The detailed questions, of course, you will fill in to conform with the particular question that is going to be discussed.

Introduction

I. What are we discussing? Write out the exact wording of the question decided upon in the preliminary discussion period.
II. Who is going to discuss the question? List the members so that you can introduce them to each other or to the audience, if one is present.
III. Why are we discussing it? Compose for extemporaneous delivery a brief statement about the general background and significance of the question, and indicate the limitations of the question and definitions of particular terms that the group has decided upon in its preliminary session.

Body

I. How may we analyze the problem?
   A. What are the central issue or issues involved?
   B. What is the extent and significance of each issue?
   C. Why is it a problem?
   D. What are some likely causes?
   E. What are some possible effects?
II. What are some criteria we can apply for our understanding of the entire problem that will aid us in summarizing our analysis?
III. What are some answers that can be given?
   A. Do these answers represent alternatives?
   B. Does each of them relate to the nature of the problem as we have discussed it?
   C. Do they meet the suggested criteria for evaluation?

Conclusion

I. How may we best summarize what we have accomplished?
   A. Have we arrived at further understanding?

B. What is the extent of our agreement or disagreement with each other?
II. What may we do further in exploring this question?

This outline is a suggested one for your use in preparation. It may or may not be used by you when you actually conduct the session. For that purpose you may want to revise it into this form:

1. State the question.
2. Introduce the members.
3. Give a brief introduction to the question.
4. Start the discussion by getting the group to begin the analysis.
5. Summarize the analysis (or call for a summary from the group).
6. Call for suggested solutions, exploring them only as extensively as time and the inclinations of the group permit.
7. Summarize the proposed solution or solutions (or call for summary from the group).
8. Close the session.

As a Critic

Evaluation of the discussion should come from the participants and from those who listen to it. They may approach criticism from a different perspective, but their areas of evaluation are essentially the same. You will find for this unit an Inventory Page for each participant to fill out for himself, and a sample Comment Page that both your instructor and individual class members may use as a guide in evaluating the entire group. Here in brief form is an outline of what to listen for in making your evaluations:

I. Items making for success of the discussion.
  A. *Content:* Consider the significance of the problem-question, the way it was worded, defined, and developed by the group. What did the group accomplish? What was the quality of reasoning as measured against the criteria for reasoned statements included in Unit IV?
  B. *Techniques:* Consider the organization and management of the discussion from the points of view of leadership and the individual participation. Was the participation balanced? Were conflicts resolved? Was the discussion properly introduced; did it move along from point to point; was it adequately summarized at the conclusion?
II. Items needing improvement.
  A. *Content:* Specify whatever shortcomings were evident in the group's handling of the entire question and in the treatment of the various issues involved.

B. *Techniques:* Specify ways by which the leader and the individual participants could improve their preparation, planning, and individual performance.

Sample Discussion Outline

Introduction

I. The question is: "Should proposed Federal aid to education include church-supported schools?"

II. The members of the panel are:

III. This question poses a significant problem that requires definition.

    A. Since education is important for the well-being of a nation, provision of adequate educational facilities is necessary.

    B. The present administration proposal for Federal aid to education does not include church-supported schools.

    C. Federal aid refers to financial assistance given through congressional appropriation to the several states and administered by them for the benefit of public schools.

    D. Church-supported schools include Catholic, Protestant, and Jewish schools at the elementary and secondary levels.

Body

I. The history of Federal aid to education can be examined.

    A. Federal activity in public education dates back to the Land Ordinance of 1785.

        1. In each township one section was to be set aside for public schools.

        2. This practice was generally adhered to as the nation developed.

    B. Since that time there have been 23 acts of Congress, the latest being the Library Service Act of 1956, and the National Defense Education Act of 1958.

        1. The National Defense Education Act is concerned with the expansion of education in the fields of science, mathematics, foreign languages, and professional educational training.

        2. Many colleges and universities provide training programs for public school teachers under provisions of this act.

    C. A report on Federal educational support prepared by the Central Michigan School Administrator's Research Association estimates total expenditures for major programs of educational aid since 1785 to be 18 billion dollars.

        1. Two-thirds of this amount, more than 12 billion dollars, has been expended in programs which have been initiated within the past 20 years.

        2. Much of this amount has been earmarked for research activities.

    D. One example of Federal assistance has been the school lunch program.

II. Present proposals are pending for increasing aid to public schools.
    A. The administration proposal of 1961 was for the Federal Government to grant by pupil ratio money to separate states for use in public schools.
        1. This payment would vary from $15 to $29.67 per pupil depending on the per capita income in each state.
        2. This proposal has not passed.
    B. Church-controlled schools are excluded from provisions of this proposal, assumedly on constitutional grounds.
        1. Although education is not mentioned specifically in the Constitution, it is argued that giving aid to church-controlled schools would violate the principle of separation of church and state.
        2. The Tenth Amendment states: "the powers not delegated to the United States by the Constitution" are thereby "reserved to the states respectively."

III. An examination of schools in the nation shows comparisons between public-supported and church-supported education.
    A. Of the 46 million elementary and secondary school children, 85 percent are in public schools, 13 percent in Catholic parochial schools, 1 percent in Protestant and Jewish schools, and 1 percent in other private schools.
    B. Catholic parochial and public schools may be compared.
        1. Approximately 5.3 million are enrolled in parochial schools and 37.6 million are enrolled in public schools.
        2. There are 144,000 parochial school teachers and 1,410,000 public school teachers.
        3. The pay of parochial school teachers averages 5 to 10 percent less than the pay of public school teachers.
        4. The operating costs in parochial schools average $440 per pupil, and $390 per pupil in public schools.
        5. Classes in parochial schools average 20 percent larger than classes in public schools.
    C. Whereas the needs for better facilities and increased teacher pay in public schools are great, the needs in parochial schools are greater.

IV. There are some precedents for Federal aid to church-supported institutions.
    A. Catholic colleges were included in the "GI Bill of Rights" which provided Federal Government payment for tuition directly to colleges attended by veterans.
    B. Federal grants for research are given teachers and students in Catholic colleges.
    C. Federal loans for dormitories are made directly to Catholic colleges.
    D. Parochial schools are included in Federal school milk programs for elementary and secondary schools.
    E. Abraham Ribicoff, former Secretary of Health, Education, and Welfare, stated that there are more than 50 Federal programs under which institutions with religious affiliation receive Federal funds through grants or loans.

V. Arguments about aid to church-supported schools indicate the issues that are involved.
    A. Proponents say that by extending aid, pupils rather than the churches or schools are directly helped.
    B. They also say that "double taxation," or paying both taxes for public school support and tuition for church schools, is unjust.
    C. Further, church schools must compete with public schools for teachers.
    D. Others say that the main problem is how to control the use of the aid so that it would serve the public interest without infringing upon freedom of private schools.
        1. Church schools now have freedom in choosing curriculum and books.
        2. If aid were given, that freedom might have to be restricted.
    E. Opponents say that aid to church schools is wrong in principle.
        1. Education of children is a state function and must be supported by the state.
        2. Public money cannot be given for support of church schools because that means state support of religion.
        3. Support given two types of systems is uneconomical and inefficient.
VI. The issues concerning aid to church-supported schools may be summarized.
    A. Precedents exist for Federal support for both public and private education.
    B. Church-supported schools have need for additional support if the general quality of education is to be maintained and improved.
    C. If aid is to be given church-supported schools, the conflict over constitutional principle must be resolved.
VII. Various alternative answers may be suggested.
    A. No Federal aid should be given church-supported schools either directly or indirectly.
    B. Present programs of Federal aid which allow some indirect aid for church-supported schools should be continued without additional expansion.
    C. The present Federal aid proposal should be altered to provide aid for pupils in church-supported schools.
    D. Federal aid to education should be increased, but the determination of how much, if any, should go to church-supported schools should be left entirely to the decision of the separate states.

Conclusion

I. The last alternative answer represents the general consensus of the panel.
II. Further investigation, study, and discussion of this solution are needed.

References

1. *Congressional Digest*, February, 1963.
2. Greene, Edith, *The Federal Government and Education* (Washington, D.C.: U.S. Government Printing Office, 1963).
3. *Newsweek*, February 13, 1961.

4. *Newsweek,* March 27, 1961.
5. *Time,* April 12, 1963.
6. *U.S. News and World Report,* April 1, 1963.

PARLIAMENTARY PROCEDURE

Although the purpose of most discussion groups is to arrive at mutual understanding, there are occasions, rather loosely termed "business sessions," when groups take official action determined by voting. In many committee meetings and in most business sessions, decisions made by the group take the form of a "yes" or "no" representing the answer given by at least the majority. Such occasions are characterized mainly by adherence to a formal set of procedures called parliamentary procedure.

We shall not set forth here a code or manual for parliamentary procedure. When you are in a position of leadership that requires you to conduct a formal business session, you will surely want to become thoroughly acquainted with one or more of the excellent manuals of parliamentary procedure that are available. Furthermore, if you are a voting member of an organization, you should acquaint yourself with the basic rules of procedure so that your participation will be intelligent and the decision you express through your discussion of the issues and the vote you cast will be fulfillments of responsible, democratic action.

When Henry M. Robert first composed his well-known *Rules of Order* nearly a century ago, he was impelled mainly by dismay over the chaotic, unintelligent manner in which many business, social, and civic meetings were conducted. Were he alive today, he might be equally appalled by the common misunderstandings and misuses of the fundamental, sensible procedures he set forth for fair and efficient handling of items of business. Although parliamentary complications can and do arise and a really skilled parliamentarian is an unusual specialist who is highly sought after, there is nothing really mysterious or unwieldy about the orderly means by which this kind of decision-making is done.

Reasons for Parliamentary Procedure

The main reason for knowledge and use of parliamentary procedure is to make for orderly, efficient conducting of business. The procedures, properly applied, also help insure that the will of the majority is advanced without denying full recognition and protection of the minority will and the rights and privileges of the individual member. It is not by accident that these formal procedures are called *parliamentary* procedure, for they evolved from procedural practices of legislative bodies in democratic societies.

Conducting Meetings

The president of an organization or the chairman of a business session is the presiding officer. This means that he conducts the meeting but does not influence decisions that only the group has a right to make. In conducting meetings, he has two general patterns or programs to follow, the *agenda* or the standard *order of business*. The agenda is a statement of one or more items of special business, published in advance, that allows the group to concentrate on the more important matters requiring immediate consideration. The order of business, sometimes called the orders of the day, includes a sequence of events announced by the presiding officer during the meeting:

1. The meeting is called to order. This frequently includes a roll call of members.
2. A reading of the minutes of the last meeting is called for. This is followed by a call for corrections or additions to the minutes and a statement of their approval.
3. Committee reports follow. The usual sequence is to have reports of officers, then those of standing committees, and finally those of special committees.
4. If unfinished business (often called "old business") is left over from the previous meeting, it is taken up until disposed of.
5. New business is called for. Items are usually introduced by individual members.
6. Following the conclusion of formal items of business, the presiding officer calls for announcements, requests, or any miscellaneous items for the good of the group.
7. The meeting is adjourned either by passage of a formal motion for adjournment or by announcement by the presiding officer.

Motions

You will want to consult codes or manuals of parliamentary procedure to learn details about such vital matters as nomination, election, and duties of officers; bylaws; handling of committee appointments, duties, and reports; and keeping minutes and other records. In such works, however, most reference is made to types of motions and how they are handled. Formal motions are the main vehicles by which business is conducted. In most manuals you will find a convenient chart or table of types of motions, their order of precedence, and ways by which each is handled by the chairman and the membership. If you refer to one of these tables during a meeting, you will be able to find answers to most of the questions that arise about any one motion. We shall list some of the more common motions for you as an introductory means of identification.

A *main motion* introduces a principal item of business. A member rises, says "Mr. Chairman," and is recognized by the chairman who addresses him by name. The member then says "I move . . ." and states the item of business. The chairman calls for a second to the motion and declares it an official item to be considered.

A motion to *amend* modifies another motion, usually a main motion. The amendment may add words, remove words, change the wording, divide into separate items, or substitute for the motion to which it applies. The amendment is seconded and becomes an item of business that must be disposed of before the principal motion is dealt with further.

A motion to *refer to committee* delays action by the group. It refers the item of business to a special or standing committee so that further study or recommendation can be made before the group considers it again.

A motion to *lay on the table* removes an item of business from immediate consideration by the group and delays action until a motion to *take from the table* restores the item for group consideration.

A motion to *reconsider* restores an item of business that has already been voted on as a means of further considering that item and perhaps taking different action upon it.

A motion to *rescind* is a means of negating action previously voted on by the group.

Normally debate on a debatable motion continues until the group is ready to vote on it. Any motion to *close* or *limit* debate requires a separate vote before the principal item is voted on. Moving the *previous question* has the effect of closing debate. If it passes, the pending item comes up for immediate vote.

The group can change its own rules of procedure, provided the action remains consistent with its own bylaws or constitution. The most frequent device used to alter standard procedure is a motion to *suspend the rules* and substitute a specified temporary procedure for handing a particular item.

If an error in procedure is committed by the chairman or membership, it becomes both the privilege and the duty of any one member to call a *point of order* so that the chairman can correct the error that has been made.

Each member should be aware of what is going on at all times. He should know especially what item is being voted on, and what procedures are being followed. If he is in doubt, he should ask the chairman by making a *parliamentary inquiry* or raising a point of information.

A motion to *recess* interrupts a session temporarily; a motion to *adjourn* concludes the meeting.

A simplified table of motions and rules is presented here to give some details about ways of handling motions. However, you need to consult a manual to find exceptions and special applications of these and other less frequently used motions.

Motions and Rules

Motion	*Seconded*	*Amendable*	*Debatable*	*Vote Required*
Main	Yes	Yes	Yes	Majority
Amend	Yes	Yes	Yes	Majority
Refer to Committee	Yes	Yes	Yes	Majority
Lay on Table	Yes	No	No	Majority
Take from Table	Yes	No	No	Majority
Reconsider	Yes	No	Yes	Majority
Rescind	Yes	No	Yes	Majority
Close or Limit Debate	Yes	No	No	Two-thirds
Previous Question	Yes	No	No	Two-thirds
Suspend Rules	Yes	No	No	Two-thirds
Point of Order	No	No	No	None
Parliamentary Inquiry	No	No	No	None
Recess	Yes	Yes	No	Majority
Adjourn	Yes	No	No	Majority

Again we stress the necessity for study and use of guides in learning uses of parliamentary procedure. It is learned best through practice, but that practice must be correct. Whether or not exercises in parliamentary procedure are a part of your assignment, we do want to stress the value of knowing and using this important tool of democracy.

References for Optional Unit C

All of these have widespread use as textbooks for courses in discussion; each is helpful for general reference. You will find most interesting the differences among the various definitions of discussion and the similarities in instructions about the steps of preparation and the organization of discussion programs.

1. Barnlund, D. C., and F. S. Haiman, *The Dynamics of Discussion* (Boston: Houghton Mifflin Company, 1950).
2. Cortright, Rupert L., and George L. Hinds, *Creative Discussion* (New York: The Macmillan Company, 1959).
3. Howell, William S., and Donald K. Smith, *Discussion* (New York: The Macmillan Company, 1956).
4. McBurney, James H., and Kenneth G. Hance, *Discussion in Human Affairs* (New York: Harper & Brothers, 1950).
5. Wagner, Russell, and Carroll C. Arnold, *Handbook of Group Discussion* (Boston: Houghton Mifflin Company, 1950).

Any of these references is helpful for use in parliamentary procedure:

1. Auer, J. Jeffery, *Essentials of Parliamentary Procedure* (New York: Appleton-Century-Crofts, Inc., 1959).
2. Davidson, Henry A., *A Handbook of Parliamentary Procedure* (New York: The Ronald Press Company, 1955).
3. Robert, Henry M., *Robert's Rules of Order Revised* (Chicago: Scott, Foresman and Company, 1951).
4. Sturgis, Alice F., *Standard Code of Parliamentary Procedure* (New York: McGraw-Hill Book Company, Inc., 1950).

Evaluating Speeches

LISTENING AND CRITICISM

This section may be assigned at any time during the course. Preferably you should read it early in the term and refer to it throughout. When you are given assignments in making written reports on classroom speeches or on speeches heard outside the classroom, you will want to review the directions given for the composition of those reports that are included in this section.

Completing such assignments will enable you to sharpen your listening skills. It should also help you to evaluate your own speeches better, both before and after you give them. In making such critiques, you will be applying the same kinds of critical judgments that you can expect intelligent, discriminating listeners to apply to your speaking efforts. The transfer to self-evaluation should not be too difficult. Developing your skill in self-evaluation may well be one of your more important achievements in this course, for after you leave it, most of the time the only evaluation your speeches will get will be that which you yourself give them.

This section includes information and suggestions about listening and the criticism of speeches. An additional source of useful information about efficient listening is Ralph G. Nichols and Leonard A. Stevens, *Are You Listening?* published by McGraw-Hill Book Company.

Listening

We have said that an important part of what you learn in a public speaking class is the value of listening. No speech is complete without that group of listeners collectively termed the audience. It has a vital part to play in any communication situation. The speaker has the primary obligation to do his very best, but audiences also have responsibilities. A listener who assumes that all he has to do is soak up what he receives is evading his responsibility. Responsible listeners weigh, consider, and evaluate the worth of what they hear, and act accordingly.

Not everything you hear spoken is worth the time and effort you expend to hear it. We hope that is not true of any of the speeches you hear in this course. We know it will not be true of most of them. What you listen to during this term should give you an excellent opportunity to sharpen your awareness of ideas, to weigh their worth, and to evaluate the content and delivery of spoken messages. In doing these things you will be gaining a higher level of listening ability than most people have.

Levels of Listening. The "lowest" level of listening is listening for conformity's sake, only because others are doing so and the listener would seem out of place if he did not at least pretend to look at and listen to the speaker. So he follows the social convention of being a part of a group, but gets little or nothing out of the speech.

Another level of listening is listening for entertainment. On this level the listener seeks only the enjoyment of the speech, and its value is entirely recreational. For those speeches whose legitimate end is entertainment, this is a perfectly appropriate kind of listening. Only a very small minority of speeches are speeches to entertain, however, and the listener who perks up his ears for nothing but the humorous or exciting anecdotes can miss much that might be profitable to him. The fact that some misguided speakers cater to this type of listening, muddying their message and subverting their real purpose by dragging in joke after joke on the slightest provocation only argues the more strongly for higher levels of listening. Listeners are as responsible for these perversions of public speaking as the speakers who perpetrate them.

The third level is listening to and accepting the message in order to justify what is already known or agreed to. It seems to be human nature to hear what we want to hear, to listen to people we like, to accept ideas that are in line with our own sets of beliefs and attitudes. Again there is nothing wrong with this type of listening *per se*. You should have a set of values, principles, and standards that you cling to and for which you seek and enjoy reinforcement. They are the core of your character, and speaking and listening that will strengthen and solidify that core are necessary and proper. But no values, principles, or standards should ever be held so absolutely that you completely close your mind to opposing points of view. Man has not yet devised a truth that is not to some extent relative. Moreover, most public speaking is done on issues where there is anything but absolute certainty of what is right and what is wrong. In some cases listening only for confirmation of one's own previously formed prejudices and beliefs is not really listening at all.

The next level of listening is listening to learn. You do this in the lectures and discussions you attend in your various classes. Your main motive is to gain something new, to understand and remember it, and often to do further study. In the section of this book devoted to the organization of the course we have said some things about the nature of this type of listening. You will do well to review at this point the suggestions made there about *creative* listening.

The other level of listening is listening to make a decision. This kind of listening requires making a more complete evaluation of what is heard and accepting it as a basis for future belief or action. It demands greater control of one's emotions, more concentration, and more thought than any other. It is the highest level of listening.

Your listening should contain elements of each of these five levels, but your goal is to gain greater proficiency in the last two—listening to learn and listening to decide. The listening assignments in this course are designed to accomplish this goal through four possible means:

1. Listening to lectures and discussions in connection with each of the units in the course to learn as much as you can about public speaking and to put this knowledge to use.
2. Listening to the various speeches given by your classmates and learning all you can from their experience and the suggestions for their improvement.
3. Listening to a particular speech of a student in order to compose a written report of criticism.
4. Listening to a speech given by a speaker outside a classroom in order to compose a written report of criticism.

Influences on Listening. Most persons listening to a public speech have little difficulty identifying to whom they are listening and what the nature of the occasion is. They can get without much trouble an idea of what the speech is generally about and form impressions of the speaker from the very beginning of his performance. Part of their reaction to the speaker and his speech is conditioned by their previous attitudes toward the speaker and his subject. If the speaker is well known, has an outstanding reputation, or is built up as an authoritative figure by the person introducing him, their expectation of hearing a worthwhile speech is greater. If you as a listener have some knowledge of and opinions about the subject of the speech, your chances of paying close and careful attention to his message will be greater. If you are fortunate enough to listen to a speaker who can combine a valuable message with an impressive, highly effective delivery, your chances of benefiting from the entire listening experience will be greater yet.

We need more and better criticism of speech resulting from intelligent listening. This is especially true since, as we said toward the beginning of this book, so much of our communication is oral that some persons dismiss it without giving it the kind of qualitative judgment it should receive. Too many persons, some of them well enough educated in other fields and perceptive in their judgments of other achievements, have little apparent means of delivering a sound judgment about a public speech. Often the range of reactions to any one speech may include such remarks as "It was a good speech," or "I didn't like it"; "Isn't he a great speaker; I was impressed by his voice and his gestures," or "I just didn't like his looks"; "Brilliant! He knew what he was talking about," or "It sounded like a lot of nonsense to me."

Could any one of these "critics" back up his statement? You should expect him to be able to, just as you expect a speaker to be able to prove any one of his points. Even though the soundest criticism includes general, subjective statements, the crucial question remains—upon what are these judgments based? How did the listener-critic arrive at them?

Your own motives, attitudes, beliefs, opinions, previous knowledge, and present feelings—the whole complex that is your personality at the moment of listening—will influence your responses to the speech. The physical surroundings in the speech situation also have their effect. A comfortable, well-lighted enclosure with favorable acoustical properties will help influence more favorable reactions in any speech situation. The audience that is present is part of the speech situation, too. If other members of the audience appear restless and inattentive, you will probably be less attentive. If they cheer and applaud, you will more easily respond in the same way. Responses of others and of the entire group are contagious.

The influences that come from within you and those that may affect you from outside can either help or hinder the fairness and competence of your listening and your critical judgments, just as these influences may help or hinder the speaker's chances of success. Intelligent listening, however, requires a degree of intellectual detachment. As an intelligent listener you should concentrate on certain things in the speech situation and try to avoid being unduly influenced by elements that are less important. The content of the speaker's message and the speaker himself are most important. What the speaker is saying and how he is saying it are the central things to which you should give your concentrated, voluntary attention. Your focusing of attention can be helped by an attitude of expectancy, an open mind toward what the speaker is trying to accomplish and continuous assessment of his degree of success in accomplishing it. If you are able to do these things, then you can rightly assume what should be the major responsibility of any intelligent listener: deciding the worth of the message. The intelligent listener, once he has given the speech a fair hearing, can ask himself the questions: "Shall I accept this or not? What would be the consequences of what I have heard if I incorporate this knowledge into my learning, or if I accept what the speaker is proposing as part of my behavior?"

Having a constructive attitude toward the speech and giving voluntary attention to the speaker and his message are prerequisites for intelligent listening. Beyond that, we shall suggest certain points of concentration that should be of help to you. This is not a complete listing, nor should you think of it as a formula for accomplished criticism, but it should at least give you a start in the right direction.

What to Listen for. We suggest that you concentrate first and foremost on the subject matter of the speech, next on the adaptation of the speech to the audience and the occasion, and finally on the speaker's delivery. Your specific points of concentration in each of these areas can be determined by asking yourself a series of questions the answers to which may sometimes be arrived at concurrently, and usually cumulatively, while you listen to the speech. In respect to the speech itself, you should ask four major questions.

What was the speaker's central idea? The central idea may or may not be stated explicitly by the speaker, but whether it is stated or not, you should think it through yourself and put it in your own words. Whether or not you forget the details in the speech, you should be able to identify and remember the central idea. If someone should ask you what the speaker said, your answer should be a concise statement of his central idea, phrased in your own words, representing the main thought you were able to get from the speech as a whole.

How did he develop the central idea? If the speaker has used an introduction that not only won your favorable attention but led into the subject, and if he has used a conclusion that reinforced the central idea of the speech, you will be better able to identify and begin evaluating how the structure of the speech and the development of the ideas it contained merged into what can be called the content of the speech. Being able to distinguish the main points in the body of the speech will help you answer the question about development. If the speaker used identifiable transitions that help you identify the upcoming points, he has made it easier for you to follow this aspect of his developmental pattern.

What developmental materials was he using and how was he using them?
The main points of a speech need development, and determining what kinds
of developmental or supporting materials the speaker was using is an important part of your concentration. Determining the pertinence of the supporting material to the points being made and the soundness of the statements and the reasoning they reveal is the foundation for forming a critical
judgment about the worth of the message. You can observe and distinguish
between statements the speaker designed mainly to add to your interest and
hold your attention and those that he used to advance his thought development. You can make judgments about his style and the language that added
color to the message, and about the words, phrases, and sentences that conveyed his meaning accurately. You can begin to judge the balance between
the attractiveness of what he said and the soundness of the content of his
speech.

What was his specific purpose; how far did he go in accomplishing it?   Again,
the speaker may not have stated explicitly what he wanted to accomplish.
After all, his specific purpose was formulated for his own benefit in helping
him prepare the speech, not necessarily for the audience to be able to
identify immediately. If the speaker has planned his specific purpose in terms
of potential audience response to his message, he should have a means of
trying to determine for himself how successful the speech was. You, as a
listener, can also have some means for helping determine the degree of success of the speech by deciding *after* the speech is completed what the speaker
was trying to do. You can do this best by asking yourself the questions:
"What did he expect me to learn?" "What did he want me to believe or do?"
"How, then, did I react?" "How much did I learn, or how much was I
influenced as a result of the speech I have just heard?"

The speaker composed his speech using materials and a pattern of organization as a means of making his message known and of accomplishing
a purpose by presenting that message to you in person. You, as a listener,
are not as aware of his actual techniques of organization as he was in planning the speech. Actually, your evaluation of the organization and the materials being organized tend to merge into one judgment about the entire
content of the speech.

Your next area of concentration has to do with how the speaker and
the speech were adapted to the audience and the occasion. You cannot
separate your evaluations of the content from this determination, but you
can keep another series of questions in mind as you listen.

Was the subject appropriate to the audience and occasion?   The decision
you make about this is whether the subject and the subject matter applied

to the interests and needs of the people who were present and who came to hear the speaker for a particular reason. If you can assume that you are a typical member of the audience, you can decide how much the speech meant to you or how much it could mean to any similar audience to which it might be given.

How significant was the subject? This can be answered not only in terms of the value you may or may not have gleaned from the speech, but also in relationship to the significance of the issue in comparison with other issues facing you and society in general.

What language and style did the speaker employ? Was he able to bring ideas to life through his use of words and phrases? Did he speak at a level you could comprehend without insulting your intelligence or appealing to motives or emotions of a lower order than you would like to acknowledge?

The final element to consider is the speaker's means of delivering the message. Delivery is not the least important element in the speech situation, but we do want to emphasize that you as an intelligent listener should not concentrate mainly and certainly not exclusively on the speaker's techniques. He may have put on a good show, but if that is all he did, or if that is the only value you gained from the speech, your listening experience has been a very limited one. Yet the speaker's delivery can either help or hinder his total accomplishment. You can ask yourself some questions about it. These can be stated rather briefly and simply:

How did he use his voice? Try to determine whether it helped or hindered your reception of the message.

How did he use action? Try to determine whether it added to your reception or whether certain parts of it distracted you.

This advice should aid you in all the listening you do in this course. Now we shall turn to consideration of speech criticism, since the criticism of any one public speech derives from the listening you have accomplished and becomes the record of your evaluation of the particular speaking effort.

Criticism

A written criticism in the form of a speech report is a detailed critical analysis of the principles and techniques of speech used by a speaker in a given speech situation. The word *critical* as it is used here may need explanation. It should not be taken to mean "finding fault." More properly, criticism means pointing out both good and bad points of the speaking effort, both praising and blaming the speaker and his speech. Your report should give a balanced, qualitative judgment based on your exact and complete observations. Your written criticism should not be carping, neither should it be "constructive" in the sense of excusing every fault and lamely ending up with pleasant but meaningless general advice. It should be fair in making an accurate report and sound evaluation of what you have heard and seen.

Professors Lester Thonssen and A. Craig Baird classify general types of critics and discuss thoroughly the qualifications of the critic and the functions of his criticism.[1] We shall describe some kinds of critics from the point of view of their general attitudes and approaches.

Kinds of Critics.   The *impressionistic* critic, as his title implies, gives his general impression of whatever he is criticizing. His judgment is his subjective feeling about the quality of a given work or performance. If he is a sensitive and well-qualified observer, his judgment may have real merit; however, it is liable to error. While we encourage you in your speaker reports to state your honest feelings about the quality of the job done, we want those feelings to be based on something more than an offhand expression. Such general comments as "The speech was good," "It was well organized," "His delivery was excellent" mean little if they represent only the total impression received. A critic must go deeper to determine what was "good" about the speech, in what ways it was well organized, and what made the delivery excellent.

The *historical* critic is concerned with correctly placing the object of his criticism in its historical context and explaining how it was the product of its time and how it might have influenced events. This kind of criticism, of course, you cannot do to any great extent in your reports, even if you should want to, for a few days is hardly sufficient time to get a historical perspective. It may sometimes be possible to determine what was "in the air" that caused the speaker to give the speech and even to predict possible effects of the speech on its immediate surroundings, but for most of the speeches you hear you cannot go much beyond identifying the particular speech occasion and the relationship of the issues of the speech to what is going on in the world outside.

The *analytical* critic figuratively, if not actually, takes the thing he is criticizing apart and examines it piece by piece. His criticism is often very

---

[1] Lester Thonssen and A. Craig Baird, *Speech Criticism* (New York: The Ronald Press Company, 1948), pp. 16–24.

valuable, but possibly just as often it misses the forest for the trees. Nevertheless, analysis is an important part of any criticism. The critic must examine the parts that make up the whole as a basis for making an evaluation. Discovering first what was done, then how it was done and why is a necessary part of the critic's task. But he should not stop there. Taking a watch apart and leaving the separate parts scattered all over the table top will not give you all the answers about its workings. Neither would identifying the separate elements in a speech without more completely evaluating their effectiveness and their worth supply you with the answers you need for making a thorough judgment of the speech. We want you to be analytical in your criticism, but also want you to go a step further.

The last kind of critic, the *judicial* critic, is the one that we would like you to be. He does a bit of what the historical critic does, attempting as best he can to place the object of his criticism in its historical context. He also does much of what the analytical critic does, examining closely and critically the parts of the whole. But he does something more than either the historical or analytical critic, which is to make a final qualitative judgment. The significant difference between his final judgment and that of the impressionistic critic is that it is a carefully considered one, one that has been based upon careful observation and analysis, and hence is far less liable to error.

Criteria for Criticism.   Speech criticism deals with all of the constituents of a speech performance: the speaker, the speech, the audience, and the occasion. In discussing your listening, we advised you to give most attention to the speech itself, to concentrate secondarily on the speaker as a person, and to concentrate least of all upon environmental influences in the speech situation. In making a critical evaluation, however, your main concern is with the speaker—not just his reputation, appearance, or delivery, but what he has accomplished by giving the speech. The audience and the occasion are important to the critic not for themselves, but as a means of understanding and evaluating the speaker's total performance. Among other things, the speaker is judged on how well he analyzes the audience and occasion and comes up with a speech and manner of speaking that are appropriate and effective. The speech, as the principal instrument used by the speaker to accomplish his purpose, gets a great deal of attention from the critic, but it is analyzed principally to show how well the speaker understood and practiced the principles and techniques of public speaking. Speech is first of all a useful art and only secondarily a fine art. It is wonderful, of course, if the speech is a thing of beauty, but that is only one of the criteria for evaluating its worth. The effect of the speech upon the immediate audience is another criterion, but the final worth of the speech cannot be measured solely on the basis of the immediate results it achieved. The rantings of a demagogue may be most effective, but the value of his cause to society is open to serious question. As James H. McBurney and Ernest J. Wrage have pointed out most emphatically, judging a speech only by its results sells short the value of public address.[2] The judicial critic cannot avoid ethical considerations of the speaker's means and the possible consequences of what he advocates when he attempts to evaluate the individual speech as a useful art.

As a college student preparing yourself for the coming battles of adult life, you should find the tasks of listening assigned you in this course immensely useful. They are useful not only for your own personal improvement of speaking and listening skills, but also for sharpening your thinking processes, gaining acquaintance with significant ideas, and developing an ability to evaluate them. The tasks of criticizing speeches should also prove to be a valuable contribution to your learning. You strive to learn intelligent speaking and listening in order to communicate well. You strive also to gain the ability to make judicial criticism of oral communication so that you may appreciate more the contribution that public address has made and is making to our society.

COMPOSING THE WRITTEN REPORT

Use a heading for your speech reports as follows:

1. Name of the speaker and his position or title.
2. Date, time, and place the speech was given and the nature of the occasion.
3. Size and general description of the audience.
4. Speech subject.
5. Specific purpose of the speech.
6. Central idea of the speech.

After this heading, develop in essay form your evaluation of the following suggested items and whatever other points that contribute to a sound critical analysis. The statements you make are not to be general impressions. Give reasons for your conclusions. These items, you will note, parallel the general items you find listed on the Comment Pages.

[2] James H. McBurney and Ernest J. Wrage, *The Art of Good Speech* (New York: Prentice-Hall, Inc., 1953), pp. 22–32.

Adaptation of Speech to Occasion

Evidence of how well the speaker analyzed the occasion and provided the right speech for it should be considered. Did he correctly gauge the audience's level of understanding and knowledge of the subject? Did he understand the audience's attitude toward himself and his speech prior to speaking and make provision for these attitudes in his speech? If he showed evidence of adapting to the audience and occasion as he was speaking, and his speech in general gave the impression that it was designed especially for this specific audience and occasion, you may judge that he accomplished this item well, and adapted his subject area to the particular occasion.

Content

What did the speaker say? You cannot repeat all of it, nor would that accomplish your critical evaluation. You can state briefly the substance of his message and certainly should be able to identify and evaluate his use of specific kinds of supporting materials. You can comment upon the wording of the speech and the use of language that revealed the content. In many ways the content of the speech is the most important item of all. Understanding the substance of what was said and evaluating its significance and worth are the main reasons for anyone listening to a speech, and hence should be main items considered in any criticism of it. Keeping the speaker's central idea in mind is a necessity at this stage of your evaluation. The content of the speech is actually the amplification of the central idea.

Organization

You cannot report the organizational pattern of a speech with the complete detail you would use in outlining your own speeches. However, the pattern you discern in the speeches you hear will help you decide whether or not you are able to follow along with the thought development of the speaker, determine how he is developing his central idea, and judge how well he is accomplishing his specific purpose. You should be able to identify and evaluate the type of introduction and conclusion being used, the kind of development employed in the body of the speech, and whether the main points are distinct, tied together with transitions, and arranged in an order that aids the audience in understanding and assists in the accomplishment of the speech.

Delivery

The speaker's delivery will have important bearing on his success as a speaker. This includes his general appearance and his ability to reflect confidence and vitality and to express himself with a sense of conviction and sincerity. Also included are his particular uses of voice and action. You will want to evaluate his vocal quality; his use of the variable elements of loudness, pitch, rate, and quality; and his clarity of diction and care in pronunciation. In evaluating his use of action you will want to consider his posture, movements, gesture, facial expression, and eye contact.

Final Evaluation

Basing your conclusions on what you have said before, you should now be able to make some judgment about the worth and estimation of the effects of the speech. Part of your judgment will be based on an assessment of what was done in comparison with the criteria for excellence in public speaking. Part will be based on your assessment of the audience's reaction. If the speaker did or did not gain the desired response from the audience, to what do you attribute his degree of success? You can further attempt an evaluation of the total worth of the message that you have heard and its implications for you or any other audience that might hear it.

SAMPLE WRITTEN REPORTS

Student Speaker

Here are two reports of a student speech given in a speech class. They are reproduced as they were handed in to an instructor. The first report received a failing grade, the second received a high grade. Read through both of them and you can see why. Although both students had about the same reaction to the speaker and drew similar conclusions, the second student did some analysis and made a judicial criticism while the first speaker did not. The first student reported his points of view without giving reasons for them. The second speaker described what happened, compared the performance with speech standards throughout, then drew conclusions that had some basis.

First Report

1. Helen Carson, student.
2. January 29, 1964. Speech class assignment.
3. Twenty students.
4. Insurance.
5. To inform us about insurance.
6. We need to begin planning for insurance programs now.

Helen adapted to the audience and occasion quite well because we all know her. Her subject was interesting.

The content of the speech was good, if someone wanted to learn about insurance. Some material was used to show why insurance is needed, what kinds of insurance are available, and what the advantages are. This kind of material is all right if the audience wanted to accept it. There were some statistics used, but I don't remember where she got them. They were good, so were the examples.

The speech was organized in a way that was appropriate for the subject. The points were well worded and clear. The introduction and conclusion were well done and accomplished their purposes. The transitions led from one idea to another. The central idea was clear and the separate points were well supported.

The audience was attentive and reacted to the speaker and her purpose. All in all this was a very good speech.

Second Report

1. Helen Carson, student in beginning public speaking.
2. January 29, 1964, speaking assignment for Unit V, given in classroom.
3. Twenty students of beginning public speaking, and the instructor.
4. Insurance.
5. To get the audience to believe in the value of having insurance coverage.
6. Insurance is necessary for protection against unexpected financial burdens that can harm us and our families.

Helen began her speech by telling us that in two or three years we will be on our own: getting married, having children, acquiring property. This will involve heavy responsibilities and certain risks. We must be prepared to meet the responsibilities and to protect ourselves and our families against the unexpected. This introduction helped show how the speech would apply directly to us. Although the twelve men in the class might be thought to be more directly involved as future heads of families, the eight women would also probably be concerned, especially with family welfare. Helen gave us a reason to listen and to want to hear more. Throughout the speech she continued to adapt to the audience by her friendly, conversational style of delivery and by using supporting materials clearly within the understanding of her listeners. Her frequent use of "you," "we," and "us" helped identify herself with us. Our attitude was probably one of open-mindedness; we were willing to learn, and were fairly open to persuasion. We did not have any particular set opinions about the matter. She did nothing that would have destroyed this attitude, or in any way have alienated us.

Since we might not accept Helen as an authority on insurance, she properly relied on other authorities for most of the material in her speech. She referred to statistics issued by the Prudential Life Insurance Company and Mutual of Omaha, and quoted directly from *Fortune Magazine* and a Mr. Richards who was identified as a field representative for the Business Men's Assurance organization. These materials were used to inform us about the risks of not having insurance, and about some of the material values of sound insurance planning. The quotations contained reasonable arguments showing the benefits of insurance; we could assume that these sources were competent although they might be biased in favor of the central idea being developed. The statistics could speak for themselves in showing comparative costs and benefits of both life and health insurance plans.

Most of the speech consisted of hypothetical examples of what could happen to us in the future. These were related mainly to the strong motive appeals of personal security, although concern for family welfare and the appeal to economic motives were also evident. Each main point was developed enough in the limited time to make it clear and to persuade us to action. She used language effectively, avoiding technical terms that might not be clear to us and choosing words that were concrete and explicit. The phrase "insurance can be our best assurance" was fresh and striking, although "a nest egg for the future" was rather trite.

The body of the speech was divided into three main points. The first was that we should understand the reason for insurance and should be concerned about it now. This was developed by examples and factual information. The transition to the second point was "Think of the difficulties that could arise if we don't have insurance." The second point told us what some of the difficulties might be. Here statistics, examples, and a quotation were used to clarify and reinforce the assumption. The next transition was a question, "What kind of insurance should we have and what will it cost?" Factual information and indirect quotations were used here. In each instance the speaker told us the source of the information, then interpreted it to show the soundness of insurance planning.

The introduction led into the theme of the speech by emphasizing the need to think now about our financial security. The first sentence, "In two or three years most of us will be on our own," certainly got our attention. Following a brief orientation, Helen led into the body of the speech by introducing the first main point about reasons for insurance. The conclusion briefly summarized insurance benefits, then appealed directly to us to investigate further, to ask our parents about their experiences, and to talk to different insurance representatives in order to get more information. The last statement, "Insurance planning shows your concern for the future," emphasized the motivation developed in the body of the speech. The arrangement of ideas made sense. The sequence was closer to a problem to solution order than to any other pattern of arrangement.

Helen always makes a pleasing appearance before the class. Her animation and pleasant smile help make the audience warm up to her and keep them alert. She appears to have gained a great deal of confidence since her first speeches and seemed almost completely at ease in her posture and movement. Possibly she used too few gestures, but they were saved for the emphatic points that most needed them and appeared to be natural and well timed.

Early in the term, our instructor pointed out the need for Helen to speak louder. It was hard to hear her in the back of the room when she gave her first speech. She has improved very much in this respect, although she would still have to use much more force if she spoke in a larger room. She has gained a great deal of vitality and animation in the use of her voice. The instructor also called attention to her excellent diction, which the rest of us could pay close attention to as a model for our own improvement. She has variety in pitch and uses pause well in emphasizing points and transitions in her speech. She has also shown improvement in slowing down her rate of speaking so that her ideas can be followed more easily.

The class was attentive and learned something new. I think the main effect of the talk was to get us to thinking about the subject and to urge us to take action in the future. We probably won't go right out and buy a policy now, but most of us will, I believe, begin to become more aware of the need for planning. Helen probably achieved her purpose, for most of us at least. I would judge her speech to be sound and effectively presented. The instructor spoke highly of her improvement in organizing and delivering her talk, and the class discussion about its content that took place after she gave it seemed to confirm my own reactions.

"Outside" Speaker

Speeches delivered to an audience outside the classroom are of a different nature. The audience is usually not a "captive" one and is there to learn something from the speech rather than to learn about public speaking. The speaker is more likely to be experienced and is somewhat of an authority in his field. He represents a particular profession or cause and is more closely identified with his message. The speech is likely to have an entirely practical function of informing or persuading the audience.

When you attend a public speech or lecture given on campus, you will be gaining a great deal from the content and challenge of ideas being presented. You will also have an opportunity to hear and see a speaker in action delivering the kind of public speech that you might possibly be called upon to give some day. Further, you will have an opportunity to apply critical criteria that will be valuable to your learning in this course.

We suggest that you go to each speech on which you intend to report with a speaker report note sheet, so that you can take notes while the speech is going on. Remember that you are a member of the audience as well as a reporter, and that your own reactions are a part of the speech situation you are evaluating. In other words, you are approaching your task with an open mind and a receptive attitude. After you have heard the speech and before you begin to write your report, study your notes carefully. Think through what you want to say before composing your rough draft of the report. When you have finished it, review the rough draft to make sure that you have covered completely and accurately what is called for in the assignment. Then make the final copy to hand in to your instructor. After he has evaluated your report and returned it to you, read through it again to see how his comments and suggestions can be applied.

Following is another report of a speech submitted by a student. Even though the student reacted unfavorably to the lecture, she did make an effort to be fair and thorough in her analysis and judgments. As a matter of fact, she conferred with a number of other members of the audience whose judgments she respected, in order to determine whether their reactions were similar to hers. From what she learned, others were just as unhappy with the speech as she was, although probably few of them—even among the professors who were present—made as complete an evaluation as this reporter did.

Speaker Report

1. Dr. X, Professor of Philosophy at Z University, author and lecturer.
2. January 8, 1964, 8 P. M., University Auditorium.[3]
3. Audience of about 350: cross-section of university students, about 25 professors from different departments. The occasion was the third in the annual university lecture series.
4. The speech subject was suggested by the announced title, "Stumbling Blocks in Education."
5. To make the university student audience believe that they must overcome traditional "stumbling blocks" in their education and aim toward a "search for truth."
6. A university education is not serving time and following a set routine in an institution; it is the product of an alert, inquiring mind seeking knowledge and truth.

Dr. X had evidently planned the speech for this kind of audience; his subject, specific purpose, and central idea appeared to be most appropriate for them. The adaptation of his message and his adaptation to the speech situation will be discussed throughout the remainder of this report.

The speaker apparently intended to make an indictment of higher education and suggest ways of improvement, yet he did not consistently use authoritative

---

[3] The date and certain other identifying details in this report have been altered by the authors. The substance of the report is reproduced with the kind permission of Sister Mary Blaise.

or reasoning materials as one would expect in a speech to convince. The proof seemed to rely on his own say-so rather than on the reasoned development of his points of view. He objected to knowledge being considered an end in itself. He gave as an example the study of *Hamlet*, where he felt that the real point the student should realize from his study should be that "drama can reflect his inmost thoughts and his inmost life." What this actually means was not explained. History, he asserted, is wrongly used when it is used to solve present-day problems. He felt that acquisition of techniques is not an end in itself. He felt especially that teachers were hampering influences in this regard, as the student was so engrossed in trying to understand the teacher's point of view and methods of learning, that he was unable to absorb what the teacher was supposed to be teaching. The relationship of this observation to what one usually associates with the term "techniques," was not made clear.

He objected to the "tools that divert the true course of education," principally attacking the textbook by saying that it reduces education to a technique. Yet he offered no supports of this statement, or any cure for the situation. He introduced the term, "acquaintance to recovery," and described it as meaning the general survey of a large number of literary works without delving into any one thoroughly. In discussing the lecture system, he stated that all the devices of the textbook reappear, but offered no alternative form of teaching. A strong feeling against postponement of knowledge was expressed by the speaker. He vehemently attacked teachers who teach erroneous material, or what is "not quite true," on the basis that the student is not ready for the truth. "The student is ready for anything," Dr. X asserted. Departmentalism, specialization, and extracurricular activities, he said, encourage all the evasions, but he did not elaborate further on this point, or offer supports for the statement. Finally, he attacked the grading system. He stated, "education cannot be predicted." His attack on the grading system permeated the entire speech. In the final part of his attack he stated, "The student has no time for learning with tests, assignments, and grades to worry about." I wondered about the consistency of this statement, especially since he had not told us at any point of what learning consists.

By themselves, these various assertions appeared to be challenging ones. Many of the members of the audience had taken courses in teaching methods, which courses he also attacked in his speech. Besides this, instructors and students in the educational system he attacked were able to draw from their own experiences and compare his opinions with the reactions they themselves had to the entire system.

Much of the difficulty I had in following his thought development came from the organization of his material. I could not catch the words of his opening remarks. Although the audience was quiet and attentive at the beginning, they could hear only a blur of sound as the words were run together. Apparently the introduction consisted of an announcement of his subject and a statement of his purpose. There was no effort to establish an atmosphere of friendliness, to arouse favorable attention, or to lead into the subject of his speech.

After adjusting to the manner of delivery, we were able to determine some things about the intended organization of the body of the speech. The speaker mentioned three stumbling blocks of true education: knowledge, history, and acquisition of techniques. He developed each of these topics by going into various points of the present educational system which he called "tools that divert the true course of education." There were nine of them, according to my best count. Since all of them have been discussed previously in this report in connection with another point, it would be unduly repetitious to mention them here again. As I said before, the development of these items consisted mainly of generalizations; few specifics were given.

Instead of a conclusion, Dr. X told an irrelevant, humorous story. No summary was given, no conclusions were drawn, no direct appeal was made to the audience. The idea conveyed by the final sentence was that he realized that he had offended his audience, and that this had been his intention.

Dr. X's method of delivery was unsatisfactory for an audience of students, or most any audience for that matter. He talked rapidly and with little vocal or facial expression. His rapid-fire delivery was like that of a TV commercial announcer and did not communicate well with the audience. The only time his tone of voice changed was when he used sarcasm. Although he condemned the lecture system, he appeared to be using some of the worst features of it himself. He read the entire speech, and failed to look at his audience. He used no movement, but stood stiffly behind the lectern while reading. Although I was trying, I could not, even with great effort, keep interested in what he was saying.

The audience, as they came in, were talking and smiling, showing their curiosity about the subject and willingness to enjoy an attack on the existing educational system under which they were laboring. Many members of the audience were armed with paper and pencil. They were there to take down pertinent information. They were attentive when the speaker began, but when they had difficulty following him, they let their pads and pencils lie unused in their laps, and began to look around in a bewildered manner. Even before the end of the speech, small groups were stealing out the exits. Over half of the audience left before a panel could begin questioning the speaker, and those who did stay began drifting out when the answers to the panel's questions proved vague, sarcastic, or irrelevant.

The audience was, first of all, disappointed because they could not follow the speech. They were aware that Dr. X may have had worthwhile information and opinions to impart, and they were eager to hear him, but they could not maintain the high degree of concentration and attention necessary to get the pattern of his talk. They had their curiosity aroused by the advance publicity given the lecture, and would have made an ideal, receptive audience had the delivery of the speech been more effective. There was no reference to the audience, nor any connection brought out between what he was saying and the direct application to the audience before him. There were no conclusions drawn, no real proofs offered, no remedies suggested. The audience wanted to be convinced; they had the attitude of open-minded interest. They did not agree or disagree in advance, but wanted to hear first and judge later. Their main judgment appeared to be an adverse one toward the speaker and his material. The purpose of the speech was therefore lost.

In applying my observations to the original speech purpose, I believe that Dr. X let a great opportunity slip by. He had a large, attentive group, who, if convinced, might have some day helped to change the educational system into a form more acceptable to his way of thinking. Yet he alienated them throughout his speech, as typified by his final statement presented as a quotation from Brahms, "If there is anyone I have neglected to insult, I apologize to him." He made no converts in his audience.

There may have been things of value in the speech. If I had had the opportunity to read the message rather than hear it spoken, I might have gained much more from it. I would judge the message to have been composed more as an essay than a public speech.

INDEX

273